MUSIC AND MUSICIANS
IN CHICAGO

Da Capo Press Music Reprint Series

MUSIC EDITOR
BEA FRIEDLAND
Ph.D., City University of New York

MUSIC AND MUSICIANS
IN CHICAGO

GATHERED AND COMPILED BY

FLORENCE FFRENCH

DA CAPO PRESS • NEW YORK • 1979

Library of Congress Cataloging in Publication Data

Ffrench, Florence, comp.
  Music and musicians in Chicago.

  (Da Capo Press music reprint series)
  Reprint of the 1899 ed. published by the compiler,
Chicago.
  Includes index.
  1. Musicians, American. 2. Music—Illinois—
Chicago. I. Title.
ML200.8 C5F4 1979   780′.9773′11   79-9802
ISBN 0-306-79542-6

This Da Capo Press edition of *Music and Musicians
in Chicago* is an unabridged republication of the first
edition published in Chicago in 1899 by Florence Ffrench.

It is reproduced, with a 7% reduction of type size,
from an original in the University of Chicago Library.

Published by Da Capo Press, Inc.
A Subsidiary of Plenum Publishing Corporation
227 West 17th Street, New York, N.Y. 10011

MUSIC AND MUSICIANS

IN CHICAGO

—THE—

CITY'S LEADING ARTISTS, ORGANIZATIONS AND ART BUILDINGS

PROGRESS AND DEVELOPMENT

ILLUSTRATED

GATHERED AND COMPILED BY

FLORENCE FFRENCH

Representative of the MUSICAL COURIER for Chicago and the Central Western States.

FURTHER CONTAINING ARTICLES OF GENERAL MUSICAL
INTEREST BY

WILLIAM ARMSTRONG	CHARLES E. NIXON	S V STEELE
MRS. O. L. FOX	F. W. ROOT	MRS. REGINA WATSON
F. G. GLEASON	W. H. SHERWOOD	HARRISON WILD

There is no archItect
  Can build as the muse can:
She is skillful to select
  Materials for her plan.

She lays her beams in music,
  In music every one,
To the cadence of the whirling world
  Which dances round the sun.
    —From Emerson's "*The House.*"

Published by FLORENCE FFRENCH, 224 Wabash Avenue, Chicago.

REGAN PRINTING HOUSE, CHICAGO

PRELUDE

O WIDESPREAD was the interest created, so thorough the praise accorded to the special Chicago edition of THE MUSICAL COURIER two seasons ago, that the supply of the issue became quickly exhausted and a heavy premium price was reached for copies. Under such circumstances the need of a re-issue was at once recognized and I felt constrained to supplement the material then gathered, and in an improved and more permanent form, to give, so far as lay in my power, the rich record of music in Chicago, its development and general progress, a more extended circulation.

Most interesting is the story of the musical advancement made by this great Western metropolis, its failures, disappointments, difficulties and varying vicissitudes, culminating in the vast triumph that has made Chicago, musically, as well as in other directions, second to no city on this continent, with the possible exception of New York.

No attempt has been made to give other than a most concise account of the history and general happenings of the years since music first began to take its place in the daily life of Chicago. The lives and careers of those who made this history, best tell its varying details and it is with these it is consequently the purpose chiefly to deal.

Surely too, should be well received, the illustrated sketches of Chicago's principal musicians and of those who in any way have associated themselves with or contributed to the city's musical upbuilding. To all such the connection of the compiler, as Western representative of THE MUSICAL COURIER, a paper whose fame and influence cover the chief countries of the civilized world, affords unquestionable assurance of widespread circulation, as well as that permanence necessary to make their names, qualifications and careers known to the musical people of the world.

FLORENCE FFRENCH.

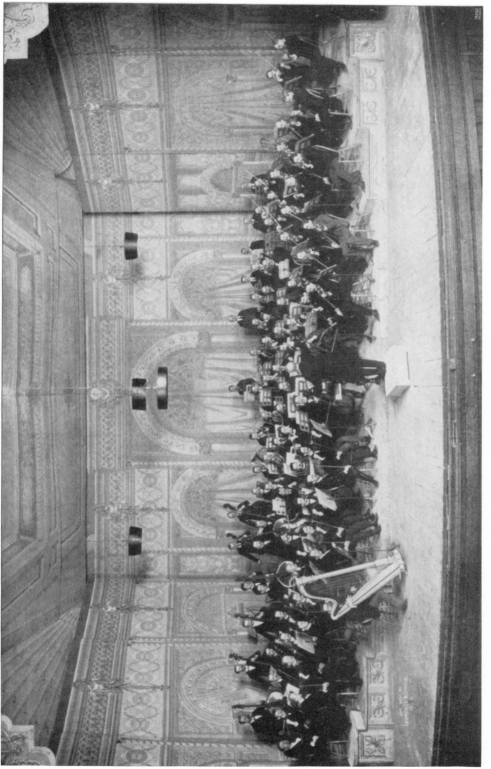

THE CHICAGO ORCHESTRA.

MUSIC AND MUSICIANS
IN CHICAGO

From the First Concert (1836) to the Present Day

Like all movements that are destined to prove of a permanent character, the musical growth of Chicago has been gradual and steady. Almost imperceptible were the primary steps, but day by day, month after month, year after year, a closer hold upon the home life became apparent, until today music is an integral portion of the life of Chicago. That growth it is the purpose to portray, to show what was done here in the early days, how as the city increased and prospered music strengthened and broadened; in fact, to follow its development through the course of the years, detailing not alone easy progresses and pleasant successes, but also some of the drawbacks and difficulties, successfully overcome. Thus each chapter in its different way contributes to the proud position reached today and the noble promise of the years to come.

There . are seven acts or scenes which need to be noted in the drama that has been played in this remarkable theater of population:

1. The old settlers' dance and church music.

2. The music of the Civil War.

3. Hans Balatka and the music of the Germans, confined mainly to the north side of the city. Of Mr. Balatka it may be here mentioned that with Milwaukee music he had been connected as far back as 1851, in which year he had been director of Haydn's "Creation," as given by the Milwaukee Musical Society.

4. Crosby's Opera House, and the birth of love for opera that led up to the erection of that edifice.

5 Central Music Hall erected, Florence Ziegfeld's College of Music established, and the singing associations that were formed after the great fire, with light opera, "Pinafore" companies, etc.

6. Jubilees, opera festivals and other large musical events conducing to the erection of the Auditorium and the interests that have centered in that noble building.

7. The larger field and nobler ambition to which all of these have tended, the Fine Arts building and the establishment of permanent opera in English.

From the simple music of the frontier-village church and the merry fiddles of the early settlers' dances, to the Apollo Club, the Thomas Orchestra and grand opera at the Auditorium, represents the span of musical art life in Chicago. Counted by years, the period between the two conditions is not long, and there are yet resident in Chicago those who have participated in the settlers' dances and have lived to be able to make generous subscriptions to the opera; but these intervening years have meant an infinite amount of toil and tireless ambition by many earnest cultivated people devoted to the interest of good music.

To write a complete and particularly detailed history of music in Chicago would be a very difficult task, and to obtain the records which have made it possible to compile the present work has been no easy one. The growth of art within a distinctively commercial community, possessing no leisure class, is often a hard matter to clearly delineate and when, as with music, it is chiefly developed in the home life of the people, to exemplify its progress stage by stage is well nigh impossible. Thus in this necessarily circumscribed review of the musical history of a great city that which is salient and memorable has been recorded and dwelt upon, rather than the mere details which if entered upon would but embarrass so limited a recital of Chicago's musical experience and culture.

Within the memory of the "old settlers" it is held that aside from the very primitive music of the first church "meetings," the two brothers Beaubien were the musical leaders in the then little frontier settlement, Chicago. Music had inspired Mark Beaubien with a love for the fiddle, and Jean Baptiste Beaubien with the ambition to own a piano. This piano as the first to come to Chicago was treated with great honor. Time has not dealt so harshly with it, for it is said to be still in existence in the house of Mrs. Ogee, a descendant of the Beaubien family, at Silver Lake, Kansas. The fiddle which Mark Beaubien had treasured became a legacy to John Wentworth, by whom it was presented to the Calumet Club, and it is now in the possession of the "Old Settlers' Association."

A musical convention of the various religious denominations was held in May, 1848, at the First Baptist Church. How high were its objects may be gathered from the following resolutions, which were adopted as representing the sentiments of the convention:

Resolved, 1. That music is naturally in the soul and, if properly exercised, is one of the most powerful of all means used for the elevation, spiritually, of mankind.

2. That instruction in vocal music should begin in public and private schools, and it is the duty of those who have the management of them to provide for such instruction.

3. That exercise in vocal music is conducive to health and all who have at heart the physical as well as the spiritual welfare of mankind will advocate its study.

4. That like all choice blessings which are bestowed on mankind, through the beneficence of God, music, as well as other gifts, must be cultivated to insure the benefits resulting therefrom.

5. That the musical ear, when possessed to any extent, may be improved by study but cannot be produced where originally deficient.

6. That it is the duty of choirs to study sacred music and assist in imparting to religious services that spirit of devotion which their duty properly performed enables them to do.

A further resolution was also added that congregational singing was the most desirable method to be used by religious bodies.

Referring to these early times in the city the *Chicago Magazine* in 1857 recites the difficulties which confronted the early choir, "as those who could sing were timid, and those who could not sing were unfortunately filled with ardor to praise the Lord."

In this necessarily somewhat cursory glance over the musical history of Chicago the reader is placed in possession of the leading facts and is made acquainted with those conditions and surroundings from which the gratifying results, up to the present, and the possibilities of even greater musical achievements in the future, are directly due.

The records of the past are undeniably most creditable to Chicago, the foundations laid by the musical pioneers are broad and deep, and what has been builded thereon challenges even most critical attention as an enduring and symmetrical creation, well within the most conservative interpretation of what constitutes true musical art.

Music in Chicago is in no embryonic condition, the experimental stage has been long passed, and the primary conditions of development have been so plainly demonstrated as in the direction of sound and thorough education that Chicago's position as the western center of musical culture, refinement and influence is not only self-evident but is now generally admitted.

FIRST CONCERTS BY THE EARLY MUSICAL SOCIETIES, CHOIR ASSOCIATIONS, ETC.

With Notes Upon Various Miscellaneous Entertainments

The first concert of which there is any reliable record was that of the Old Settlers' Harmonic Society on Dec. 11, 1835, in the Presbyterian Church at the southwest corner of Lake and Clark streets, where the grade was then about ten feet lower than it is nowadays. The program on that occasion, unquestionably a very long one, is not without interest and is therefore reproduced:

Allegro movement in the overture to
    Lodoiska ....*Krietzer*
Wreath (glee for three voices....*Mazinghi*
While with Ceaseless Course the Sun..
    ....*Webbe*
Di Tanti Palpiti.................*Rossini*
Behold, How Brightly Breaks the
    Morning ....*Masinello*
Sprig of Shillalah, with variations—
    violin solo ....*Lewis*
O, Lady Fair (glee for three voices)..
    ....*Moore*
Nightingale (favorite military rondo).....
O, Sing Unto the Lord (anthem)...
    ....*Whitfield*
Soldier Tired (celebrated movement in
    Artaxerxes) ....
The Muleteers (duet)..................
La Flora ....*Mozart*
Canadian Boat Song (glee for three
    voices) ....
Away with Melancholy (variations,
    violin obligato)..................*Lewis*
Deep Blue Sea (glee for three voices).....
Dead March in the oratorio, "Saul".......
Schoolmaster (glee for three voices—
    **basso obligato, violoncello accompani-
    ment**)
        To commence at half-past six.
          Tickets, 50 cents.

The Old Settlers' Harmonic Society does not appear to have been permitted to experience any of the sufferings of old age, for after a second concert which was given at the Presbyterian Church in the first month of 1836 no further mention of it is discoverable.

The first record of a public performance which can be traced was one at the Mansion House, whose proprietor was a Mr. Dexter Graves, on Feb. 24, 1834, and was given by a Mr. Bowers, a conjuror and ventriloquist. This was followed by the Boston Arena Company, Chicago's first circus, a profitable visiting enterprise which advertised the city far and wide as a most excellent show town. But music was not yet. On July 22, 1837, however, a negro minstrel troupe known as Christy's Minstrels gave a performance at Rice's Theater.

The Chicago Sacred Music Society was organized in 1842, with the following named subsequently well known citizens as officers: B. W. Raymond, president; Benjamin Smith, secretary; T. B. Carter, treasurer; Seth P. Warren, C. A. Collier, directors; W. H. Brown and E. Smith, executive committee. T. B. Carter is the first teacher of music of whom one finds traces, but a few years later, in 1844, are noticed H. Cramer, on Clark street between Washington and Madison, and Charles Sofftje, who made his home with John H. Kinzie.

Some mention is necessary of a society called the Choral Union, which was formed in 1846 and remained in existence for about two years. Its officers were: A. D. Sturtevant, president; A. S. Downs, secretary; J. Johnson, first leader; S. P. Warner, second leader; I. A. Hosington, third leader.

From the Choral Union arose Dec. 4, 1849, the Mozart Society, of which George Davis became president. Mr. Davis had already been most active in connection with the earlier musical organizations and the general promotion of all musical culture, being himself a popular singer of the time. The society's inauguration concert program given on Oct. 24, 1850, is worth reproduction:

Potpourri, Fille du Regiment....*Donizetti*
    Orchestra.
Song, with vocal quartet accompaniment...
Violoncello solo.........................
    Carlina Lenson.
Comic song and chorus.........*Weinman*
The Chicago Waltz................*Lenson*
    Composed for the occasion—Orchestra.
Vocal trio ....
    Messrs. Davis, Lombard and Dunham.
Polka—French song ....*Lenson*
    Orchestra.
Medley overture—Negro Airs..*Dyhrenfurth*
    Orchestra.
French Grand Chorus...........*Weinman*
(With full orchestral accompaniment, ar-
ranged from "Preciosa.")

To Julius Dyhrenfurth, violinist, was attributed by George P. Upton, the Chicago *Tribune's* first music critic and the author of a number of valuable books on music, the honor of first establishing musical culture in the West. It was in 1847 that Dyhrenfurth arrived in this city, and on Dec. 27 of that year he attended the New England festival, where George Davis, Frank Lumbard and others sang. Frank Lumbard was one of the Lumbard brothers, Frank and Jules, who for a considerable time before had been delighting the pioneers with "Old Shady." One of the veteran Chicago newspaper men tells of hearing Frank Lumbard's voice at an Ingersoll meeting for Hayes in 1876 at the old Exposition Building, when every note was perfect, every syllable distinct, "although I had not been able to catch a single syllable or sound coming from the mouth of the orator—I was too far away. At that time Frank Lumbard was getting old, his voice was of the political mass meeting variety, very gratifying to old farmers." Twenty years previous to that, at the initial performance in the New Metropolitan Hall, which was opened Dec. 26, 1854, with a concert by Frank Lumbard, assisted by the best musical talent in the city, the editor of the *Press* said: "This is the finest hall in Chicago. We would rather hear Frank Lumbard sing one evening in plain Saxon than hear all the Italian artists in Christendom screech and squeal until doomsday." If some-

what rash in their judgments, honesty then was a distinguishing feature.

The Philharmonic Society was formed in 1850 by John G. Shortall, Edward Stickney, Joseph Stockton, Edward Tinkham, John Le Moyne and others. Eight concerts were given, beginning Oct. 24, 1850, in the dining-room of the Tremont House, and then afterward in Metropolitan Hall and Bryan Hall. The last named stood on the site of the present Grand Opera House on Clark street. This series was the real initiation of organized musical culture, and Hans Balatka was the leader of the society.

Strangely named were the traveling concert troupes of those days, frequently called after families, such as the Berger, Peak, Sequin, Hutchinson family, the Alleghenies, etc. Sol Smith Russell, when eleven years old, is recalled as singing "Lanigan's Ball" in the Peak family bell ringers. Then the songs which were especially dear to the people were "Hazel Bell," "Nellie Gray" and "Rosalie, the Prairie Flower." The latter song is fondly commemorated, according to an old-timer in his lately printed recollections, in the name of "a shady street leading from Fifty-seventh street in the south division of the city to the Midway Plaisance, which, if one of the shortest, is certainly among the prettiest, most convenient and charming residence localities in Chicago."

P. T. Barnum, the circus king, brought musical companies here about 1840, when the Saloon was evidently the favorite hall.

As to vocal music, it seemed to have come into use in the first place as a relief to the tediousness of the wait between the acts or various portions of the program of dramatic performances. Singing of this character is spoken of as far back as 1839 at the Rialto on Dearborn street, and Joseph Jefferson junior, then a mere child, was a popular singer of the time.

Jan. 5, 1843, Mrs. Strangman, organist of the Catholic Church, gave a concert at the Saloon before mentioned and secured a good attendance.

The presence of an organ in Chicago is first mentioned as at St. James' Episcopal Church.

In the May of 1848 Mr. McVicker appeared in song and in dance. Difficult was it for those who in his later days were accustomed to sit through afternoons with that eminent, peculiar and great Chicagoan, enjoying conversations upon sociology, municipal affairs, history and personal recollections, basking, from the fund of his keen memory, in the most entertaining tales of old-time Chicago, to refrain from occasionally recalling to him the odd contrast afforded upon his entry into life in Chicago as a singing and dancing comedian and the dignity and state with which he unwittingly surrounded himself in later days. Incidentally Mr. McVicker was accustomed to declare that he owed more to David Swing than to any other mortal.

Jenny Lind was here with Barnum in 1851, a tour interesting in another way also, as she was accompanied by Mr. Theodore Thomas as solo violinist. Already for fourteen months in connection with Dr. William Mason and others he had been conducting a series of chamber concerts in New York.

Adelina Patti and Ole Bull made their first appearance in Chicago on April 21, 1868, at the Tremont Music Hall. As showing the extraordinary character of the entertainment given for those days in Chicago, with tickets of admission only $1 and $2 each, the program of the concert is here given:

Overture from Rossini's grand opera, "William Tell," performed by M. Strakosch.

Madame Sontag's celebrated cavatina, from Linda di Chamouni, "Luce di quest 'anima," sung by Adelina Patti.

"The Mother's Prayer"—a fantasia religioso, composed and executed by Ole Bull.

"Ah non giunge," the celebrated rondo finalle from "La Sonnambula," sung by Adelina Patti.

Paganini's famous "Witch Dance," performed by Ole Bull.

"The Banjo," a new capriccio characteristic, composed and performed by Maurice Strakosch.

"Comin' thro' the Rye," the famous Scotch ballad, sung by Adelina Patti.

Grand National Fantasie, for the violin alone, performed by Ole Bull.

Jenny Lind's "Echo Song," sung by Adelina Patti.

"The Carnival of Venice," by Ole Bull.

The record of musical events and occasional performances thus far brings us to the early attempts to give opera an appreciative hearing in Chicago. The first opera season here was, probably, the shortest on record, for it consisted but of a portion of one evening's entertainment and lasted only one hour. It was the night of July 30, 1850, that a company of which Mr. Manvers, Mr. Ghibelei, Mr. Lippert and Miss Bienti were members was announced to appear, with the assistance of a local chorus and orchestra. The bill for the opening night was "La Somnambula" and the place of presentation Rice's first theater, which was located on Randolph street. A goodly audience was present and all went well until the second act, when an alarm of fire arose, and less than an hour later the theater was burned to the ground with a loss made of $4,000.

Later in the same year appeared the following in the *Democratic Press* from the manager of another operatic troupe:

"The undersigned, acting in the name and in behalf of Madame De Vries and Signor Arditi, known by the name and style of the Artists' Association, has the honor of calling the attention of the musical community and of the citizens of Chicago in general to the fact that he has made arrangements with Mr. Rice, the manager, to have the Italian Opera Troupe on Thursday evening, October 27, at the Chicago Theater to perform the opera, in three acts, of Lucia di Lammermoor. The undersigned begs leave to introduce the following artists: The grand prima donna, Signorina R. De Vries; the favorite tenor, Signor Pozzolini; the tenor, Signor Arnoldi; the comprimaria, Madame Sidenbourg, late of Madame Albani's troupe; the unrivaled baritone, Signor

Taffenelli ; and the eminent basso, Signor Colletti. Also a grand and efficient chorus and grand orchestra. This great company numbers over forty members, the whole under the most able direction of the distinguished maestro, Signor Arditi.

"G. POGLIANI."

On Oct. 17, 1854, the New York Italian Opera Company stopped over for a one-night's entertainment on its road to St. Louis, New Orleans and other Southern cities. As for the financial success achieved, it was evidently not of any extraordinary character, for opera remained an absent amusement until an English company came to McVicker's Theater Sept. 27, 1858, and remained there for one week. Rosalie Durand was the soprano, Miss King alto, Frederic Lyster bass, while as for the tenor roles they all were sustained by Miss Georgia Hodson. During the following February sixteen nights of Italian opera were given. In the cast was Brignoli, of whom there is more to be said later. This was followed in April of the same year at North's Theater and again in July at the Met-ropolitan Hall with English opera given by a company which included as soprano Anna Miller, and with Aynsley Cook as bass. In the following December Italian opera opened at the Metropolitan Hall for one week and English opera at McVicker's for a period of two weeks, and in the same year (1859) the Castle and Campbell Opera Company was heard at a little theater formerly on the site of the Title and Trust Building, Washington street.

In the days which led up to the dark and stormy period of the Civil War a fine concert which was given to dedicate Bryan Music Hall, built where the Grand Opera House now stands, Sept. 17, 1860, is an occurrence well remembered by many veteran citizens.

Although what may perhaps be appropriately termed the progressive musical education and entertainment of the city was seriously interfered with during the period of the war, as was the experience in all art work in other cities, yet there were many notable musical happenings in Chicago during that time.

MUSIC IN CHICAGO DURING THE CIVIL WAR

Growth of Musical Organizations — Music Both Popular and Classical

When the war cloud burst in 1861, the popular pulse responded chiefly to the strains of martial music. The fife and drum roused men to form battalions to feed the red carnage of a hundred battlefields. But while the shrill music of civil strife was sounding Chicago had two sons who spoke to the nation in more pleasing and still more inspiring cadences. From Chicago it was that George F. Root, who was so lately with us, sent forth "Tramp, Tramp, Tramp, the Boys Are Marching," and "Just Before the Battle, Mother," to bedew the eyes of patriots and uphold the mighty arm of Abraham Lincoln. From Chicago it was also that Henry C. Work paid to the genius of Tecumseh Sherman and to the courage of his army the immortal tribute of "Marching Thro' Georgia." It was the brain of the latter that gave to the sorrowing nation that refrain of comfort singing

"Brave boys are they,
    Gone at their country's call,
And yet, and yet we cannot forget
That many brave boys must fall."

In speaking of what the Germans of early Chicago, and the great German-American community in later years, have done for the cause of music in this city, no one at all adequately acquainted with the subject can refrain from instantly recalling the busy life and invaluable work of Professor Hans Balatka.

In his personal work and influence alone, truly Hans Balatka was a musical force. In October, 1860, he had given a new lease of life to the Philharmonic Society, into association with which he had gathered as officers and members those who were most prominent in the society and musical circles of the city. The first president of the society was E. J. Tinkham, who three years later was succeeded by John V. Le Moyne, who held the position four years. Of the officers of the society whose active energies and labors contributed most to its success may be named Thomas B. Bryan, Julius Dyhrenfurth, John G. Shortall, Charles Larrabee, William H. Bradley, J. M. W. Jones and Otto Matz. Devoted entirely to instrumental music, singers of high reputation were added to the attractions of the concerts. In the first season, when seven concerts were given, the success of the society was wonderful. Madame Fabbri, one of the most noted Italian artists of the time, sang at two of the concerts. The sixth of the series also calls for special mention. It took place on April 13, 1861, the day following the bombardment of Fort Sumter. Notwithstanding the intense excitement which prevailed the Philharmonic concert drew an immense audience to the Bryan Hall. The completion of the program was approaching when Mr. Balatka roused the audience to an enthusiastic outburst by the playing of a number not on the program, "The Star Spangled Banner." There was a rising of the audience even as of one man and so great was the cheering that it absolutely drowned the music. A demand that the national song should be repeated brought with it the unfurling on the stage of the Stars and Stripes. Then following came an ovation which may be imagined but which cannot be described. At the final concert of the series on May 14 Mrs. Carrie Matteson once more sang the same song, flag in hand, and with a

result but little less striking than on the preceding occasion. Fashionable Chicago rejoiced in its Philharmonic Society and testified its appreciation by overflowing audiences year after year for seven winters until 1868, when the desire for orchestral music found a temporary lull in the more pronounced attractions of Italian opera. During those years much notable music of the great composers had been offered, including Beethoven's symphonies, first to eighth (third excepted), the third symphony of Mozart, Gade's fifth and seventh, Schumann's B flat and the Triumphal of Ulrich.

The Philharmonic Society offered its final concert in Metropolitan Hall on April 3, 1868, to an audience which, however appreciative, lacked the primary essential of encouragement toward further effort—numbers sufficient to pay expenses. The society, however, had served its purpose and done a great work.

Notwithstanding the exciting and troublous times of the Civil War, art and art life held its own in Chicago, and there were devotees and patrons of both painting and music, who, at much personal and pecuniary sacrifice, kept the work up, at least to the holding of the standards which had been achieved.

A letter of the pianist and composer, Louis Moreau Gottschalk, written in December, 1864, gives a good picture of our city at that time. Some extracts are culled: "Chicago is always *the* city of the West. Moore and Smith's new hall is inaugurated. All tickets were sold in advance and there was a great deal of enthusiasm. They talk of making a gigantic canal from the Atlantic coast which will thus enable European vessels to land directly at Chicago, eleven hundred miles in the interior of the country. Fifteen hundred houses are at this moment being built. The new Academy of Music which a very young man by the name of Crosby is building at his own expense (his colossal fortune of over two millions of dollars having been made in two years from speculations in whisky) will be inaugurated on the 17th of next May by the Italian Opera Company now in New York. The new hall will hold comfortably three thousand persons and rivals in richness of ornamentation that of New York. The inhabitants of Chicago pretend they will establish a permanent Italian opera company in the West. Notice to artists without engagements. Nothing can give you any idea of the feverish enterprise which exists here; everything is done in grand style, the stores are palaces, the hotels towns.

"A newspaper here attacks me because I play exclusively on Chickering's pianos, and thinks it shocking that I place maker's name on a plate that decorates the side exposed to public view. He adds facetiously that it is asserted that I intend to wear, suspended to my neck, a placard, upon which will be inscribed the name of my favorite maker." Mr. Gottschalk then goes into the divers merits of various makes of piano, explaining at the same time that a special make is possibly in some ways better adapted to the special talents of the individual.

The epoch marked by the erection and dedication of the Crosby Opera House and Art Gallery is one within the history of Chicago to which citizens who remember it justly refer with pride and admiration, and a history of the city, especially one dealing with the development and progress of art in Chicago, would be sadly incomplete without a full recognition of the great benefits conferred by Mr. U. H. Crosby and his brother, Mr. Albert Crosby, the fine arts patron and collector, at immense personal expense.

"If as an individual Uranus H. Crosby could do little to promote the progress of musical art among the people, yet he devoted a very large part of his private fortune to give to Chicago such a temple of the arts as put the city well away ahead of any place in the United States, save New York, and in point of beauty of construction and some exceedingly happy interior lines and arrangements "Crosby's" easily challenged comparison with any house in New York and was superior to most of them, as stated by Mr. Louis Gottschalk in his letter.

The site chosen for the opera house was a large double lot on the north side of Washington street, between Dearborn and State streets, and an adequate idea of the dimensions of the interior of the house may be gained when it is stated that the depth of the lot extended north to the alley just near the Unity Building. The late Mr. W. W. Boyington was selected as architect, and a brother architect, Mr. Frederick Baumann, was made superintendent of construction. Together they erected the stately white marble palace, which from its dedication to the time of its destruction in the great fire of 1871 was the recognized home of music and the fine arts in Chicago. Popularly speaking, the cost of the opera house was roundly estimated as $1,000,000, but it probably cost not more than half that sum, and some books have put the expenditure at no more than $376,000. Be that as it may, "Crosby's" gave to the public of Chicago a spacious and delightfully arranged auditorium, a large and well filled art gallery, containing many of the most notable art works, such, for instance, as the "Yosemite Valley," portraits by Healy and similarly rare and costly gems, while the building also afforded commodious and much-needed facilities for artists and teachers in a large number of studios and small halls. The palatial building, with its elaborate French roof and imposing sculptural grand entrance, was the pride of the fast growing metropolis, and the people gladly thronged it to hear opera as it was heard in cities at that time far more advanced. The assassination of Lincoln postponed the opening until April 20, 1866. The first opera given in that really great theater was "Il Trovatore," the artists being Clara Louise Kellogg, Zucchi, Lotti Susini and Brignoli, while the operas that followed were "Lucia," "Poliuto," "Martha," "Norma," "Sonnambula," "Faust," "Puritani," "Lucrezia," "Ernani" and "Fra Diavolo." In all respects the theater was a grand one, and of cheap seats there were a great many, and it was in the Crosby Opera House that hundreds had an opportunity to listen greedily to the music of Europe's greatest composers and singers. Night after night, season after season, there they sat, with their pleasant anticipations realized of hearing the great Christine Nilsson in "The Huguenots" and other of her famous roles.

But the opera house seriously embarrassed Crosby. With a rapidity characteristic of the West he landed on his financial feet, offering the

fair and straight was composed of ten of Chicago's most prominent citizens. Mr. Coolbaugh, the banker, was the chairman, and in charge of the wheel was Mr. John C. Dore. In one box the prizes were placed, in another the tickets. A blind man was in charge of the box containing the prizes—of minor prizes there was a number sufficient for each and every member of the Crosby House Art Association— while another had charge of the tickets for each number. Finally the prize of the opera house was drawn. It was a day or two later that the winner appeared in A. H. Lee, of Prairie du Rocher, Ill., who held the winning ticket out of the 210,000 numbers, but

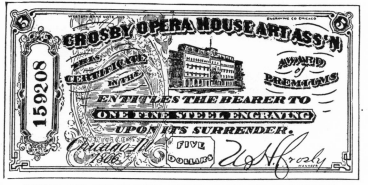

TICKET FOR THE FAMOUS CROSBY OPERA HOUSE LOTTERY.

scheme of a mammoth lottery for the house. This proposition dazzled America and delighted Chicago. Each ticket was to cost $5. The opera house, the lucky number drawn, would be his. A million for five! There was yet another lottery under the same auspices in which each ticket was but $1 and the prize to be won $10,000. But to return to the first mentioned. The West went at it to get that opera house. There were several delays and postponements, but finally the drawing was brought about January 23, 1867. It was a memorable occasion and the opera house was filled to overflowing with an excited throng. The committee to see that everything was

of which several thousand had been retained by the owner, Mr. Crosby, as chances undisposed of. Rich indeed was the prize, the pride of Chicago. The winner, Mr. Lee, welcomed a cash offer by Mr. Crosby, who again entered into possession. Here a mention of those who occupied the opera house stores fronting on Washington street will not be out of place. At 60 Washington street was the firm of J. Bauer & Co., at 67 were Root and Cady, while on the opposite side of entrance were H. M. Kinsley at No. 65 and W. W. Kimball at 63. The lottery event was one of the most daring and successful advertisements the city ever had, and it is very probable was responsible for an additional 100,000 in population.

German and English operas followed this speculative action of Crosby. Jarrett had astonished New York with the splendor and wickedness of "The Black Crook," "The White Fawn," "Undine," "The Grand Duchess" and "The Red Horseman." Other spectacular shows with brilliant tableaux followed, and as they were withdrawn in New York they were transferred to the stage of Crosby, where Bichl, the orchestra leader, attuned them to the best of music. Later his medleys for "The Field of the Cloth of Gold" and "The British Blondes" won the applause of all discriminating Chicagoans. For some reason it is hard to follow the regular theatrical orchestras of Chicago. They made far more bad music than good, there was a superabundance of cornet and trombone and the selections usually were but mediocre. But as to Bichl, it must be acknowledged that he was a talented theater orchestra leader. With him only the pretty things were culled, and he certainly knew how to arrange a most tuneful potpourri. Mr. George Stevens was one of the few thoroughly musicianly directors of that time. He was for many years the leader of the orchestra at Wood's Museum.

None the less Crosby's Opera House was ahead of the city at that time. It often stood vacant, for Chicago could not be at fortissimo all the time. Yet in those days there was no other building in the city that could have done justice to Parepa Rosa. Madame Parepa, when she appeared there in 1868, was supported by Castle and Campbell. Frequently has it been said there could not be a sweeter or more pleasing tenor than was William Castle in those days. Later tenors came here in trios—Lefranc, Capoul, Campanini, Tamagno, Wachtel, Brignoli—but Castle, who is still in Chicago as a director of the Chicago Musical College, had a voice which compared favorably with all and any of those mentioned.

When Nilsson came to Chicago for the first time she gave a concert at Crosby's, with the famous contralto, Annie Louise Clary, Brignoli and Vieuxtemps, the violinist.

But Crosby was not without enemies. In Chicago there was one named Wilbur F. Storey, who owned the Times, and made it celebrated as a newspaper. Crosby's Opera House was blacklisted by him and its usefulness seriously crippled.

Editor Storey had always opposed the interests of the opera house in the Times and when the "British Blondes" arrived and created a furore the attacks of the Times became bitter and personal. In return Lydia Thompson and Pauline Markham furnished the city with one of its biggest ante-fire sensations in "the horsewhipping of old Storey," as it was called. This episode occurred on Wabash avenue, near Harmon court, the two women being defended by two men, George Henderson and Archibald Gordon. Storey, however, who was with his wife, although already a white-haired man, made a brave and somewhat successful resistance against all four of his assailants. At the trial in the police court next morning the defendants were fined $100 each, but Lydia Thompson received an ovation at the opera house and drew bigger houses than ever.

There are a large number of other ante-fire events which call for recognition. In the fall of 1867 Haydn's "Creation" was given at St. Patrick's Church, on which occasion Robert Hall, organist of the church, was conductor, and he had the assistance of a full orchestral accompaniment under the leadership of A. J. Vaas. Soloists were Messrs. Nilsen and Sloan and the Misses Heinrichs, Robinson and Sommers. Another event to be recorded in the same year was the grand charity ball arranged and managed by P. S. Gilmore, of Boston, the leader of Gilmore's Brass Band. There was an orchestra of 100 musicians. A season of grand opera was given in October of the same year by Max Strakosch, the leading stars being Brignoli and La Grange. Its success was great, although some fault was found with the orchestra and the chorus. Following opera came four concerts by the Mendelssohn quartette, at all of which full audiences gathered.

Very ambitious was the attempt of Henry Ahner in 1857—he was well known as a gifted musician—to establish a full orchestra, but he failed in the achievement. Julius Unger followed in the same path, and with a better result, for he gave a number of concerts, in which he was assisted by Mrs. Emma Bostwick. Of infinitely greater influence, however, upon the musical future of this city was the establishment in 1858 of the Musical Union for vocal and instrumental music. The officers of the union were J. S. Platt, president; J. G. Lumbard, vice-president; C. M. Cady, conductor; A. L. Cole, librarian, and D. A. Kimbark, secretary and treasurer. Every year to 1866 a series of concerts was given, the power of the union became marked and its success appreciable. Operettas were many and a large number of miscellaneous concerts were heard, but of far greater worth were the oratorio productions, which included the "Messiah," "Elijah" and "Creation." The organization dying out under its old title of the Musical Union, Hans Balatka recognized the possibilities, and taking the principal members reorganized under the name of the Oratorio Society, a name which was well sustained throughout the winters of 1868, 1869 and 1870. Then happened the great fire, and this proved the forerunner of disaster. Reorganized after considerable difficulty on the west side of the city, a concert was projected, when on the evening preceding—it was in the winter of 1871—a fire consumed the building, and the society also went out of existence.

An auspicious opening to the year 1868 was the reappearance in Chicago of Ole Bull, after ten years' absence. His concerts were given in Farwell Hall, January 6 and 7, and were the reopening of his American tour. Max Strakosch was once more in the city at the end of May, 1868. La Grange and Brignoli were his principal artists and he also had Stella Bonheur, the French songstress; Sarti Lorini and the clarionet soloist, Cicconi. There were two concerts given, one of operatic selections and the other Donizetti's "Don Pasquali." In the first a chief feature was made of the grand romantic symphony for two pianos, entitled "The Sailor's Dream," composed by Brignoli and performed by him and Madame La Grange. During this time also a number of good concerts were being given by Mr. Goldbeck, who is still living in Chicago, in which the artists engaged were all local. Among the latter may be mentioned Mr. Lewis, violin; Mr. Root, cabinet organ, and Mr. Goldbeck, piano. Mrs. Matteson, Frank Lumbard and Mr. Nelson were the favorite singers.

In June of this same year Der Saengerfest, the sixteenth annual gathering of North America, was held in this city and aroused immense enthusiasm. Unquestionably it was a notable advance upon any that had preceded it, for from outside cities alone there came an attendance of over 2,000 presidents. Even from Europe came a number of delegates, while many of the prominent musicians of Germany sent, together with their letters of regret, original compositions to be performed at the festival. The concerts, which were begun with a jubilee overture of C. M. von Weber by the Chicago orchestra of 100 musicians, under the directorship of Hans Balatka, were given in the skating rink on Wabash avenue. One thousand voices composed the chorus. Momentous indeed was this meeting in the history of the city's music, as the Germans would say, being the *hauptsache*. German singing festivals were already remarkable for the range and varied resources of their musical repertoire. "From the sensuous waltzes and inspiring galops of Strauss to the incomprehensible 'music of the future' of Wagner; from the quasi sensational instrumentation of Meyerbeer to the fugues of Bach; from the Bacchanalian songs of Offenbach to the masses of Mozart and Haydn; from the light musical pictures which are given by the Turner Hall orchestra every Sunday in Chicago to the Mendelssohnian symphonies by Liebig's orchestra in Berlin on the same Sunday—there is nothing in a musical way that is impossible or unknown to the German." The situation was thus expressed by a writer of the time.

In September, 1868, Max Maretzek, with a combination company for Italian and German opera, gave a three weeks' season with a fair amount of success. Weber's "Der Freischutz" for the first time in several years was the event of the season, but it was hardly satisfactory, the chief failing being the need of another prima donna in addition to Madame Ritter and Madame Cellini, who consequently were forced to do duty both on the German and Italian evenings.

In September, 1868, also the Orchestral Union concerts were instituted by Hans Balatka, and the first series of five was given in the Library Hall. He succeeded in bringing together an orchestra of forty-seven instruments. Public rehearsals were held, and to these latter season ticket holders possessed the right of free admission. The first concert, while unremunerative in a financial sense, was a decided success from a musical standpoint. Mr. Goldbeck greatly distinguished himself in his concerto for piano with orchestra accompaniment, which was decidedly his most ambitious effort up to that time. In November a three weeks' season was given by Riching's English opera troupe, which included Chicago's favorite tenor, William Castle, among its members, and also Mrs. Bernard, Mrs. Sequin, Miss Abell, Messrs. Campbell, Peakes, Bernard and Sequin. One of the principal successes of the company, "The Lily of Killarney," was sung for the first time in Chicago for the benefit of Mr. Castle.

During this year a couple of highly successful concerts were given by Ole Bull, and Parepa Rosa appeared for a single concert at the Library Hall in December. In the company were Carl Rosa, the violinist; Brookhouse Bowler, the English tenor; Ferranti, the buffo, and George Colby, pianist, as well as the famous cornet player, Levy. Although the night of the concert followed a terrific gale and snowstorm, still a great audience attended, one worthy in every respect such an artist as Parepa Rosa. In such circumstances no great difficulty was experienced in inducing another concert by the same company at the close of the following week.

Dull times followed, and in 1871, after a long season of inaction, U. H. Crosby determined to give his theater a boom, and, it was said, spent $80,000 in its refurnishing and redecorating. A reopening with Theodore Thomas' orchestra was advertised for Monday, October 9, 1871. A veteran Chicago newspaper man tells how "at 3 a. m. of Tuesday, October 10, 1871, I was on my way to the lake front, carrying my red Boosey books of the opera. I looked up Washington street and saw a sheet of crimson flame. My opera house—like so many others, having a dollar to spare, I had gambled and with fond hope that I would prove the fortunate winner—where, too, so many happy, inspiring and ennobling hours had been spent—my opera house was gone. I wish that the conflagration had spared me that sorrow and its attendant calamities to popular music."

Theodore Thomas and his orchestra had been engaged to reopen the renovated and magnificently decorated Crosby Opera House on that memorable Monday of the historic fire. Of this occasion George P. Upton wrote in the *Tribune*: "The opera house had been brilliantly decorated and renovated throughout, until it had no equal for beauty and richness in the country, and Mr. Thomas was to dedicate it anew. It was lit up for the first time on the evening of October 8, and two or three hours later it was in ashes. Mr. Thomas and his orchestra reached the Twenty-second street depot just after the great fire broke out, and the conductor immediately made his arrangements to go South, resting that night in Joliet.

Just a year later, October 7, 1872, Mr. Thomas returned to Chicago to open the new Aiken's Theater, giving a series of eight concerts, assisted by George L. Osgood. Many important works were given, and music of Raff, Berlioz, Liszt and Wagner, up to that time practically unknown in the city. Under the management of Messrs. Carpenter and Sheldon five concerts were given in 1873. Later in the same year a Wagner concert was given and the opportunity to hear that which was already recognized as the music that was to be was enthusiastically embraced. On March 17, being still under the same lecture course management of Messrs. Carpenter and Sheldon, three concerts in conjunction with Rubinstein, the mighty piano king, were received as the concerts of such an organization deserved to be. At the end of October of the same year another Thomas season began, the Kingsbury Hall being dedicated with a series of eight concerts, in which M. W. Whitney, the bass, was assisting soloist. For the last concert also part was taken by the Apollo Club, and the result was so successful that the club arranged a series of four concerts in February, 1874, in all of which music of the highest order was given.

MUSIC AND MUSICAL CONDITIONS AFTER THE GREAT FIRE

Entertainments in the Churches—Formation and Work of the Leading Choral and Orchestral Societies, the Apollo Club, the Beethoven Society, and the Chicago Quintette Club

The theaters and public halls destroyed in the great fire included Crosby's Opera House, McVicker's Theater, the Dearborn Theater and Wood's Museum, all on the south side of the river, and the Turner Hall and German Hall on the north. The loss of the opera house, which was held in especial pride and affection, has been hitherto touched upon. During the winter following all the concerts, and in fact every sort of standard entertainment, were given in churches. Two sections of the city had been established, the south and the west divisions, and these were separated by a considerable territory, over which the fire ruins still held sway. For the south side the center of musical activity was the Michigan Avenue Baptist Church, near to Twenty-second street, while for the west side the Union Park Congregational Church on Ashland ave. was a similar center. All through that never to be forgotten time, the winter of 1871-72, the Thomas concerts and all other musical happenings took place at either one or the other of those two churches. Hans Balatka Oratorio Society, which had done much good work also came near to destruction as an effect of the fire, for its library was totally lost, the members scattered and the leader for the time thoroughly discouraged, had removed to Milwaukee. The managers, however, Orlando Blackman and A. R. Sabin, endeavored to resuscitate the organization. With kindly generosity the Handel and Haydn Society, of Boston, came to the Chicago society's aid and donated a considerable number of books, including sets of "Israel in Egypt," "The Messiah," "David" and other oratorios, as well as miscellaneous selections. A perfectly new start was made. J. A. Butterfield was elected conductor and W. S. B. Matthews for organist. At last a performance of Handel's "Messiah" was given May 16, 1872, in the Union Park Congregational Church. On this occasion the solo artists were Mrs. Clara Huck and Mrs. George B. Carpenter, sopranos;

S. C. Campbell and James Gill, bassos, and J. H. Bischoff, tenor. A creditable chorus was provided of about 150 voices and an orchestra numbering twenty-two. A repetition of the program was given a few weeks later in the Michigan Avenue Baptist Church. Sufficient success was won to appear to offer good augury for the future, but evidently this the fates forbade. Interest was difficult to sustain. Rehearsals were resumed in the autumn of 1872, and a miscellaneous program prepared for a concert in the First Congregational Church on a Thursday evening in January, 1873. But just an hour before the concert was to have begun the building took fire and was burnt to the ground. Not alone was the newly gathered library destroyed, but the opportunity of obtaining some financial support was gone also. Its decease was slow and gradual, for Orlando Blackman continued rehearsals, even with his few members, just so long as it was possible.

The Apollo Musical Club is at once the most deservedly popular, as well as the largest, local musical organization of the city. Its history is certainly worthy of extended attention.

To Silas G. Pratt belongs the honor of the idea which, nourished and fostered by himself and a number of gentlemen he had interested, bore full fruit in the foundation of the Musical Club. An initial meeting was held in the summer of 1872 in the music store of Lyon & Healy, which then was situate on the corner of Sixteenth street and Wabash avenue. The purpose avowed was the formation of a society composed of male voices and modeled on the German Maennerchor to devote itself to the study of male choruses and part songs. A proper organization was made, the name and constitution of the Apollo Club, of Boston, being adopted. Before the first concert, which was given in January, 1873, a chorus composed of the following gentlemen had been formed: S. G. Pratt, George P. Upton, Charles T. Root, Charles N. Pring, Warren C. Coffin, Frank A. Bowen, Philo A. Otis,

George C. Stebbin, F. S. Pond, Charles C. Curtiss, Fritz Foltz, J. R. Ranney, E. H. Pratt, William H. Coulson, Louis Falk, Harry Gates, C. C. Phillips, J. S. Marsh, W. W. Boynton, S. E. Cleveland, Theodore F. Brown, H. Rocher, A. L. Goldsmith, William Sprague, A. R. Sabin, William R. Allen, John A. Lyndon, William Cox, L. M. Prentiss, Frank G. Rohner and Frank B. Williams.

The first officers of the society were George P. Upton, president; William Sprague, vice-president; F. A. Bowen, treasurer; C. C. Curtiss, secretary; W. C. Coffin, librarian; Fritz Foltz, S. E. Cleveland, P. A. Otis, musical committee, and A. W. Dohn, conductor.

In regard to A. W. Dohn, he had formerly been conductor of the Mendelssohn Society, and when the Apollo Club had been in existence but a few weeks S. G. Pratt resigned. Mr. Dohn was immediately chosen to the directorship. Twofold were the new society's objects, social entertainment following as a direct outcome of excellence in singing. No public concerts were given, at first only associate members being admitted, but these at one time reached the goodly number of 1,500. Following is the program of the first entertainment which was given at Standard Hall, January 21, 1873: "Loyal Song," Kuecken; "Always More," Seifert; "Beware," Gerschner; "Champagne Song," Schroeter; "The Miller's Daughter," Haertel. In every sense of the word the concert proved a success and at the club's second concert on February 25, 1873, Standard Hall was overcrowded with an audience composed of every one then best known in the city's social life. On this occasion the soloists were Fritz Foltz, Mrs. O. K. Johnson, Mrs. O. L. Fox and Mrs. Anna Mehlig, the last named presiding at the piano. Regarding Mrs. Mehlig, her appearance on this occasion was an unexpected one. Recognized among the audience she was induced to take the place to which she was so well accustomed. With the third concert given on April 16, the good promise of the two preceding ones was well sustained and considerable augmentation in the chorus discovered. An extra concert closing the first season was given on June 5 and was a very fitting finale. Concerning this occasion the Chicago *Tribune* said: "The club has now finished its first season. Its success has been very remarkable, considering that it has been in existence so short a time. The spirit and enthusiasm of its members and the equal spirit and invincible determination of its excellent conductor, Mr. Dohn, promise still more successful efforts in the next season."

For the opening of the second season an occasion was made to inaugurate the new Kingsbury Music Hall, the first distinctively musical hall to be constructed since the fire. The concert took place on September 30, 1873. Great progress was shown in the chorus work, and the public was afforded a chance to hear three such singers as Mrs. Huck, Mrs. Farwell and Mrs. Johnson, and three most accomplished instrumentalists in Mr. Goldbeck, Mr. Lewis and Mr. Eichheim.

In conjunction with the Theodore Thomas Orchestra a series of concerts was begun February 17, 1873, at McCormick's Hall. The vocal numbers of the opening concert were by Schumann, Schubert and Beethoven. In Schumann's "Omnipotence" the Apollo Club had the assistance of the Germania Maennerchor, forming together a chorus of eighty male voices. An extra concert took place February 18, 1874, at which Schumann's "Paradise and the Peri" was produced. Again the accompaniment was furnished by Theodore Thomas' Orchestra and the following were the soloists: Miss Clara Doria, Myron W. Whitney, Mrs. O. K. Johnson, Mrs. O. L. Fox, Miss Ella A. White, Mrs. T. E. Stacey, Miss Anne Lewis, Messrs. Toltz and Ruehling. At the end of 1874 the president of the club, George P. Upton; the vice-president, William Sprague, and the conductor, A. W.

Dohn, resigned, and Theodore F. Brown and Carl Bergstein became respectively vice-president and conductor. Mr. Bergstein retained the position for only a short time, and William L. Tomlins accepted the musical directorship of the club. Most fortunate did the appointment prove in every regard. Born in London, England, February 4, 1844, Mr. Tomlins had even in early youth shown a rare genius for music. At nine he was a choir boy, at eleven he had taken up the harmonium and he received an appointment as organist. Two years later he became choir master also, and at seventeen conducted his first oratorio. Careful tuition was in no ways neglected, for he had the benefit in his studies of the personal direction of Sir George Macfarren, at that time president of the Royal Academy of Music. He was an attendant also of the Tonic Sol Fa College, and at twenty-two became a member of its governing board. How strong were his musical endowments, how rare was his possession of the ability to lead and direct and how capable of responsibility was evidenced in Mr. Tomlins' appointment, when only twenty-three, as government inspector and examiner of music teachers in the public schools. His particular department was that of theory of music and harmonium playing, but he was also vested with authority over the other examiners in musical subjects of less responsibility than his own. In January, 1870, when he was twenty-five years of age, he came to New York and met with the vicissitudes usual to the musician who is locally unknown. In addition to some vocal teaching he obtained some work as organist and conductor. At this time Mason & Hamlin were introducing a masterpiece of reed work, containing seven full sets of vibrators and every facility for orchestral effect. Mr. Tomlins' mastery of the harmonium was brought to the firm's attention and an engagement was at once offered him to go on tour with a concert company using the new instrument. His success was immediate and the greatest interest everywhere followed his playing. At last Chicago was visited. Mr. Tomlins was conductor of the Richings-Bernard Old-Folks' Concert Company, and already had been afforded such opportunities to display his abilities as a vocal teacher that he was recognized as the artistic genius of the company. Just when he arrived in the city a change in the directorship of the Apollo Club became necessary and Mr. Tomlins was offered and accepted the position. Since that time he has been an inseparable factor in Chicago's musical advance. His first concert as leader of the club was given on November 17, 1875. To him difficulty was only another name for opportunity. He found a small male chorus of extremely limited capacity, and he saw that if his work were to be conscientiously performed the society must recommence *ab initio*. Difficult music was for the time being dropped, simple part songs being taken up instead. Every phase of choral work was considered and given proper study. He fought opposition and had to meet criticism, but, convinced that he had set out on the correct road, he pursued the even tenor of his way and scored victory. The history of the Apollo Club became the story of Mr. Tomlins' efforts. Recognition, if slow, was decided, and as a strength and an influence no one can claim a higher place than W. L. Tomlins. Music to him was a method of speech, every intonation meant a something. He inspired confidence, and what he undertook ensured success. Of his later work, more hereafter.

For officers in 1875 the Apollo Club possessed G. W. Chamberlin, vice-president; E. G. Newell, secretary; William Cox, treasurer; E. D. Messinger, librarian, and William L. Tomlins, musical director.

Its board of management was composed of W. S. Elliott, Jr., L. M. Prentiss, G. W. Chamberlin, L. D. Collins and E. G. Newell, music committee; R. M. Clark, Philo A. Otis and R. S. Clark; social committee, C. F. Matteson, W. S. Elliott, Jr., Philo A. Otis

and F. S. Pond. That a ladies' chorus should be added was a fixed idea with Mr. Tomlins, and, once convinced of its necessity, to the achievement to such a character as his was but a matter of time. A number of ladies were trained, and a first appearance made at an extra concert given for the benefit of Mr. Tomlins on June 8, 1876. On the day following the Chicago *Tribune* had this to say: "Mr. Tomlins has succeeded with his mixed chorus exactly as he has with his male chorus, namely, in perfect enunciation, fine phrasing and shading, promptness of attack, steadiness of time and development of power. The enthusiasm of the chorus was unlimited, showing a very remarkable magnetism and inspiration on Mr. Tomlins' part." A move was made to the club's new rooms in the American Express Company's building on Monroe street November 27, 1876, and in those quarters the club remained until the Central Music Hall was opened in 1879. Very decided was the advance made as year followed year, and there was a generous contribution to the public musical exchequer in the production of the most important works of the day. Handel's "Acis and Galatea," in December, 1878, was one of the first achievements by the society, but it was only the forerunner of a great number of others of little minor importance. What the Apollo Society has done for the city it is impossible to estimate. Local artists have been given opportunities and the public has had the chance afforded to hear the greatest musical works of the day interpreted by the artists who had made the various characters their own.

Even as the Apollo Club brings before us involuntarily and inseparably William L. Tomlins, so does the Beethoven Society recall the great work of Carl Wolfsohn. This society founded as an organization of active members, male and female, for the production of choral works and with an associate membership to afford a fitting audience and all due appreciation, takes its place as a factor in musical advancement second only to the Apollo Club.

Carl Wolfsohn was visiting Chicago in the winter of 1872, and to that circumstance the Beethoven Society owed its life. A musical scholar of rarely rich attainment, to whom his art was a life enthusiasm, a man of great personal magnetism, Mr. Wolfsohn was able to inspire others with like sentiments and aspirations. His own enthusiasm was transmitted to every member of the Beethoven Society, and the work done was a remarkable testimony of what enthusiasm under proper regulation is able to accomplish.

Mr. John G. Shortall was organizer of the Beethoven Club, and among the educated women connected with it were Mrs. Augustus Eddy, Mrs. Arthur Caton, Jessie Haskell, now Mrs. Fuller, and Miss Nina Lunt.

The mixed chorus of which Mr. Wolfsohn took charge culminated most successfully in the Beethoven Society the first great mixed chorus this city ever had, and whose purpose was the cultivation of the highest standard of choral work and the elevation and advancement of the public musical taste in every direction of the art. Not alone was he able to produce a highly trained chorus, but in his monthly reunions and piano recitals were afforded musical treats of the highest order. An active membership of 200, in which were many of the best voices in the city, makes it altogether unnecessary to speak of the standing of the club.

Three choral concerts were given each year by the Beethoven Society, and there were also monthly reunions, at which chamber music was given, opportunity being at the same time afforded for social intercourse. As at each of these latter evenings at least one new work of importance was given, the educational and stimulative effect on the members is not difficult to understand. During one of the earlier seasons, a recollection that lingers fondly in every memory, Mr. Wolfsohn completed the remarkable undertaking, previously performed in New York and Philadelphia, of playing the entire thirty-three sonatas of Beethoven, for that time a most remarkable feat. This was in the spring of 1874, beginning on April 11 and finishing on June 13, in a series of ten recitals in Standard Hall, at the corner of Michigan avenue and Thirteenth street. The following season Schumann, even less familiar than Beethoven, was taken up in a similar way. Ten recitals were given in the Beethoven Society rooms, Nos. 168 and 170 State street, beginning March 13, 1875, and closing May 15. As a relief to the monotony of the piano, no matter how great the executant, forty-four of the songs of this composer were sung during the series, and of these many were first productions. During 1876 Chopin was the chosen master, and, however conscientiously carried through, the increased burden upon the pianist seemed to be productive of less popular approval. Toward this result it may be that satiation with piano music, as a consequence of Mr. Wolfsohn's prodigious labors, was a cause. Resultant upon Mr. Wolfsohn's work and coincident with the popularity he had created for piano music, were the visits of several of the greatest virtuosi of the time. Enthusiastic, our great Chicago Beethoven exponent failed to observe, or, observing, failed to heed, the signs of the time. In 1877 he projected a series of twenty-four historical piano recitals to cover the whole range of pianoforte literature, but he found it a simple impossibility to retain a sufficiency of public interest and the series was never completed. Through all this time the monthly reunions rich in all that was best in chamber music and possessed of the same social features as when the society was originally launched, went on uninterruptedly. For eleven years the Beethoven Society remained in existence, and by its work an imprint was left that time will not efface. Still at last the active members were reluctantly forced to admit the better results elsewhere obtained, and acknowledging the justice of the criticism made, which, it must be acknowledged, had become unsparing, they resigned. Such was the end of the Beethoven Society.

How great was Mr. Wolfsohn's contribution to Chicago's cultivation of chamber music is fully acknowledged, and it becomes necessary to speak of several others who took only little less part in that process of musical education at that time. Of these Mrs. Regina Watson was one of the most prominent leaders for the benefit of music in the city. She quickly made and retained a reputation for musicianship and scholarship.

Interesting in connection with the Beethoven Society was the debut of Fannie Bloomfield, then ten years of age, and who has since made herself famous as Mrs. Bloomfield Zeisler. One of the leaders in the crusade for a higher musical standard was William Lewis, who, anterior to the fire, had been prominent as a violinist in the musical evenings of Root and Cady, the chief sellers of musical works at that time. A Devonshire man by birth, he was the inheritor of much musical talent from his father, who was a violoncello player of acknowledged ability. The son first distinguished himself as a singer and it was while a chorister at Exeter Cathedral at the age of ten that the organist found him worthy of a thorough musical education. Later the viola was studied with Mr. Wonacott, a man of much reputation in his art, but in 1850, with his family, he came to America and it was in the year following at a musical convention in Monroeville, Ohio, that he obtained the notice of M. C. Cady, who proved a true friend. A number of good engagements were secured, and were filled with gratifying success. A vacation taken by the Continental Vocalists, of which he was a member, gave him the chance to obtain some lessons from Theodore Thomas in New York. In 1862 he came to Chicago and for a time was engaged in merchandise, but his bent was evidently in a different direction, and he was also at this time a member of the Philharmonic Society. He accepted a position with the firm of Root & Cady and was about to become a partner in the firm when the great fire brought what was almost financial ruin and which the panic of a couple of years later completed. The firm of Root & Lewis was then formed, but in 1875 with George F. Root and Chandler & Curtiss the firm became absorbed with the Root & Sons Music Company. Three years later Mr. Lewis retired and with E. C. Newell founded the Chicago Music Company, which added to its business, in later years, the sale of pianos. As a violinist Mr. Lewis was at the time thus described: "The possessor of a natural genius for the violin which, patiently and laboriously cultivated, has made him an acknowledged artist in his line." In William Lewis Mr. Wolfsohn found a congenial co-worker. Soon after this arrived Eichheim the 'cellist, and it was to these three great artists that the reunions of the Beethoven Club were much indebted.

The Chicago Quintette Club an organization for chamber music, was for a long time the most important and certainly the longest lived of any organization of its kind in the city. Its members were Miss Agnes Ingersoll, M. Eichheim, Herman Allen, William Allen and Mr. Pellage. To the first mentioned and to Mr. William Lewis, who gave the ablest co-operation, the Quintette owes its existence and its success. Founded Jan. 6, 1879, it gave for the first time in Chicago, Rheinberger trio in B flat opus 121, trio in D opus 34, quintette opus 114 and quartette for strings opus 89, Rubinstein sonata opus 13, sonata opus 39, quartette opus 66, Brahm's trio opus 8, Reinecke quintette opus 83, Kiel trio opus 33, Scharwenka trio opus 1, quartette opus 37, Onslow sextette in E flat, Raff quartette for strings opus 192 No. 2, quartette opus 202, No. 2; trio No. 3 opus 155, Jadassohn quintette opus 70, trio opus 59, Ries suite piano and violin No. 3, Saint Saens trio opus 18, sonata for piano and 'cello.

The success of the quintette was immediate, its audiences somewhat limited at first in numbers soon increased until the entertainment offered took its proper place as one of the leading musical features of Chicago's artistic life. Of those who composed the quintette club more extended mention is here well in place. Miss Agnes Ingersoll, born in New York, had a natural talent for music carefully cultivated by an elder sister who was a pupil of the famous Zundel. Piano studies were taken under S. B. Mills, of New York, and afterwards with Robert Goldbeck, of this city. Her further education, both theoretical and practical was obtained abroad from Reinecke, of the Conservatory of Leipsic, Jadassohn, of the same city, as well as other work in Berlin and in Paris. Her connection with the Quintette Club has been before referred to but she has at all times been a leader in concerts and other musical entertainments throughout the city.

In no city of this continent is a true artist surer of an appreciative audience than in Chicago and in no department of music has this been more thoroughly demonstrated than in that of the piano. Few have been the years in which some great celebrity has not been heard and the tour of a master nowadays would be strangely incomplete were a visit to this city omitted. This commenced many years since, for in 1872 visits from Teresa Carreno and the incomparable Rubinstein delighted everyone in whom artistic instinct had found the smallest foothold. Carreno appeared under the auspices of the Weber piano house in connection with her husband, the great violinist, Emil Sauret, at the Michigan Avenue Baptist Church. Rubinstein on Dec. 2, at Aiken's Theater at the same time as Wieniawski, the violinist. Rubinstein's mighty power moved the crowded audiences delighting to honor the great virtuoso, to an extent that can never be forgotten by anyone who was so fortunate as to hear him. In 1874 at an Apollo Club concert Miss Julia Rive was heard for the first time in this city, and did much to popularize the study of the piano. The Thomas Orchestra brought Madame Madeline Schiller in the year following. Hans von Bulow, as eccentric as mighty in his genius, was followed by Madame Essipoff. Then at the opening of Hershey Hall, Jan. 21, 1877, the great-

est of our American pianists, William H. Sherwood, began a connection with music in this city that has continued uninterruptedly up to the present time and in which his good and powerful influence is universally recognized.

It was in 1876 that the Hershey Music school was opened and Clarence Eddy produced with Messrs. Eichheim and Lewis much music of the highest character. Mention of the Hershey school makes necessary some reference to its distinguished founder, Miss Sara Hershey, who is famous alike as musician, pianist and vocal instructor. She was born in Pennsylvania and received her education in the city of Philadelphia. With strong musical inclinations from her very childhood she first took up music as her profession at Muscatine, Iowa, but still continuing her studies and frequently going east for that purpose.

In 1867 she went to Berlin placing herself under Professor Sterns in the Conservatory and taking vocal instruction from Jennie Mayer. Then followed study with Kullak and in vocalization with Dr. Engel; declamation was taken up with Schwartz, the leading German elocutionist and the royal court actor Beandahl in Berlin. Over three years were spent in the latter city and then on to Milan where singing was pursued with Professor Gerli and in the class of Lamperti. Having every reason to believe herself conversant with the Italian method of opera singing she next spent some months with Madame Sainton Dolby in London, England, studying oratorio work and the English methods generally. Her determination had been made to settle in Chicago, but the great fire temporarily altered this. She remained in New York for two years at concert and church work and also in teaching at the Packer Institute, Brooklyn. For some time she had charge of the Pennsylvania Female College at Pittsburg and therefore it was not until 1875 that Mrs. Hershey came to Chicago and then immediately she founded the Hershey School of Musical Art.

OPERA AND FESTIVAL

Development of the May Musical and Opera Festivals—Erection and
Dedication of Central Music Hall—Dr. Florence Ziegfeld and
the Chicago Musical College—Conditions Leading to the
Founding of the Auditorium by Ferdinand W. Peck—
Its Construction and Dedication—Grand Opera
and Classical Concert

The various musical festivals have undoubtedly borne a most important part in the city's musical history and when at times interest has seemingly been flagging these have once more roused it into spirited life. Gilmore's band at the musical festival organized June, 1873, in celebration of the opening of the newly erected terminal by the Chicago, Rock Island & Pacific Railroad Company and the Grand Pacific hotel, was the first of these occasions. For the four concerts which were given the band was augmented to the number of one hundred with such material as was easily procurable and the services of a local chorus of one thousand voices directed by J. A. Butterfield were also utilized. Mr. Butterfield was not inexperienced for his charge as the Chicago contingent had done its work a short time previously at the Boston Jubilee. Crowded audiences testified in no half hearted manner their appreciation at once of such choruses as "See the Conquering Hero Comes," "The Heavens are Telling," "Hallelujah," and at the same time the fact that superior to all misfortunes Chicago enterprise and pluck were ready not alone for work but also for enjoyment and life.

Several years later in the great hall then known as the Moody and Sankey Tabernacle, 238-246 Monroe street, Theodore Thomas and the Apollo Musical Club jointly managed by Carpenter and Sheldon and with a chorus trained by William L. Tomlins, a musical festival was given far more ambitious in design and of greater practical influence in its execution. In

addition to the chorus of the Apollo Club, which for the occasion was enlarged to four hundred voices, a chorus of school children was used, but the latter addition proved to be unsatisfactory. The Thomas Orchestra consisted at the time of sixty musicians and Mrs. H. M. Smith, Williams Winch, Myrom W. Whitney and Miss Anna Louise Cary were the soloists. The choral features of the festival are worthy of recall. At the first concert "Calm Sea" by Rubinstein, male voices, "Ye Spotted Snakes," by Macfarren, female voices, "Hunting Song," by Benedict, full chorus and the first half of Mendelssohn's "St. Paul." In this also was for the first time introduced in Chicago Siegfried's "Funeral March" from Wagner's Gotterdammerung. At second concert Gounod's cantata, "By Babylon's Wave," Arthur Sullivan's "On Sea and Shore," and "Bridal Chorus," from Lohengrin. Third concert, Beethoven's "Second Symphony," scene from second act of "Orpheus" and a considerable portion of Handel's "Israel in Egypt."

On the opening, Dec. 4, 1879, of the Central Music Hall its desirability in all ways as the hall for all essentially musical entertainments became at once acknowledged. Built under the personal supervision of the late George B. Carpenter, whose energy and enthusiasm had originated, there he remained as lessee and manager until his death. Many new and very desirable features were possessed by the Central Music Hall in addition to its great merit in location.

Dear are the recollections of the Central Music Hall to all music loving Chicagoans. Here Adelina Patti first appeared on her return to America, and concerts were given there also by Carlotta Patti, Emma Thursby, Julie Rive-King, Teresa Carreno, Chevalier de Kontski, Clara Louise Kellogg, Bernhard Listemann, Camilla Urso, Brignoli, Remenyi, Joseffy, Wilhelmj, Cary and numerous other most celebrated musicians. Central Music Hall has also been largely identified in Chicago's musical advancement because Dr. Florence Ziegfeld there for so many years made his headquarters. His college, the Chicago Musical College, may be fairly called the parent of all the others. Easy is it to be believed that his pupils have formed a major portion of the musical forces that have made the whole West melodious. For thirty years or more he has imported a good share of the musical talent that has found a home in Chicago, and which in turn has established schools of its art. For over thirty years he has united with the cause of music the good will of the influential classes of Chicago and his seasons of concerts, usually in the Central Music Hall or previous to that in the First Methodist Church, have been noteworthy for their enormous aggregate attendances. Dr. Ziegfeld was the means of bringing to Chicago Louis Falk, Eliodoro de Campi, William Castle, L. Gaston Gottschalk, J. J. Hattstaedt, Carl Hild Jacobsohn, Josephine Chatterton, August Hyllested, while later there have been Hans von Schiller, John Ortengren, Felix Borowski, Bernhard Listemann and Arthur Friedheim. And these are but a few of a great host of accomplished musicians for which Chicago is indebted to Dr. Ziegfeld.

Dr. Florence Ziegfeld enjoyed the friendship for many years of Allen C. Fowler, chairman of its board of directors, one of the grandest looking and one of the noblest of men. Mr. Fowler is said to have given to Ziegfeld's public entertainments and commencements a distinction and elegance that attracted all people of refinement.

The North American Sangerbund held its twenty-second grand festival in this city June 29 and 30, July 1, 2 and 3, 1881. Max Bruch's Odysseus was the first concert, the second an afternoon miscellaneous, the third, Mendelssohn's "Elijah" (the first part) followed by a miscellaneous concert in which in addition to the North American Sangerbund of 1,500 voices, Miss Annie Louise Cary, Mme. Peschna Leutner and Mr. W. Candidus, took part. The fourth, fifth and sixth concerts were also miscellaneous in character and for the concluding concert on the Saturday there were given the introduction and third scene from Lohengrin and Beethoven's symphony in D minor (No. 9, opus 125). This festival marked the twenty-fifth anniversary of the debut of Hans Balatka as a festival conductor. He had done much not alone for the music of the German societies but also for music generally in the West. Born March 5, 1827, in Hoffnungstall near Olmutz, Moravia, his first instruction in the theory of music had been obtained from Ritter von Dietrich. In 1846 he was already giving lessons in music and was conductor of the "Academische Gesangverein." For a short time he was in Vienna studying under Sechter and Proch. In 1848 he came to the United States and settled in Milwaukee, founding there two years later the Musikverein, which proved one of the most successful musical associations of the United States and which for ten years under his leadership gave symphonies, oratorios and operas. Invited in 1860 to conduct Mozart's "Requiem" in the cathedral of Chicago the success won induced the lovers of music to establish a Philharmonic Society with Mr. Balatka as leader. His services as a conductor were soon in great request, he being given charge not only of the "Musical Union" and the "Oratorio Society," but also of the Germannia Mannerchor, Orpheus and "Liederkranz." Series of symphony concerts, oratorios and general concerts were given by him each year. It should have been mentioned that preceding the festival just spoken of he had conducted ten festivals of the North American Sangerbund, the first being at Cleveland in 1856. Towards the success of this festival his remarkable energies and indefatigable work were the main factors.

Opera appeals to a constituency far larger than the merely musical. The social side of the question is strongly pronounced and then there is the happy combination of the musical with the dramatic. The advent of Theodore Wachtel was the first event in the annals of opera to follow the fire. This took place at the Globe Theater on Desplaines street, Feb. 12, 1872, the first performance being Trovatore. Then an interval to Jan. 6, 1873, when at the Academy of Music an English company appeared. Pauline Lucca at McVickers a month later, when Mignon was given for the first time with Madame Lucca and Clara Louise Kellogg in cast was an occasion long remembered. In January of the following year, 1874, Christine Nilsson sang in opera here, among the other artists being Campanini, Del Puente, Capoul and Miss Cary. Aida was the leading attraction but Nilsson as Marguerite in Faust and as Mignon were attractions of little if any less interest. Madame Albani was the prima donna of 1875, in which year on Jan. 21, Chicago heard Wagner's Lohengrin for the first time. Madame Pappenheim and Charles Adams gave a German season at Hooley's in November, 1877. Wagner's "Flying Dutchman," "Tannhauser," and "Lohengrin," "The Huguenots," and "Robert the Devil" of Meyerbeer, and Beethoven's "Fidelio." There was little of operatic moment until the season of Jan. 13 to Feb. 1, 1879, when, associated with Manager J. H. Haverly, Col. J. H. Mapleson brought his company from Her Majesty's Theater, London. With an orchestra of fifty-seven chosen musicians, a chorus of forty and a troupe double the size of any preceding, Etelka Gerster, Ma-

dame Lablache and the world's operatical leading as principals, success was never for a moment in doubt. I Puritani gathered the greatest crowd and for two weeks the receipts were nearly $60,000. Mapleson found the field so productive that Chicago became at once a leading object point of all his American tours.

It was during the 1879 Mapleson opera season that a squabble among the principals afforded the newspapers good and considerable copy. Madame Gerster was the prima donna on the opening night and having chosen her dressing room it for that reason became known as "the prima donna's room." For the second night the opera was "Le Nozze de Figaro"—chief parts being taken by Madame Roze and Minnie Hauk. The idea of occupying the prima donna's room evidently appealed to Miss Hauk and as early as 3 o'clock in the afternoon she ordered her boxes and dresses placed there. An hour later Madame Roze sent her maid to secure the room and it being found to be occupied, her husband removed Miss Hauk's baggage and had it placed in the room opposite. Still later Miss Hauk's agent, discovering her dresses not to be in the room they were supposed to be made another change and had the room padlocked. Madame Roze arrived at 6 o'clock and finding the room locked at once sent for a locksmith and had everything of Miss Hauk turned outside the room, which she proceeded to personally occupy. Minnie Hauk was also early and when she found her intent defeated went straight back to her hotel, absolutely refusing to sing a note. It took the manager of the company and the attorneys two hours to alter her determination but finally when the opera was nearly half over she was at last persuaded to take her part.

The season of 1880 was, however, somewhat unfortunate, and the following year, although Gerster was once more in cast, no phenominal success needs to be chronicled. In 1882 in Haverley's new theater, now the Columbia, although Minnie Hauk, Paulina Rossini and Emma Juch were present, the public only responded moderately to the financial call. 1883 was an operatic epoch, for in that year on Jan. 15, Col. Mapleson brought Adelina Patti. Whether or not a great monetary profit was won is a matter of secondary importance and necessarily the expenses, however inadequate the supporting company, were enormous. No matter aught else Patti was to be heard as Valentine in the "Huguenots" and as Violetta in "La Traviata," and no deficiencies could make the occasion other than memorable. The Abbey Opera Company, formed for the opening of the New York Metropolitan Opera House, gave a two weeks' season in 1884, at Haverley's Theater with Christine Nilsson, Scalchi, Marcella Sembrich, Signor Campanini, Novarro and Katschma. Seemingly oblivious of the size limitations of the house an orchestra and chorus consisting each of eighty had been transported here, but only about half of this number could be utilized. No comparison with former operatic companies, however, would be possible for in the way of completeness of detail nothing to approach the present season had before even been attempted. Notwithstanding all these advantages but one novelty was given, Ponchielli's "Giaconda," in which Madame Nilsson was in the title role. At the same theater and combating with similar difficulties the Damrosch German Opera Company gave a three weeks' season at the Columbia in 1885. It was another red letter occasion in our music, for a number of the principal operas of the German school were given more thorough presentation than ever before. In this regard it will not be out of place to call attention to Halevy's "Jewess," Meyerbeer's "Prophete," and Wagner's "Lohengrin," "Tannhauser," and "Die Walkure." Of the last named for the first time in Chicago three wonderful performances were given with a cast immeasurably superior to the ideal performances of the Royal

Opera House in Munich. Well worthy is it of record, Fraulein Anna Slack as Sieglinda, Frau Materna as Brunhilde, Fraulein Marianne Brandt as Fricka, Herr Anton Schott as Siegmund, Staudigl as Wotan and Koegel as Hunding. Walter Damrosch was the director of all the performances.

The first Chicago May musical festival was given in May, 1882, in a hall hastily put together in the Exposition building, but with a capacity for 6,000. Mr. George P. Upton, to whom the city is musically deeply indebted, was responsible for the following in the program books: "The idea dates back nearly three years and was discussed by a few gentlemen of musical taste with Mr. Thomas in 1879. Not only was the Chicago Festival decided upon but it was associated with the New York and Cincinnati May festivals all under the same leader, employing the same solo artists and utilizing the same orchestral material. The names of those who composed the Chicago Musical Festival association are given: W. F. Blair, A. J. Caton, G. C. Clarke, J. M. Clark, J. C. Coonley, Rev. F. Courtney, W. S. Crosby, George L. Dunlap, N. K. Fairbank, Marshall Field, Charles D. Hamill, C. M. Henderson, Samuel Johnston, Edson Keith, J. P. Kelley, Henry W. King, Rev. J. H. Knowles, G. H. Koch, Franklin MacVeagh, E. G. Mason, E. G. McCagg, A. C. McClurg, C. H. McCormick, jr., George M. Pullman, B. L. Smith, A. A. Sprague, George Sturges, J. Van Inwagen, Christian Wahl, W. S. Warren. These gentlemen were seconded by the following guarantee fund subscribers in addition to those hitherto given: C. E. Adams, W. T. Baker, Alfred Cowles, R. T. Crane, John Crerar, C. R. Cummings, Wirt Dexter, J. W. Doane, H. F. Eames, L. J. Gage, Charles Gossage, W. G. Hibbard, W. B. Howard, C. L. Hutchinson, J. R. Jones, S. A. Keith, E. F. Lawrence, A. J. Leith, J. T. Lester, H. T. Macfarland, James R. McKay, A. B. Meeker, B. P. Moulton, Thomas Murdoch, S. M. Nickerson, J. W. Oakley, Potter Palmer, H. H. Porter, O. W. Potter, George A. Seaverns, Perry H. Smith, G. C. Walker, M. D. Wells, H. M. Wilmarth.

For president N. K. Fairbank was chosen; vice-presidents, George L. Dunlap and A. A. Sprague; secretary, Philo A. Otis; treasurer, George Sturges. Music committee, Charles D. Hamill, J. F. Kelley, Philo A. Otis, J. D. McIntosh, W. S. Warner.

The musical staff was: Musical director, Theodore Thomas; chorus director, W. L. Tomlins; sopranos, Frau Friedrich-Materna (from the Imperial Opera, Vienna), Mrs. E. Arline Osgood; contraltos, Miss Anna Louise Cary, Miss Emily Winant; tenors, Signor Italo Campanini, William Candidus (principal tenor from Opera House, Frankfort - on - the - Main), Theodore J. Toedt; bassos, Myron W. Whitney, Franz Remmertz, George Henschel; organist, Clarence Eddy. To a chorus provided of 900 voices, 250 of whom were from Milwaukee, eight months of the most thorough training was given by Tomlins. The orchestra numbered 169, 110 being from New York and Cincinnati. While financially the result was not a success, the whole total receipts being $57,006 and expenditures $66,215, the festival nevertheless meant much for Chicago's music.

Justly proud indeed might Mr. Thomas be of the showing he had made since with his New York orchestra he had first appeared in this city in 1869. Every year with the exception of 1871, to which a reference is made elsewhere, he had visited Chicago and had introduced here Beethoven and Wagner, fitting foundation for the long list and the much varied music that lies between those two masters. It was in 1873 that the Apollo Club chorus was added to his forces and two years after that found a mixed chorus of upwards of 200 voices to which we were later indebted for the Tabernacle concerts and the Apollo Club festival, the latter an undoubted progenitor of the musical festival of which we

are speaking. At the first morning concert of the festival on May 23, 1882, in the first part of the program was given Beethoven's symphony in C minor, No. 5 Op. 67, and following the intermission, scenes from Lohengrin. At the second concert the "Messiah"; in the second portion of the third Beethoven's symphony in D minor, No. 9, Op. 125, with for the final chorus Schiller's "Ode to Joy." At the last evening concert the program was Schumann's Mass in C minor, Bach's "Tragic Overture," Berlioz's "Fall of Troy," and the "Hallelujah Chorus" from the "Messiah." For the first matinee Wednesday afternoon, May 24, 1882, the concert was an extremely ambitious one. Composing the program were selections from Le Nozze di Figaro, Mozart, Euryanthe, Weber, Mozart's symphony in C, and in addition to other numbers the Ball Scene from the dramatic symphony, Romeo and Juliet, Op. 17, Berlioz and a movement of the Ocean Symphony of Rubinstein. At the second matinee the program was a popular one and at the last on Friday afternoon a Wagner program was provided with selections from Rheingold's "Walkure," "Siegfried," and "Gotterdammerung." In all these concerts the solos were in most efficient hands, the sopranos being Frau Friedrich Materna and Mrs. E. Aline Osgood; contraltos, Mrs. Annie Louise Cary and Miss Emily Winant; tenors, Signor Italo Campanini, Mr. William Candidus and Mr. Theodore J. Toedt; bassos, Mr. George Henschel (his first appearance), Mr. Franz Remmertz, and the elder Myron W. Whitney. At the organ was Mr. Clarence Eddy, solo trumpet by W. F. Dietz.

Two years later came the second May festival and again for the official program George P. Upton writes: "In all its elements the efficiency of the orchestra, the strength and ability of the chorus, the eminence of the solo artists and the greatness of the works to be performed, the festival of 1884 marks a step in advance of that of 1882. In this we have the trio of artists who created their respective roles in both the first and second Bayreuth festivals. Frau Materna, Herr Scaria, court singer Imperial Opera, Vienna, and Herr Winklemann, from the Hofapernhaus, Vienna, so that Mr. Thomas is enabled to still further enrich his programs with selections from Wagner's later works and scenes from the older ones, 'Lohengrin' and 'Tannhauser' which he has never given here before. By the aid of these artists, reinforced by Madame Christine Nilsson and other soloists, he is also enabled to present the larger part of 'Tannhauser,' with a choral and orchestral setting also, which will insure the most remarkable performance ever heard in this country." Other assisting artists were Miss Emma Juch, Miss Emily Winant, Mr. Remmertz, Mr. Toedt, Charles W. Barnes, George H. Broderick and Mr. Heinrich. Among the performances given were "The Creation," "'Tannhauser," Berlioz' "Requiem," Gounod's "Redemption" and extended selections from "Die Walkure." A feature of the second matinee and indeed of the festival was the singing of nearly one thousand children trained by Mr. W. L. Tomlins. There is but one way to characterize the result, an eloquent vindication not alone of the children's capabilities, but also of their trainer's astonishing power in the musical enlightenment and development of young voices. Too much of the festival was devoted to the German to obtain public approval and the result was once more a loss of nearly $6,000, the receipts being $65,747.77 and the expenditures $71,565.17.

About this period Siedl gave a two weeks' season of German opera at the Chicago Opera House producing for the first time "Die Meistersinger." His prima donna was Lilli Lehman and the tenor Max Alvary.

With the chronicling of Chicago's first opera festival another epoch is reached of the very greatest musical moment and to which extended notice is a necessity. The festival was given from April 13 to April 25, 1885, and consisted of fourteen performances.

As was officially announced the Chicago Opera Festival Association was organized and incorporated April 16, 1884, to provide grand opera for the people at popular prices and to raise the performances to a higher standard of excellence. The board was composed of A. A. Sprague, Henry Field, John R. Walsh, R. T. Crane, George F. Harding, Louis Wahl, George Schneider, Eugene Cary, George M. Bogue, Ferd. W. Peck and William Penn Nixon. The officers were: President, Ferd. W. Peck; first vice-president, William Penn Nixon, second vice-president, Louis Wahl; treasurer, George Schneider; secretary, S. G. Pratt; executive committee, Eugene Cary, A. A. Sprague, Ferd. W. Peck, George M. Bogue, William Penn Nixon. One feature and the most marked of the enterprise was the building of an opera house with comfortable accommodation for an audience of 6,000 at the north end of the Exposition building. There was an immense stage 80x100 feet. The decorations were elegant, the appointments all that could be desired, with the new scenery, etc., a total cost for the mere fitting up being reached of $60,000. The artists from Mapleson's Italian Opera Company were as follows: Prima donna, soprani contralti, Madame Adelina Patti, Madame Fursch Madi, Mdlle. Dotti, Madame Scalchi, Mdlle. Emma Steinbach, Mdlle. Seruggia and Mdlle. Emma Nevada (her first appearance). Tenori—Signor Giannini, Signor Rinaldini, Signor Cardinalli (first appearance), Signor Vicini, Signor Bielletto and Signor Nicolini. Bassi—Signor Cherubini, Signor Caracciolo, Signor Manni, Signor de Vaschetti and Signor Serboli (first appearance). Baritoni—Signor de Anna (first appearance), Premiere danseuse, Madame Malvina Cavallazzi, coryphees, etc.; festival chorus of three hundred, orchestra of one hundred musicians, director, Luigi Arditi. During the first week Patti appeared three times, in "Semiramide," "Linda de Chamounix" and "Martha" for the Saturday matinee. Other operas presented were

"L'Africaine," "Mirella," "Lucia" and "Der Freischutz." In the second week Patti was heard in "Aida" and in "Faust;" "Sonnambula," "Il Trovatore," "Puritani," "Lucia," and "Lohengrin" being also given. Extraordinary was the financial success obtained, gross receipts amounting to $132,999 for the fourteen performances, leaving above all expenses a good balance for the association's treasury. Artistically, certainly there was much wanting, but no one present will ever forget the wild enthusiasm of the Patti nights, which were a deserved testimony to the association's performances at more reasonable prices than had hitherto obtained.

Before passing for the present from the subject of opera a glimpse may be taken of some operatic occurrences in the city other than of really grand opera. Joseph Maas was at Hooley's Theater in an English company in 1873 and again in 1876. Marie Roze was here in 1878 and again at Haverley's in 1880. Castle and Brignoli gave English opera at the Grand Opera House in September, 1880. French opera under the management of Beauplan was at McVicker's for two weeks in March, 1881, the artists being M. Tournie, M. Pellin, M. Armandie, M. Escala, M. Baldi, M. Corriveani, M. Atol, M. Jourdan, M. Mange, M. Feitlinger, M. Mussy, M. Rossi, M. Fleury, M. Jullien, M. Vie, Mdlle. Emlie Ambre, Mdlle. Delphrato, Mdlle. N. La Blanche, Mdlle. J. Pilliard, Mdlle. Feitlinger, Mdlle. Lagye, Mdlle. De Marie, Mdlle. De Villray.

The determination of Ferdinand W. Peck to create the noble Auditorium for Chicago was largely due to the magnificent success achieved by the Opera Festival Association in the spring of 1885. In fact it was in the special building constructed for the festival that Mr. Peck and his architect, Mr. Adler, fixed the lines that were to mark their great granite auditorium, which Mr. Peck then set out to promote and build. Milward Adams was sent to Europe to gather information. Night and day, year after year, in his offices at the southeast corner of Clark and Washington streets, where Gottschalk had played his "Last Hope," Ferdinand W. Peck measured, argued, pleaded, solicited, ordered, invested, and at last was in a position to erect his huge monument, the Chicago Auditorium.

The program of the ceremonies on the occasion of the dedication of the Auditorium, Dec. 9, 1889, before the president, Benjamin Harrison and a most distinguished audience, comprised a "Triumphal Fantasie," composed for the occasion by Theodore Dubois and given on the organ by Clarence Eddy. Address by the Mayor De Witt C. Cregier. Address by Ferd. W. Peck, president of the Auditorium Company, and to whom the building owed its birth. Cantata composed specially for the occasion by Frederick Grant Gleason, and sung with a chorus under the direction of William L. Tomlins. Address by President Harrison. "Home, Sweet Home," by Adelina Patti. "America" by the Apollo Club. Dedicatory address by Joseph W. Fifer, governor of Illinois. Hallelujah chorus from the "Messiah," by the Apollo Club.

Of the inspiring and indeed deeply imposing scene presented at the dedication ceremonial the well known local writer, John McGovern, said: "In a democracy Ferdinand W. Peck has been a Pharaoh, building like Cheops; if you entered Chicago from the south you saw the spike among the nails, and you said 'that is the Auditorium and Ferdinand Peck built it.' At that opening and dedication ceremony I sat confused, bewildered, almost terrified with delight, in the deep yellow velvets and among the soft lights innumerable of that celestial place. The storm without made not a noise within our strong place— our fenced city of art. I went forth into the mist and darkness, childishly proud and happy; and, as I went, it seemed to me I shone with the radiance out of which I had lately come."

MUSIC AT THE COLUMBIAN EXPOSITION.
(WORLD'S FAIR) CHICAGO, 1893

Music at the World's Fair demands more than a mere passing mention. To the necessities of a proper choral building $50,000 was devoted by Director General Davis in his initial report and to this somewhat limited amount ample justice was certainly done in the building which was produced.

The director of the orchestral part of the plan as formulated made only one choice possible and Theodore Thomas, one of the foremost masters of music in the world, was chosen for the position, while to William L. Tomlins, another necessary choice, was given the control of the choral. The attendance at the concerts given was unfortunately not of such a character as the high class music presented should have justified. A reason advanced was that the average visitor was a mere beginner, to whom Wagner and Liszt were unknown quantities. Consequently the magnificent concerts were comparatively neglected, due to no fault either in the concerts themselves or in Mr. Thomas, but to the natural deficiences of the musical tyro.

The intention of the music bureau was expressed in very decided terms to give an exhibit of the art of music in orchestral concerts twice a week, with choral concerts, bi-monthly, of oratorio festivals in three series, these to be supplemented with concerts by the various Swedish and German societies, organ recitals and an absolute necessity, daily popular orchestral concerts. A brass band had been the highest musical delight hitherto of the majority of the visitors, and the whole program as arranged was aptly described by Joseph Kirkland, of the Chicago Tribune, as "Xenophon to a kindergarten."

The initial trouble—a commercial unpleasantness into which it is quite unnecessary to enter—made matters muddy at the very outset of the fair. Paderewski and what piano he should use was the main bone of contention. Mr. Thomas was a man whose friends were legion, and the idea that any individual should think him capable of mercenary motives, or a discrimination amounting to professional corruption was not for a moment to be tolerated. In August he resigned his position and his manly, dignified, yet withal entirely good humored communication to the board is worthy of a place in these notes of Chicago's music:

"Chicago, August 4, 1893.
"James W. Ellsworth, Esq., Chairman Committee on Music—

"Dear Sir: The discouraging business situation, which must of necessity react upon the finances of the Fair, and which makes a reduction of expenses of vital importance to its interests, prompts me to make the following suggestions by which the expenses of the bureau may be lessened. The original plans of the bureau, as you know, were made with the design of giving, for the first time in the history of the world, a complete and perfect exhibition of the musical art in all its branches. Arrangements were made for regular orchestral and band concerts; for performances of both American and European master works of the present day under the direction of their composers; for concerts by distinguished European and American organizations; for chamber concerts and artists' recitals; for women's concerts, etc., besides a general review of the orchestral literature of all kinds and countries, in symphony and popular concerts throughout the season.

"The reduction of expenses at the Fair has obliged the bureau to cancel all engagements made with foreign and American artists and musical organizations and to abandon all future festival performances, thus leaving very little of the original scheme except the bands and the great Exposition orchestra, with which are given every day popular and symphony concerts. My suggestion is, therefore, since so large a portion of the musical scheme has been cut away, that for the remainder of the Fair music shall not figure as an art at all, but be treated merely on the basis of an amusement. More of this sort of music is undoubtedly needed at the Fair, and the cheapest way to get it is to divide our two fine bands into four small ones for open air concerts, and our Exposition orchestra into two small orchestras which can play such light selections as will please the shifting crowds in the buildings and amuse them.

"If this plan be followed there will be no further need of the services of the musical director, and in order that your committee may be perfectly free to act in accordance with the foregoing suggestions and reduce the expenses of the musical department to their lowest terms, I herewith respectfully tender my resignation as musical director of the World's Columbian Exposition.

"Should, however, any plans suggest themselves to you, in furthering which I can be of assistance, I will gladly give you my services without payment.

"Very respectfully,

"THEODORE THOMAS,

"Musical Director."

The fact that Paderewski had given his services without asking for return, even for the necessary expenses he might be incurring, was at this very time made public. Thomas' detractors considered it wisdom to remain silent, and the whole unfortunate incident closed. The resignation of Theodore Thomas was accepted, and Max Bendix was offered and accepted the vacant directorship, fulfilling its arduous duties and heavy responsibilities in a manner to which absolutely no exception could be taken.

The New York Symphony Orchestra brought on sixty pieces under Mr.

Walter Damrosch. In American composers' series were given Mr. Chadwick's second symphony, a serenade by Arthur Foote for strings and a suite, opus 42, by E. A. MacDowell. For some time Mr. Thomas was a victim of ill health and during that period Mr. Arthur Mees, an energetic young American, who had served as assistant conductor and orchestra working superintendent took his place and with much credit.

Mendelssohn's "Elijah" was given by the Apollo Club, with Madame Nordica, Mr. Whitney Mockridge and Mr. Plunkett Green as the soloists. The conductor was Mr. Tomlins, for Mr. Thomas was at the time still laid up.

The Columbia Chorus of 1,250 voices and an orchestra of eighty-five appeared for the first time on May 25 in Haydn's "Creation" under the leadership of William L. Tomlins. Recital Hall was opened for chamber music on May 23 by the Kneisel Quartette and proved a distinct musical success. On June 14, 1893, "The Messiah" was given by the Apollo Club, again under the direction of Mr. Tomlins. Soloists were the following: Mrs. Agnes Thomson, Mr. Edward Lloyd and Mr. Ericssen F. Bushnell. It was the most successful concert up to that time given and the chorus, about 500 strong, took chief honors even though such a master of oratorio as Mr. Edward Lloyd was singing. The same club gave Bach's "St. Matthew's Passion" on June 6, which was memorable chiefly for the wonderful exhibition of English singing recitative by Mr. Lloyd. On that occasion the chorus, only numbering 250, failed to reach its usual standard. A popular concert with Mr. Lloyd once more among the soloists captured a very fine audience on June 17. From the 19th of the same month until the 25th there was a choral festival in which took part the choral associations of St. Paul and Minneapolis under S. A. Baldwin. Led by Mr. Arthur Weld, the Arion Society of Milwaukee, which was associated with the Cincinnati Festival Chorus under Mr. Thomas, but trained by Mr. W. L. Blumenschein, gave some successful concerts. Among other events given were Mendelssohn's "St. Paul" and Handel's "Utrecht Jubilate." Also were given Handel's "Judas Maccabeus," selections from Berlioz' "Requiem" and "Judas," every one of which found good recognition. For "Lohengrin" there were the following soloists: Emma Juch, soprano; Miss Lena Little, alto; Edward Lloyd, tenor, and Emil Fischer, basso. June 26 "A German Requiem" of Brahms' was given under Mr. Thomas for the first time in Chicago in the Music Hall.

The Welsh Eisteddfod, or harp festival, of September, was a feature of such interest to the thousands who gathered at that wonderful Exposition, in bringing before them the music and ceremonies of the famous Druid age in ancient Britain, that it is well worthy of particular mention.

Still, it must be acknowledged that the World's Fair, even if, for reasons Mr. Thomas' letter has made clear, it did not gather in Chicago all those who are greatest and highest in the musical life of our century, as was the prime intention, yet was able to afford to the people of the great West opportunities of enjoyment, the memory of which no years can ever efface.

MUSIC IN THE GREATER CHICAGO

Grand Opera and Classical Concerts, Musical Entertainments, Both Artistic and Popular

In 1888 the Chicago Symphony Society under Hans Balatka gave its first season, a concert on March 9, being preceded the day before by a public rehearsal. This year was the sixteenth of the Apollo Club. Massenet's cantata "Eve" was given Dec. 3, 1887, the customary "Messiah" on the 20th of the same month, the overture, choruses and postlude to "Oedipus Tyrannus" with Mendelssohn's "Hymn of Praise" on March 1, 1888. Then in the month following a somewhat miscellaneous concert with Madame Carreno as pianiste. The Chicago Chamber Music Society, which had succeeded the Chicago Quartette after an existence of eight seasons with Emil Liebling, Agnes Ingersoll and William Lewis as directors, continued its musical successes of the year before.

Five trio concerts were given by Carl Wolfsohn and met with gratifying success. 1888-9 saw Theodore Thomas' eighth season of summer garden concerts with an orchestra of fifty-five performers. Much good music was given and our American composers were not forgotten; overture, "A Journey in Norway;" S. A. Baldwin;

Vorspiel, "Otho Visconti," F. G. Gleason; "Love Song and Wedding Bells Song," "Opteous Processional" and finale to scene second "Montezuma" and symphonic introduction to the Auditorium Festival Ode.

Three very successful concerts were given by the Boston Symphony Orchestra. For the Apollo Club concerts April 23 and 24 "Frithgof's Saga," Bruch; "Eve," Massenet, with Mr. Charles Santley as baritone and W. R. Root as tenor. Miss De Vere sang "Shadow Song," Meyerbeer. Verdi's "Requiem Mass" was given May 22 and 23 with Emma Juch, Mrs. W. C. Wyman, Mr. C. A. Knorr and Mr. Emil Fischer. On Oct. 29 the Chicago Auditorium organ was dedicated by Mr. Clarence Eddy; Mr. A. Rosenbecker had charge of the orchestra. Later a good concert was given by the Germania Mannerchor, cantata "Columbus' Last Night," with Sturm for baritone solo, chorus and orchestra; "Heroic Fantasie" for chorus, organ and orchestra, by H. Schoenefeld, both for the first time in Chicago.

1891-2 saw the Chicago Orchestra's first season at the Auditorium, Theodore Thomas being conductor and Max Bendix leader. The increase in the orchestra was noticeable, its number now being eighty. At the first concert on October 17, Rafael Joseffy played concerto No. 3, B flat minor, Tchaikowsky. January 2 Paderewski played Rubinstein's concerto for piano in D minor and Liszt's fantasie on Hungarian airs. A popular concert was given January 23, with Mrs. Julia L. Wyman, B. Steindel, 'cello; Anderson and Schreurs, flute and clarionet, respectively, and Mr. Edward Schuecker at the harp. Another popular concert took place February 20 with Mr. Italo Campanini and Max Bendix (violin) as the soloists. So successful proved to be these popular concerts that a third was given on March 19 with Emil Liebling at the piano, and yet another on April 16, with Miss Medora Head at the piano, and Mr. Adolph Carpi.

April 4 and 5 for the first time in America the Apollo Club gave A. Becker's cantata "Reformation." There was also a series of three twentieth anniversary concerts given by the club, Theodore Thomas conducting. May 17 "The Creation;" 18th, Handel's cantata "Acis and Galatea," soloists, Mrs. De Vere Sapio, Mr. Edward Lloyd and Mr. Gardner S. Lamson; and on May 19 for the first time in Chicago Bach's St. Matthew "Passion Music," with Mrs. G. Johnstone-Bishop, Madame Amalie Joachim, Mr. Edward Lloyd, Mr. William Ludwig and Mr. Gardner S. Lamson.

The Bendix String Quartet, consisting of Messrs. Max Bendix, Knoll, Junker and Unger, gave a series of four concerts which were received with the greatest delight by all lovers of high class music.

A new impetus was given to operatic fervor at the end of 1891 by the Grau & Abbey Opera Company. With Miss Eames, the Ravogli sisters, Madame Albani, Madame Scalchi, Madame Lehmann, the famous brothers De Reszke and others the success achieved was pronounced, Jean de Reszke's "Lohengrin" and Raoul in the "Huguenots" being the chief triumphs.

It was on Feb. 23, 1892, that the Chicago Musical College held its twenty-fifth anniversary concert at the Auditorium, obtaining the assistance of the Chicago Orchestra, Theodore Thomas conducting. On this occasion the soloists were Lewis Falk at organ and Mr. Leon Marx, violin. Mention should also be made of an additional season of seven popular concerts given by the Chicago Orchestra from April 27 to May 2.

During the season 1892-3 a greater feature was made by the Chicago Orchestra of the employing of local musicians. At its first concert Bruno Steindel, the 'cellist, was the soloist; at the fifth, Max Bendix, violin; at the sixth, Mrs Fannie Bloomfield-Zeisler; at seventh, Madame Ragne Linne. The eighth concert was a Beethoven night, and a chorus of 200 voices from the Apollo Club was added. The ninth concert was a popular Wagner night—soloists, Frau Martha Werbke-Buckard and the late Mr. George Ellsworth Holmes. Mr. William Sherwood played Raff concerto C minor, opus 185, at the eleventh, while at the fourteenth Theodore B. Spiering, violinist, was soloist. The following one was a popular concert, while in the succeeding Ignace J. Paderewski played. In seventeenth, Bruno Steindel, 'cellist; at the next Xavier Scharwenka, pianist; at nineteenth, Edmund Schuecker, the harpist, while the twentieth was a Wagner night, with Lillian Nordica, Charles A. Knorr, tenor, and George Ellsworth Holmes, baritone. Three people's concerts were also given, January 30, February 20 and March 20, which proved successful as well as profitable. This season four excellent chamber concerts were given by the Bendix String Quartet. Among other events four artists' recitals were given by the Amateur Musical Club at the Central Music Hall and a couple of good concerts by the American Conservatory of Music at Chickering Hall, the first on February 23, a chamber concert, and the second, an American composers' concert. Three Liebling concerts of a highly popular order served to emphasize the high estimation in which this accomplished artist is held by the musical public.

Since 1876 Emil Liebling has made himself a portion of Chicago's musical history and has done far more than his share in contributing to make this city the musical center it now is. The Liebling Amateurs, an organization of musicians who have benefited by his teaching, has for several years been recognized as among the musical institutions of the city.

So far as the Apollo Club was concerned the season was also peculiarly good, and as regards the German Mannerchor, its three concerts on Oct. 29, March 18 and April 15 all gathered crowded attendances.

In March, 1892, Paderewski, appeared in eight Chicago recitals, winning eight veritable triumphs.

With its second season the financial outcome of the Chicago Orchestra was far more encouraging, although still there was a large deficit. The two appearances of Paderewski were the chief occasions, and on each of these the Auditorium was crowded. Dvorak's "Requiem" was the magnum opus of this season (1893) of the Apollo Musical Club and a highly appreciable success was scored. Mrs. Agnes Thompson was the soprano, Mrs. Katherine Fiske, alto; Charles Knorr, tenor, and the late J. Ellsworth Holmes, bass.

On April 21, 1893, Henri Marteau, the violinist, appeared at the Amateur Musical Club, obtaining immediate recognition as an artist of very high gifts. During this year William Sherwood gave a series of recitals to large, and appreciative audiences and which assuredly proved his rank as the leading American pianist.

The close of the 1893-94 Chicago Orchestra season well sustained its reputation. On April 27 Tschaikowsky's symphony, op. 74, No. 6, Pathetique was given for the first time in this city. Mr. Middleschulte, the organist, was soloist. For the concert

following a Beethoven program, with Max Bendix as soloist, and for the last concert of the season, described as a popular program, Madame Emma Eames Story was soloist. Siegfried's "Rhine Journey," "Gotterdammerung" of Wagner closed an eventful season.

In April, 1894, there was a four weeks' season of opera, twenty-seven representations being given of eighteen different operas: "Carmen," five times; "Faust" on four occasions, and "Cavalleria Rusticana" on three. Of the leading artists Madame Emma Eames appeared ten times; Mme. Calve, eight times; Mme. Melba, eight; Mme. Arnoldson, seven; Mme. Scalchi, nine; Mme. Nordica, five; Jean de Reszke, twelve; Edouard de Reszke, eleven; M. Lassalle, nine; Signor de Lucia (who failed altogether in the pleasing of Chicago audiences) seven; Signor Ancona, eleven; Signor Vignas, seven, and M. Plancon, four.

In February, 1895, the violinist Ysaye had a very successful appearance. Mr. Cesar Thomson, the Belgian virtuoso, was also heard in a couple of concerts. Max Bruch's "Arminius" was heard from the Apollo Club on February 7, with soloists Mrs. Julia Wyman, Mr. Riedel and Max Heinrich, but hardly up to the standard the club had made.

It was in March, 1895, that Mr. Rafael Joseffy made his first appearance in three years with the Chicago Orchestra. Beyond all question it was the event of the season and it was so recognized. Doubts as to his playing were general up to the moment when he took his place at the piano and in conjunction with Mr. Thomas afforded us an opportunity of hearing Brahms' second concerto as only Joseffy could give the work. His reception in Chicago must have shown this wonderful artist in what respectful regard and esteem he is held in the states of the Central West. The announcement that Joseffy will play rouses the eager enthusiasm of all who understand and take delight in piano music. He holds a place of his own, and one that those who are best acquainted with his playing declare no other artist can approach. Concerning this appearance Mr. Liebling, always happy when speaking of a colleague, thus expressed himself: "Mr. Joseffy has it all—power, delicacy, sweetness, elasticity and unrivaled speed, combined with expression to any extent."

In April, 1895, a week of German opera was given under Mr. Damrosch. The following was the week's program: "Die Walkure," "Lohengrin," "Tristan und Isolde" (first time), "Siegfried," "Tannhauser," and "Die Meistersinger." "Die Gotterdammerung" was promised, but owing to the illness of Frau Sucher had to be omitted. For some reason or other Max Alvary failed to add to his laurels. Chiefly noticeable, however, was the great work done by the orchestra, which numbering about sixty, was in power exceptionally strong.

In June, 1895, Sousa gave Chicago a week at the Auditorium covering music of all kinds and conditions, from Wagner's "Siegfried's Death" to Sousa's own setting of the latest popular song. On June 11 at Steinway Hall the Mendelssohn Club gave its first concert. With a chorus of about forty chosen voices a program was offered comprising Mendelssohn's "The Hunter's Farewell," Lachner's "Hymn to Music," Rheinberger's "The Deserted Mill," and a couple of lighter pieces. For this occasion the soloists were Mrs. Genevra Johnstone-Bishop, George Hamlin and Bicknell Young, who were supported by Max Bendix and Seeboeck at the violin and piano respectively.

April, 1896, opened another season of Abbey & Grau grand opera—in every way wondrously successful. Seidl directed "Tristan and Isolde," given with an ideal cast—Madame Nordica as Isolde, Jean de Reszke as Tristan, his brother Edouard as king, Mark Kaschman as Kurneval, Miss Brema as Bregaena, etc. Mr. Seidl also conducted a notable performance of "Lohengrin."

"Acis and Galatea" of Handel, and Rossini's "Stabat Mater" were given April 27 by the Apollo Club and in the interval between these two works a part song of Dr. Parry, "Blest Pair of Sirens," and the Templar's Soliloquy from Sir Arthur Sullivan's "Ivanhoe." Great work was done by the chorus, particularly in Dr. Parry's part song, in which a most brilliant accompaniment was given by the orchestra. Soloists were Mme. De Vere Sapio, Ben Davies and Ffrangcon Davies, baritone, who made a tremendous success, being recalled over and over again.

During this season Mr. Carl Wolfsohn, assisted by Messrs. Boegner, violin; Steindel, 'cello, and Junker, viola, gave a remarkable series of chamber concerts dealing with the works of Brahms. Not being concerts of a public character, the audiences in the recital hall of Steinway Building were limited in number, but the artistic interest was indorsed by all the leading musicians and the general desire expressed that a more public opportunity should be afforded to hear Mr. Wolfsohn upon the subject in which he had made so special a study.

The closing of the 1895-6 Chicago Orchestra season was able to record an infinitely better financial result.

At the end of 1896 the Chicago Festival Orchestra, an infant organization under the direction of that excellent musician, Adolph Rosenbecker, ceased to exist. Two concerts only had been given in Chicago, neither of which obtained any particular success and when a start was made on a tour, under the management of Messrs. Cowles and Bernhard Ulrich, even worse disaster followed, and "stranded in Kansas" was the announcement that greeted its sympathizers.

The organization of the Spiering Quartet at last gave Chicago a first-class string quartet. Nothing was wanting excepting sufficiently worthy audiences, but as experience has taught all of us, a great movement is necessarily a long time in making itself felt. Music of the highest class is not the food of the many, it is the rich enjoyment of the gifted few, and to the educated musician the Spiering Quartet reveals all that is highest in higher classic art. It is second to none in the country.

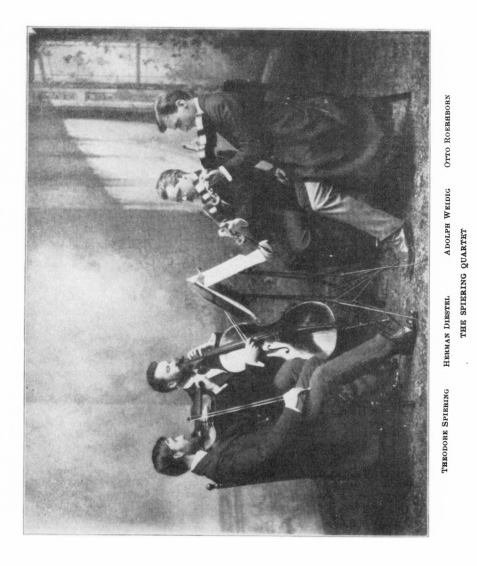

THEODORE SPIERING   HERMAN DIESTEL   ADOLPH WEIDIG   OTTO ROEHRBORN

THE SPIERING QUARTET

Considerable were the changes marking the opening of the 1896-7 Chicago Orchestra season. No longer was Max Bendix heard as concert master, his place having been filled by a protege of Joachim, Mr. E. Wendel. Theodore Spiering was also missing and missed among the first violins, and yet these were only instances of numerous other alterations. Tchaikowsky's fifth symphony was on the program of one of the earlier concerts. It was a great undertaking, in every regard satisfactorily carried through, and a decided advance upon the performance of the same work two years before.

The Chicago Manuscript Society gave its first concert on February 10, 1897, at Summy's Recital Hall. Our composers were worthily represented by Mr. Gleason, Robert Goldbeck, W. H. Sherwood, Henry Schoenefeld, Mrs. Mazzucatta Young and Mrs. Jessie Gaynor. All the works given were highly characteristic and proved not alone a pride to the composers, but also to the society and to Chicago.

A feature of the third concert of the Spiering Quartet, December 15, in Handel Hall, was the presence at the piano of W. H. Sherwood and the singing of Mrs. Clark Wilson.

December 21 and 23 were the dates of the Apollo Club's annual "Messiah" at the Auditorium. Excellent work was done by the chorus of 400. On both occasions Mr. Middleschulte was at the organ and the soloists were for the first concert Mrs. Genevieve Clark Wilson, Miss Cameron, Evan Williams and Ffrangcon Davies, while in the second concert the soprano role was taken by Miss Helen Buckley.

The first concert of the Chicago String Quartet, under the direction of Theodore Thomas, was on December 22. The quartet was composed of F. Boegner, first violin; F. Esser, second violin; A. Yunker, viola, and B. Steindel, 'cello. In the Schumann Quartet, opus 22, Mr. Leopold Godowsky assisted at the piano.

The month of December, 1896, saw the Carl Wolfsohn Jubilee, the celebration of his fiftieth year in connection with music. A chorus of old-time members of the Beethoven Club was gathered and an admirable concert was given. It was of the benefit order, the funds being used to present a bust of Beethoven to Lincoln Park in the name of Mr. Carl Wolfsohn.

A feature of very special interest at the thirteenth concert this season of the Chicago Orchestra was the playing by Mr. Godowsky of the Tchaikowsky concerto in B flat. Whatever may have been in the minds of the public, the previous doubts as to where Mr. Godowsky should rank among the great pianists, the performance upon this occasion placed him among the world's greatest virtuosi. Another noticeable work at the same concert was the second of Brahms' serenades, opus 16 in A, and remarkable for having no violin.

At the close of the sixth season of the Chicago Orchestra (1896-7) an interesting report was made. Soloists during the season were: Violinists, Messrs. Halir and Van Oordt; organist, Clarence Eddy; pianists, Madame Carreno, on two occasions, Mr Godowsky, Herr Bruening; 'cellists, Messrs. Stern and Steindel; vocalists, Madame Januschowsky, Miss Sue Aline Harrington, Miss N. E. Harrington, Messrs. George Hamlin and Ffrangcon Davies. In the eighth concert devoted to Beethoven the Association chorus of 200 voices assisted, soloists being Mrs. Genevieve Clark Wilson, Mr. George Hamlin and Mr. George Ellsworth Holmes. At the ninth concert the novelty was the ninth symphony, scenes de ballet, opus 52, Glazounow, while the soloist was Mr. L. Kramer. For eleventh concert a second hearing was given to the symphonic poem, "Edris," by our local composer, Frederick Grant Gleason. Mrs. Josephine Jacoby, who sang an air from "Samson and Delilah," was soloist. At the twelfth symphony concert Brahms' "Variations Chorale St. Anthony" and symphony in D minor, together with a notable composition of Hugo Kaun, of Milwaukee, were the chief features. The soloist, M. Raoul Pugno, the French pianist, was a very popular choice. He played the Grieg concerto, opus 16.

The season of 1897 proved to be particularly prolific in musical events of the first rank. In January (19th) for the purpose of introducing Mr. Walter R. Knupfer, the Chicago Musical College gave a most excellent concert. Hans von Schiller and Mr. Henry Schoenefeld led the orchestra, which was composed of players from the Chicago Orchestra. Mr. Knupfer played the Grieg concerto, as well as selections from Liszt and Moszkowski, Mr. John R. Ortengren sang acceptably and Mr. Bernhard Listemann won honors for his playing of Franz Listemann's "Grand Polonaise" for violin and orchestra.

March, 1897, found Grand Opera with the Schoeffel & Grau Company in full swing at the Auditorium. Madame Calve as Carmen, with Lassalle as the Toreador, and Mme. De Vere Sapio as Micheala opened the season. "The Huguenots" was given on the second night with the De Reszke brothers, and "Martha" on the third, with Chicago's Marie Engle assuring a good house. The season closed with "Romeo and Juliet," in which Miss Engle played the part of Juliet. Of this season Calve and Jean de Reszke were the leading attractions, Massenet's "Le Cid" was given a first presentation here and Boito's "Mefistofele" for the second time. It saw a repetition of Jean De Reszke's former success as Tristan and for the first time as Siegfried, as well as once more his singing of Lohengrin. Also to be recalled was Calve's Marguerite, both in Gounod's and in Boito's operas of that name, in each of which her grand dramatic power was shown to the greatest advantage.

In April Mme. Carreno won a distinguished success. With the Chicago Orchestra she gave the Rubinstein fourth concerto and the Hungarian fantasie of Liszt. Afterward at two recitals she created an enthusiasm unequaled except by Paderewski.

April 21 the Apollo Musical Club gave its third concert consisting of Dvorak's "Stabat Mater" and the "Swan and Skylark" of Goring Thomas. It was a splendid performance, the club's one hundred and thirty-fourth, and brought out a full audience. The chorus of 350 was assisted by about fifty members of the Chicago Orchestra and for its soloists had Miss Ella Russell, Mrs. Katherine Fisk, Mr. Ben Davies and George Ellsworth Holmes.

The Mendelssohn Club closed its season in May with an interesting concert, the soloists being Mrs. S. C. Ford and David Bispham. Mr. Harrison Wild, the director, was able to show excellent work with his chorus of sixty voices and Mr. Bispham added to his many triumphs in this city. Among the selections given by the club were Schubert's "The Omnipotent," Goldbeck's "Three Fishers," "Come, Dearest, Come," "The Wandering Musician" and "The Wood" and Arthur Krug's "Fingal."

"Elijah," the closing concert of the twenty-fifth season of the Apollo Club, was made a festival occasion and was given to a splendid and thoroughly appreciative audience.

Brahms' Symphony No. 2 in D major was given at the sixth concert of the Chicago Orchestra; to the delight of all local music lovers, Ysaye was soloist. Tchaikowsky's "The Voyvode Symphonic Ballade" was also on the program. In the one following Weingartner's "King Lear" was the piece de resistance. Soloists were Bruno Steindel and Ernest Schuecker, 'cellist and harpist respectively of the orchestra. The last named was for ten years professor of the harp in Leipsic Conservatory. A number of important books or studies for the harp have been written by him and his transcriptions of music for the same purpose have never been excelled. In 1896 he refused the position of court harpist in Vienna on terms the most advantageous and honorable.

December 8, 1897, the Chicago Mendelssohn Club gave its first concert of the season with Mr. and Mrs. George Henschel as the soloists. With the beginning of 1898 a new era in piano playing appeared to have arisen. In addition to the French pianist, Raoul Pugno, recitals were provided by Alexander Siloti, the Russian; Franz Rummel, a Belgian born in England, and our local great pianist, Leopold Godowsky. In the case of Mr. Rummel, the artist was in very bad health and so far from being able to do himself justice, the exhibition given was painful in the extreme.

In February M. Alexandre Guilmant was heard twice with the Chicago Orchestra and also in two recitals in the Steinway Hall. The privilege of hearing the great French organist was eagerly embraced by every student of good organ music in the city.

During March an excellent violin recital by Mr. Earl Drake in the recital hall of the Auditorium gathered to his assistance Emil Liebling, the pianist, and Sydney P. Biden, the well known young baritone.

Josef Hofman appeared with the Chicago Orchestra in April of this year. In the orchestra concert following, Ysaye was soloist and made a highly acceptable appearance in Max Bruch's concerto No. 12 for violin and orchestra. Chief interest, however, centered in the production in Chicago of Mrs. H. H. Beach's Symphony in E minor, which proved a notable success. At the next concert the symphony "Eroica" of Beethoven was on the program, a great performance with Mrs. Minnie Fish Griffin and Charles W. Clark as soloists.

At this time Mr. Leopold Godowsky was giving a remarkable series of piano recitals, each program of which was an opportunity broader and musically grander than the one preceding.

April 21, 1898, the Apollo Club held its closing concert for the season: "The Dream of Jubal," by A. C. Mackenzie, and the "Swan and Skylark," by A. Goring Thomas. Peculiar interest attached to the occasion in consequence of the retirement of Mr. W. L. Tomlins after twenty-three years' continuous service as director. This accounted for the un-usually large chorus, 450 strong, augmented by a portion of the Chicago Orchestra. In "The Dream of Jubal" the intervening text was read by Mr. S. H. Clark, of the Chicago University, but the chief impression left by the work was one of monotony. In the "Swan and Skylark" the considerable chorus failed in doing justice to its numbers. For soloists, George Hamlin took the place of Evan Williams, the tenor, who was ill; Arthur Beresford was bass, Miss Helen Buckley, soprano, and Mrs. Katherine Bloodgood, alto.

Most worthy of commendable mention are two chamber concerts given in the Central Music Hall at the end of April. Never before in Chicago were five such artists brought together as Ysaye, Max Bendix, Henri Marteau, Gerardy, and at the piano M. Lachaume of "L'Enfant Prodigue" fame. Following is the program: Quatuor opus 15, G. Faure; concerto in D minor for two violins, Ysaye and Marteau; Bach, quintet in F, Cesar Franck. With such a feast provided it is unnecessary to say every music lover in the city tried to avail of the opportunity.

About this time several bequests are directing attention to the library musical facilities. In such Chicago is a rich field. The public library is fairly well supplied, but the musical department of the Newberry library is, in this particular, unequaled on this continent and possesses but few rivals in the world. Particularly full are the collections of operas, oratorios, cantatas, symphonies and chamber music. Science and technique, instrumentation and the history of the various instruments, biographies, history and literature are all very thoroughly covered, while of librettos, special and first editions, rare works and curiosities, there is a really splendid collection. Among the latter is the original edition of Jocopis Peri's opera "Euridice," printed at Florence in 1600, and the first opera to which public performance was ever given, its occasion being the marriage of Maria de Medici to Henry IV of France. No other copy of this work is known to exist, that in the British

Museum, London, being a second edition printed in Venice in 1608. The Newberry book is bound in vellum and is in an admirable state of preservation. Purchased with the entire library of Count Pio Resse, of Florence, it was a fitting nucleus for the many treasures since acquired. Another rarity is the Musica of Boethius, the writer on musical subjects in the beginning of the sixth century, a volume which was printed in 1491. It is as unnecessary as it is impracticable to recapitulate all that this library contains. Sufficient to state that every subject in musical literature is well covered. In addition to Count Pio Resse's library before mentioned, the main collection of psalmody and hymnology as well as the library of Dr. Julius Fuchs of Chicago were purchased entire, the latter containing a number of rare scores and a peculiarly good collection of French and German works on musical science. The donation of the library of the defunct Beethoven Society through the intervention of its leader, Mr. Carl Wolfsohn and Mr. John G. Shortall, made another very valuable addition.

MUSICAL EVENTS AND GENERAL HAPPENINGS TO THE BEGINNING OF 1900

The visit of the famous French organist, Alexandre Guilmant, who in February, 1898, made two appearances with the Chicago Orchestra at the Auditorium, and who also gave a couple of recitals at Steinway Hall, was an occasion of much interest in musical circles, especially with those devoted to organ music. These last turned out in creditable numbers to hear his masterly playing, and musical Chicago generally awarded Guilmant a reception commensurate with its prompt and full recognition of his abilities and international reputation as a grand organ virtuoso. All of his programs were in many ways interesting and some of them indeed remarkable.

There is a chorus maintained at the University, and two or more concerts are given every year. The Spiering Quartet has appeared several times in connection with the Quadrangle Club. At one of these college concerts a program was given consisting of a manuscript overture by Carl Gustav Schmitt; Edward Grieg's chorus for women's voices, solos and orchestra, "At the Cloister Gate," and Mendelssohn's "Athalie." The overture by Mr. Schmitt, who is a composer well known in New Zealand, was composed for and dedicated to the Chicago University.

A song recital concert by the well known tenor, Mr. George Hamlin, proved to be one of the best art entertainments of the sort, not only within the musical season of '98 and '99, but in the memory of even the veteran concert-goer. It was given at the Grand Opera House (belonging to his father, Mr. John A. Hamlin), and drew a large and fashionable attendance. The program was decidedly unique, since it was composed exclusively of the songs of one composer, Richard Strauss, and of these Mr. Hamlin sang fifteen, none of which had ever been heard here. The piano accompaniment was played by Mrs. Nellie Bangs Skelton. Mr. Bruno Steindel, accompanied by Mrs. Steindel, played a 'cello sonata by Strauss.

While on the subject of song recitals it should be mentioned that there were two in the mid-season of 1899 which deserve both remembrance and honorable mention. They were given by Mr. Charles W. Clark, in University Hall, of the Studebaker building, presenting a program in two parts. The entire fourteen "Swan Songs" of Schubert constituted the first part, the remainder being made up of English songs. The Schubert songs were sung in German, Mrs. Nellie Bangs Skelton, accompanist.

In addition to its manifold work in the promotion of correct taste and sound knowledge, the American Conservatory has maintained a series of afternoon concerts which have proved not only pleasurable, but educational. The Rosenthal piano recitals aroused considerable attention. Mr. Rosenthal presented some exacting programs containing among other things the Liszt Concerto in E flat, the Chopin A flat, Valse opus 42, Beethoven's sonata ops. 109, Schumann's "Carnival," Chopin's "Berceuse," "Barcarole," "Deux Novelles Etudes" and the Schubert-Liszt "Linden Tree."

The seventh season of the symphony concerts by the Chicago Orchestra, concluded with the twenty-second concert May 6 and 7, presenting the following program: Symphony E flat, Mozart; concerto for piano, No. 4, G Major op. 58, Beethoven; overture, "Nature," op. 91, Dvorak; "Wotan's Farewell," "The Magic Fire Scene," "The Valkyrie," Wagner. The singing by Mr. Charles W. Clark of this great number, "Wotan's Farewell," was an exceptionally interesting feature of this closing concert.

Miss Sanford, a talented young pianiste of this city, made her appearance with the orchestra at the twentieth program of the series, which, taken altogether, added very considerably to the substantial record achieved by the orchestra in music of the highest class.

A song recital of an unusually pretentious character was that given under the direction of Mr. D. A. Clippinger by his pupil, Mr. Sidney Biden, who was heard in songs by Schumann, Franz and Richard Strauss. Mr. Emil Liebling contributed the instrumental numbers of the program.

The establishment of the Chicago Musical College in the large and commodious building specially constructed for it, which took place early in June, was an event of interest to musical people generally, not alone to those residing in Chicago, but to its hundreds of pupil graduates throughout the country. To those familiar with the history of the college under the successful administration of its able and indefatigable president, Dr. Florence Ziegfeld, since he established it in a suite of rooms in the Crosby Opera House in 1867, it is gratifying to find it occupying an entire building in the very center of the art section of the city and so arranged and equipped as to make it unquestionably one of the most commodious, appropriately appointed and handsome music schools, not only in the United States, but, indeed, in the world. The building, which is of the most modern description, is six stories high and occupies an area of thirty feet frontage upon Michigan avenue to a depth of 106 feet. In addition to many teaching rooms it possesses a concert room seating 700, and also has the advantage of a direct connection with the Fine Arts Building concert room, which will seat 2,000. In the course of extended comment upon the new building for the college, the Chicago Tribune said among other things: "This new home of the Chicago Musical College is thoroughly artistic in the just sense. Compared to it in surroundings, the most noted music schools of the continent and England make a poor showing. Growing with the city, and part of its musical life, the college in its present home has certainly kept abreast of the growth about it."

The new Studebaker Hall was opened September 29. The attendance was large and of a representative character and the musical program presented exceptionally interesting and attractive. The chief feature was the appearance of Mme. Bloomfield-Zeisler in a performance of the Beethoven E flat Concerto; Schumann's in A minor, the Scherzo of the Litolff concerto, the Mendelssohn "Spring Song," and an arrangement of the "Lucia" Sextet for the left hand alone. The accomplished pianiste was accompanied by an orchestra of fifty members of the Chicago Orchestra, led by Mr. Arthur Weld.

A sonata recital for piano and violin

was given October 8 by Messrs. Leopold Godowsky and Theodore Spiering at Auditorium Recital Hall.

Grand opera again furnished the center of musical interest when the Grau company commenced a three weeks' season at the Auditorium in the second week of November. For stellar attraction a large representation of the favorites, Mme. Marcella Sembrich, Mme. Emma Eames, Mme. Nordica, Schumann-Heink, Suzanne Adams and Marie Engel; Edouard De Reszke, Campanari, David Bispham, Vanni, Salignac, M. Plancon and Ernest Van Dyck, the last named a noted Belgian tenor. The repertory included three Wagner operas, "Tannhauser," "Lohengrin" and "Walkure;" for the rest, "Romeo and Juliet," "Faust," "Aida," "Lucia," "Huguenots," "Traviata," "The Barber," and "Marriage of Figaro."

A concert at University Hall commenced the season of the Spiering Quartet programs. It opened with Haydn's quartet and closed with one of Brahms'. The quartet has given a number of concerts in the cities and the central part of the country with a marked degree of success.

The closing month of the year 1898 was unusually prolific in good things musical, of the concert order. The Chicago Mendelssohn Club gave a very excellent program of part songs for male voices, containing the following numbers: "Hope," Mohr; "The Collier Lassie," MacDowell; "On Venice Waters," Macy; "Chorus of Spirits and Hours," Buck; "Under the Linden," Bruschweiler; "Evening Serenade," Bache; "Three Chafers," Truhn; "Gipsy Love," Arnold Krug. Mr. Max Bendix, the violinist and Mr. Gylim Miles, baritone, were the soloists of the occasion, which drew out a large and fashionable attendance, evidently impressed with the fine training and high cultivation of the club.

The Apollo Club, to the strength of about 400 singers, under the direction of its newly appointed conductor, Mr. Harrison M. Wild, opened its twenty-seventh season with two "Messiah" concerts December 19 and 21. At the second concert Mrs. Genevieve Clark Wilson, Miss Mary Louise Clary, Mr. Myron Whitney, Jr., and Mr. Whitney Mockridge were the soloists.

The favorite American pianist, Mr. William H. Sherwood, commenced a series of four recitals in Studebaker Hall, his appearance inducing a very good attendance of the lovers of piano music. In his opening program he presented the Beethoven "Waldstein" sonata, the Chopin preludes, Nos. 7 and 16, Fantasia in F minor, Scherzo in B flat minor, Schumann's "Carnival," a new Sherwood number, "Autumn," and of Rubinstein "False Note Study," "Fifth Barcarolle" and "Staccato Study in C."

From time to time ample evidence reaches both press and public, of the really progressive and permanently valuable work in and for good music, accomplished by the leading teachers and musical amateurs of the Chicago University. Particularly is this the case at the music department under the direction of Mr. Wardner Williams. The Northwestern University at Evanston offers strong possibilities, but so far has not proved its claim to any particular notice. This may be due to the lacking of a strong director, as the faculty includes such fine musicians as Hubbard William Harris, Karleton Hackett and Mrs. George A. Coe.

The first part of the year 1899 found all the musical organizations of the city in good condition, resourceful in capacities for results, and with an abundance of carefully selected work in more or less advanced rehearsal. Thorough organization supplemented art enthusiasm, the successes of the past affording the greatest stimulus to achievement in the future.

Mme. Teresa Carreno was heard as soloist with the Chicago Orchestra, and also in piano recitals.

The dedication of the large concert organ at the Studebaker hall was the occasion for a really fine concert, which was given February 24, to the evident gratification of a large, thoroughly musical and fashionable audience. Quite a number of prominent artists participated in a lengthy program. Mr. Charles W. Clark in the "Pagliacci" prologue and songs by Tschaikowsky, Mr. Emil Liebling, who gave the Chopin Fantasia op. 49, and Dr. Louis Falk, Mr. James Watson and Mr. Harrison M. Wild in organ music.

A memorable musical entertainment was given at the Auditorium on the evening of May 1, for the purpose of fitly marking the anniversary of the victory achieved by Admiral Dewey at Manila. Most appropriately the "Manila Te Deum," by Walter Damrosch, was selected for performance on the occasion. It was presented with a chorus of about 300 voices from the Apollo Club, sustained by the Chicago Orchestra, conducted by Mr. Damrosch. The soloists were Mme. Gadski, Mr. George Hamlin and Mr. Frank King Clark.

A notable concert of the year was that given by the Kneisel Quartet of Boston, finished artists who have played the very best music together for more than a dozen years. The program was, as might have been expected, unusually fine, three quartets, Mozart, in D Minor; Schumann, in F minor; Tschaikowsky, in E flat minor.

Opera in English by an adequate stock company, has proved to be a popular and profitable attraction in Chicago. The crowds of music loving people who have crowded the Studebaker theater month after month to hear the Castle Square Company in standard operas, particularly those of the lighter class, have furnished indisputable evidence that a prompt and liberal public appreciation and patronage awaits opera in English, well done —that is to say, without high priced lyric "stars," and unusually costly mounting and staging—which of course create certain limitations. The Castle Square Company organized and controlled by that most progressive of managers, Henry W. Savage,

opened at the Studebaker with a production of "Faust," which was succeeded by "Carmen." During the summer the company produced a new work, "The Tarentella," in which, since it is by Jacobowski, author of "Erminie," the public showed considerable interest. "The Queen's Lace Handkerchief" was the commencement of a series of light and comic operas, and these in turn were succeeded by more pretentious performances, such as "Martha," "Aida," "Rigoletto" and Puccini's "La Boheme." The leading people of the organization, Miss De Treville, Miss Carrington, Miss Quinlan; Messrs, Reginald Roberts, William C. Stewart and Rhys Thomas, established themselves favorably in the estimation of the public, and the management has won the recognition to which it was fully entitled for the complete and frequently handsome manner in which the operas have been put on the stage. Aside from the interests of the company or its management is to be considered the supremely important fact that a long and uninterrupted popular success such as has been attained in this instance is a sure indication of what the great masses of the public want, and is of itself a sufficient answer to the oft quoted statement that the people generally will steadily and profitably support nothing but vaudeville entertainment. Given the production of the favorite dramatic and musical works by a company sufficiently good in all essential respects, to make manifest in the language the people understand (French in France, German in Germany, Italian in Italy, as is in Europe invariably the rule), their excellences and beauties, and the public will indicate its prompt and profitable support quickly enough. As educational forces in good music such enterprises are invaluable.

Light and comic opera other than that of the Castle Square Company has been heard during the year, novelties such as "The Little Corporal" by Harry B. Smith and Ludwig Englander; Alice Nielsen in "The Fortune Teller"; "The Jolly Musketeer," by Stanislaw Stange and Julian Edwards and Sousa and Klein's "The Charlatan."

The work accomplished by the Chicago Orchestra, under the direction of Mr. Theodore Thomas, during the year which closes this necessarily limited historical summary of "Music in Chicago" (1899), was of exceptionally high character. Month after month throughout the year with the exception of the summer vacation and the time when the Auditorium was required for opera, has this indefatigable conductor and the talented instrumentalists who sustain him, rehearsed and performed programs of superlative excellence, often of immense difficulty, introducing to the musical public new and hitherto unheard masterpieces of the world's greatest composers; the concerts also affording occasion to present to large and critical audiences some of the most renowned musical virtuosi. In this list, in addition to the appearances of Mme. Carreno already noted, are to be mentioned Emil Sauer and Mark Hambourg, pianists; Lady Halle and Petschnikoff, violinists, and Van Eweyk, the baritone. To the gratification of many musical people familiar with their great abilities, and to whom their public performances are always welcome, several local artists were retained for the interpretation of important solo work. Mr. Sherwood was heard in Saint-Saens Piano-Concert, No. 2; Mr. Middleschulte in the Rheinberger organ concerto No. 1 and an original composition. Mr. Amato in the Raff 'cello concerto, and Mr. Bare in Vieuxtemp's fourth violin concerto. The "Manfred's" symphony by Tschaikowsky; the Beethoven C minor and the Schubert "Unfinished" symphony, were each given twice during the season. The works hitherto unplayed here, and presented by the orchestra for the first time, were a set of symphonic dances by Greig, the overture to Peter Cornelius' "Barber of Bagdad," Strauss' "Don Quixote," a new suite by Emanuel Chabrier, and Paul Dukas' scherzo, "L'Apprenti Sorcier," the prelude to Sylvia Lazzari's opera "Armor," Liszt's "Faust" symphony, and new selections from the works of Hugo Kaun and Arthur Foote. A specially interesting occasion was the tenth anniversary of the dedication of the Auditorium signalized in the concerts of December 8 and 9, at which Dubois' "Fantasie Triomphale," for orchestra and organ, composed for the opening ceremonies Dec. 9, 1889, was revived.

A performance of unusual interest was the singing of Haydn's "Creation" by the Apollo Club, to celebrate the one hundredth anniversary of the first production of this world-famous work. And in referring to the Apollo, now under the direction of Mr. Harrison M. Wild, it is most appropriate to note the first-class character of the program outlined for the present current season, its twenty-eighth. It was inaugurated December 11 with a performance of Saint-Saens' "Samson and Delilah," which was followed by the "Messiah" on Christmas night. The third concert in February was devoted to part songs, the soloists being Mr. Leopold Kramer, the violinist, and Mr. David Bispham. The oratorio "Mary Magdalen" by Massenet was given at the concert in April, with Miss Helen Buckley, who replaced Mme. Gadski at a few hours' notice.

In Grand Opera the Chicago musical public has had the advantage of a variety and frequency of performance, distinctively metropolitan. The organization earliest in the field was the Ellis company, of which Mme. Melba and M. Alvarez, the tenor, were the particular stars, these renowned principals being well supported by Mmes. Gadski, Mattfield, Brandes, Olitzka, Van Cauteren and Mlle. de Lussan. Messrs. Kraus, Boudouresque, Bensaude, Viviania, Stehman, De Sol, Cass, Raines, De Vries, Pandolfini, and Rosa; conductors, Sepelli and Damrosch. The repertoire included "Cavalleria Rusticana," Puccini's "La Boheme," "Carmen," "Pagliacci," "Faust," "Tannhauser" and "Lohengrin." In all, twelve performances were given, three in Italian, three in German, and six in French.

Noticeably popular was a short season by the French Grand Opera company, from New Orleans, which gave Gounod's "Queen of Sheba," "La Favorita," "The Jewess," "Trovatore," and a gala program, consisting of acts from "Faust," "The Jewess," "William Tell" and "Aida."

Twenty-two performances of grand opera by the Maurice Grau company at the Auditorium may be said to have brought the measure of musical art entertainments for the year 1899 to a close. The organization included not only most of the old favorites, but also some new aspirants for public favor, among these Mlle. Ternina, Herr Theodore Bertram and Signor Scotti. Mmes. Sembrich, Nordica, Eames, Schumann-Heink, Zelie de Lussan, Edouard de Reszke, Plancon, Campanari and Bispham, were all heard in roles more or less familiar and with more or less success. The performances generally accredited with being by far the best of the season were "Il Barbiere," "Lohengrin," "Faust," "Carmen," "The Marriage of Figaro" and "Don Giovanni."

What has been said of the frequency and popularity of the song recital is equally true of piano recitals of the highest order, to avail oneself of which there is always the amplest opportunity in Chicago, where Paderewski invariably draws admiring and enraptured thousands. But Chicago is too many sided in her musical appreciation to gauge the piano virtuosi by such an extraordinary stellar attraction as Paderewski alone, and mention has already been made of several superb and justly renowned pianists who have received a cordial and sympathetic welcome here. There remains, however, one name to add, De Pachmann—Vladimir De Pachmann the Russian—who was heard in two recitals in Central Music Hall, the program of which included sixteen Chopin numbers, and among other good things, a variety of Schumann compositions and selections from Mendelssohn, Beethoven, Schubert and Weber.

The death of Prof. Hans Balatka, which occurred early in the spring of 1899 (April 24) took from his devoted life work in this city a highly gifted musician, of whose really invaluable efforts and influence in the development and maintenance of standard and high class music in Chicago, mention has already been made. His demise was attributable to heart failure, so the end came suddenly, and up to the last of his active and most useful life he was enabled to continue his work in and for music.

Prof. Balatka was a strong personality and a splendid musician, and notwithstanding the able men who in these later days have led the active musicians and singers of Chicago to commendable rank and gratifying achievements, no one conversant with the history of musical endeavor will be able to trace its history and progress very far without encountering the individuality, the industrious, and ambitious work and far-reaching influence of Hans Balatka.

It is impossible within the extremely limited compass of the present work, to deal adequately with several phases of the city's musical life. While important, they are less conspicuously in the public eye than the features dwelt upon here. Particularly there may be specified church music, a mere narrative of the progress of which, in Chicago, would of itself make a full and interesting volume.

As to church music it is certain that in no city in the United States, excepting New York, can there be found as high an average of musical accomplishment, and an inspiration which makes for so much that is noblest in religious music, as is exemplified throughout the year in the churches of Chicago, notably so in those of the Catholic and Episcopal communions. A liberal pecuniary outlay, to sustain the dignity and beauty of the musical setting of her services, has ever been characteristic of the Catholic church in Chicago, and they are enriched by the knowledge and skill of proficients in church music. The high character and ambitious standard of the music of the Episcopal church in Chicago, has been noteworthy for years.

A consideration of the high school and academic work opens up a subject of such large dimensions that it is only possible to call attention to it, but such mere reference will convey to the reader, at least, an idea of how great is the multitude of that new, oncoming generation, which, with correct training at the outset, will soon supplement that large body of thousands of trained singers who made the great World's Fair choruses possible.

The facilities for thorough musical education which Chicago can offer are something exceptional, even for a metropolitan city. It is particularly the case here that artists and professors, who, respectively, have achieved distinction in special directions of study in the acknowledged musical art centers of Europe, have found their permanent homes, and are actively engaged in the pursuit of the profession. A veritable army of students is domiciled in the city from autumn till late spring, and even the numerous summer courses—a great advantage to many from the country—are always well filled. The commercial and pecuniary value of all this amounts each year to an aggregate something very considerable even for a great city.

Thus have things worked together for years past, and now more than ever do work together, efficiently and well, to promote the interests of music in Chicago, the city, which from her commanding position and manifold advantages, is easily the music-art mother and guide of the cities and towns of the great central west.

Brief necessarily has been this record as will be readily admitted when the broad field and splendid advance western music has made in recent years are taken into consideration. No longer is music a mere amusement. As the years have passed along it has grown and prospered, until today it has become a mighty and refining influence, which in conjunction with literature and art, is still pressing forward to further refinement and culture, having already bestowed upon the development of our general progress that dignity, elegance and tone which are distinguishing features of far older civilization.

Musical art in Chicago has not reached its present high place without multitudinous labors, and the most earnest struggles against adverse conditions, together with the most thorough determination on the part of its pioneers and those who had to carry results through, not to be overborne until good progress had been shown. Many of those who fought and struggled have been referred to briefly in the foregoing pages. Great and noble was their work, but today there are numerous followers in the same pathway; men and women daily striving to elevate the musical profession, and of many of these, short biographies will be found in the succeeding pages.

With the musicians of Chicago today endure the aspirations and hopes of the times that are past supplemented by the designs, oftentimes temporarily baffled, but finally triumphant of those who have zealously labored, together creating for us a present that sees Chicago the Wonder City, a center of music, art and science.

MRS. FANNIE BLOOMFIELD-ZEISLER

Fannie Bloomfield Zeisler was born at Bielitz in Austrian, Silesia, but came to America with her parents when she was less than 2 years of age. Her parents settled in Chicago, where she still lives. Her musical talent showed itself when she was about 6 years old, and when she, before receiving any instruction, picked out the tones of "Annie Laurie" on the piano, upon which her older brother (Dr.

Slivinski, Gabrielovitch, Hambourg, and other pianists of the first rank. This advice was followed, and in the summer of 1878 little Fannie Bloomfield went to Vienna, and for five consecutive years studied under the great master. In 1883 before leaving Vienna, she played several times in that city, earning more eulogistic comments from the critics there. In the fall of 1883 she returned to America and soon began public playing in this

AT THE AGE OF SIX

AT THE AGE OF THIRTEEN

Maurice Bloomfield, now professor of Sanscrit at Johns Hopkins University, Baltimore), did his practicing.

Her first teacher was Bernard Ziehn, of Chicago. But very soon she became a pupil of Carl Wolfsohn, of whom she received instruction until she went to Europe. In 1877, when Madame Essipoff, the great pianiste, toured this country, she heard little Fannie Bloomfield play, and pronounced her a pianistic genius which should be educated in Europe. She strongly advised her parents to send her to Leschetizky, who was then and is now one of the foremost piano teachers in the world, and among whose pupils are Essipoff, Paderewski,

country. Up to the spring of 1893 she appeared on the concert stage every winter, and has frequently been the soloist of all the prominent orchestral organizations in this country, such as the New York Philharmonic and Symphony Societies, the Boston Symphony Orchestra, the Chicago Orchestra, the Buffalo, Cincinnati and St. Louis orchestras, and at the Worcester festivals. Everywhere and always she was pronounced a pianiste of extraordinary attainments. Not satisfied with the position assigned to her by American critics, she went to Europe in the fall of 1893 and appeared at Berlin, Vienna, Leipsic, Dresden and other German cities, and was in all those places recognized by press and public alike as the greatest of woman pianistes, and as one of the greatest pianists of either sex and of all times.

While there she was accorded the honor of an invitation to be the piano soloist at the annual Lower Rhine Music Festival which took place at Cologne May 29 to 31, 1898. Playing

AT THE AGE OF EIGHTEEN

AT THE AGE OF TWENTY-FOUR

On the strength of these successes she was engaged for a tour all over Europe during the winter of 1894-5, during which she played in Berlin, Hamburg, Bremen, Cologne, Frankfort, Munich, Dresden, Leipsic, Magdeburg, Hanover, Copenhagen, Geneva and many other cities, everywhere carrying away her audiences and winning triumphs upon triumphs. In the spring of 1895 she returned to this country and played every season since then in the most important American cities and with all the great orchestral organizations. In the autumn of '96 she made a tour of the Pacific Coast with unusually brilliant success, both artistically and financially. She gave eight concerts in San Francisco alone, each surpassing its predecessor in point of popularity and the enthusiasm of the audience. In the spring of 1898 Mrs. Zeisler went to England and completely captivated the London public in a series of recitals and appearance with the great orchestras of the English capital.

there before the most critical audience of the world, in the presence of the most celebrated musicians and critics

AS SHE IS TO DAY

of all Europe, she won a singular triumph and was unanimously declared to be one of the world's greatest pianistes.

THE GERMAN MUSICAL SOCIETIES

Work of German-Americans in their Social and Musical Organizations for the Cause of Music in Chicago

No thoughtful observer of the development of good music in Chicago can be insensible to the valuable aid in this direction contributed by German singing and orchestral societies, and by the German-American element of the community generally. Precisely as the German Turner societies did much in arousing public attention to the advantages and benefits of athletic exercise, so the early German singing societies, the Mannerchors and Musicvereins, fulfilled a most important part in the creation of a sound musical taste, and indeed in the promotion of public musical education. The simple folk songs of the "Fatherland," harmonized for the male choruses, soon followed the equally simple and severely devout singing of the pioneer churches. From such unpretentious beginnings grew the carefully selected program of concerted numbers, and as the clubs gained membership, and under the training of the few—very few—educated musicians who got out west to Chicago, in musical knowledge, entertainments were given at which the work accomplished, gradually yet surely opened up the way to the cantata, and opera of later days. Of the earliest societies the two leading ones were "The Manner Gesang Verein," organized in 1850, "The Freie Sangerbund" and the "German Musical Union" founded about five years later. An entertainment that has become a recognized institution and of which tens of thousands of visitors to Chicago have carried away pleasant remembrance, the Sunday afternoon concerts at the Turner Hall has accomplished much in the direction of popularizing good music in Chicago. Its orchestra, a self governing and co-operative association, has from the first, and invariably, represented the very best of the local players, no insignificant thing to note, when so eminent an authority as Signor Arditi is quoted as saying, as far back as twenty years ago, when the Mapleson company used to come here, that he found no difficulty in supplementing the nucleus of his grand opera orchestra most satisfactorily from the Chicago musicians. Professor Vaas, formerly conductor of the Great Western Light Guard Band, and affectionately spoken of by the orchestra players of Chicago as "Papa" Vaas, was for many years the director of these concerts, the programs for which always have been and yet are admirably made up, embracing the best of such popular and classical selections as can be given in a miscellaneous concert. It became the fashion to attend the Turner Hall concerts, the social feature of the entertainments, in facilities afforded companies of friends to gather around tables for coffee, wine or a glass of beer while listening to the charm of Strauss or the inspiration of Schumann, contributing much to make it the vogue. Among the best generally known musicians and conductors who have directed the concerts at Turner Hall may be mentioned the late Hans Balatka, Adolph Rosenbecker and the present director, Professor Carl Bunge. The two really leading German-American singing societies of Chicago have been the Germania Mannerchor and the Concordia Society, the latter named going out of existence several years ago. Undoubtedly the best choral work of these societies was done up to the time of the great fire (1871) and for some years thereafter. At that time these organizations formed the nucleus of all choral work of a pretentious or public character and great was the impetus given

52

to musical affairs in Chicago by their public spirited assistance and co-operation. They would give entire operas, with a really very creditable cast of principals, and supplemented by a chorus equal, if not in some points superior, to any chorus presented with grand opera in the Chicago of the present. Operas at Crosby Opera House, such as "Der Freischutz," "Stradella," "The Magic Flute," "Merry Wives of Windsor," etc., with that gifted and charming lyric artiste, the late Mrs. Louis Huck as principal soprano, and the tenors Edward Schultze and Herman Bischoff in the cast.

The Germania Club grew and prospered, but retired practically from all public entertainment. Its membership includes, and for years past has included, what may justly be termed the elite of the German-American element. The Mannerchor, though kept well up to the mark, is perhaps more of an adjunct to the social life of the organization than anything else, while the club has grown notable for well managed social entertainments, and a lavish hospitality dispensed at its spacious and handsome modern club house on North Clark street near Lincoln Park.

In connection with the valuable work done for the interests of music in Chicago by the German-American choral and instrumental societies, and in addition to those most conspicuously identified with it, such as Hans Balatka and Adolph Rosenbecker, the names of quite a number of thoroughly good conductors and most capable musicians occur to mind among whom certainly should be mentioned John Molter, Otto Lob, Paul Grosscurth, Theodore Hoffman, Joseph Clauder, George Loesch, Charles Hunneman, Christian Nuenberger and M. Eicheim.

SAM V. STEELE.

THE CHICAGO AUDITORIUM

The Auditorium Hall, which is a main part of the Chicago Auditorium Building, all owned and managed by the Chicago Auditorium Association, owes its inception and successful accomplishment to the business abilities, courage and enthusiasm of one man, Ferd. W. Peck.

It is famous in the musical world for operas, concerts, dramatic performances and great meetings which have been held within its walls. In 1888, before it was properly roofed, the hall was the scene of the Republican Convention which nominated Benjamin Harrison as presidential candidate. The greatest singers the world has known of recent years have there been heard. Its vast capacity (there is seating accommodation for over 4,100 people) in no way interferes with the perfect acoustic properties which enable every note to be distinctly heard even in the upper galleries. The stage being utilized for seating purposes and the entire hall thrown open, gives accommodation for double the number above named, making it one of the largest as it is one of the grandest halls in the world.

Its stage equipment, modeled after the leading European opera houses, is most complete in every particular, there being twenty-six hydraulic lifts for the purpose of moving the stage platform. The height of the stage is eighty-nine feet and the perfection of its appointments may be judged from the fact that over this portion of the house alone nearly $200,000 was expended. The organ, which possesses electric action and a number of wonderful improvements, is one of the grandest in the world.

MILWARD ADAMS

Foremost among those whose active minds and ceaseless energies have made the artistic Chicago of today an object lesson to the world is Milward Adams, the manager and inspiring mind of the Auditorium. Still a young man, whose forty-two years

Adams was born, to Ohio. The latter came to Chicago in April, 1870, and eighteen months later, recognizing what an immense power the amusements of the people were in the daily life, took up amusement work as a career. Those who are conversant

of life have not only impressed that which has been brightest in Chicago's musical history, but have at the same time given fairest token of higher achievements in the years to come.

Milward Adams is a Southerner by birth, with all the warmth and impulsiveness characterizing his race. His father was a surgeon in the United States army, and when the Civil War began to make history moved from Lexington, Ky., where Milward

with Chicago's history are aware how popular in those days were concerts and lectures. Mr. Adams was brought into acquaintance with Laura Keene, Charlotte Cushman, Carreno, Thursby, Ole Bull, Wilhelmj, Rubinstein, Weinawski, Henry Ward Beecher, Wendell Phillips, Alexander Stephens, and a number of others equally well known and popular. Such associations and connections further strengthened his artistic impressions and ambitious aspirations were created to which his life since has to a large extent given testimony. Here was no man of aimless and uncertain desires; strong determination and absolute fearlessness were the distinguishing points in a character that none in a position to know the man has not honored and esteemed.

Central Music Hall, the crowning memorial to George Benedict Carpenter, a man whose life bore a remarkable resemblance to Mr. Adams, was raised as a home for the highest in music and when Mr. Carpenter untimely passed away, Mr. Adams, formerly the assistant manager, took full charge. This was in January, 1881, and the position was retained until December, 1887, when work on the projected Auditorium, of which he had been offered the management, claimed his undivided attention. For the next two years business in connection with the new home for musical art engaged much of Mr. Adams' time abroad and his untiring work, his

splendid business faculties, his energetic handling of the affairs unquestionably did more than those of any other individual toward the successful accomplishment of that truly magnificent design. Since the same qualities have been employed and the result must be as satisfactory to himself as honorable to Chicago.

Mr. Milward Adams had the management of the May Musical Festival of 1882 and 1884 in the old Exposition Building. Under his charge also came the Theodore Thomas summer night concerts, which preceded and culminated in the Chicago Orchestra. In fact, inseparably has he been connected for twenty years past in all the great musical enterprises of the city, and it is said by those who know him, and all who know Mr. Milward Adams esteem him most highly, that during that long connection with its affairs he has been brought into close connection with every great visiting artist, the greater majority of whom he numbers among his friends.

MAY ALLPORT

May Allport has been so long identified with the best in the musical and social life of Chicago, and has been so zealous in encouraging all effort in all lines of truly artistic work in that city, that some one well said the other day: "Miss Allport should never leave Chicago; she is a part of it."

Early in her musical career, she studied in Europe both vocal and instrumental music, and while there, was in some doubt as to which of these branches of musical art should be her life work. Her vocal teachers wished her to go upon the operatic stage, while her piano teachers were equally strenuous in urging their claims.

Upon her return to Chicago, she continued to study the piano, with Mrs. Watson, and she always delights in telling how much she owes to this most gifted teacher. But her many friends, and those who have had the

pleasure of hearing her play, know that the poetic insight, and dramatic fire of her interpretations are qualities which have not been acquired by study.

Her playing is peculiarly inspiring, and more than one artist, after hearing her, has told her that she has given him an idea for a story, or incited him to paint a picture.

In spite of her great endowment, Miss Allport is keenly alive to the practical side of life, and has never ignored the dry technicalities of her art. She fully realizes that all products of the imagination must be made known through a material medium, and the velvety characteristic of her technique well supports the artistic qualities of her mind.

Of late years Miss Allport has become very deeply interested in the development and fostering of the musical talent of younger, artistic workers. In 1892, she organized the society known as the "Junior Amateur Club," which was to be a preparation for the larger "Amateur Musical Club," of Chicago, of which she was one of the founders and always been an active member. At the time of the World's Fair she was asked to take charge of the piano department of the "World's Congress of. Musicians," but she was already so fully occupied with the demands of her own city, that her friends urged her not to assume this additional responsibility.

Beside being identified with the two musical societies just mentioned, Miss Allport is a member of the "Dilettanti," the "Fortnightly" and the "Little Room," but she could not strictly be called a club woman, for her talents and life are quite entirely given to the service of her friends, and of individuals whose artistic or personal needs are brought to her notice. She seldom plays in public, but finds her happiness in her studio surrounded by "her girls."

MRS. CROSBY ADAMS

Mrs. Crosby Adams, whose work in the various departments of teaching, composing and lecturing has placed her name in the front rank of musicians in Chicago, was born at Niagara Falls, N. Y., her maiden name being Juliette Graves. A quiet life on the home farm was conducive to effective study, and nature was the teacher from whom she received her deepest impressions. The grand Niagara river was a constant inspiration. To these early impressions, and the love for this great river, and indeed of all nature, Mrs. Adams attributes much of the development of her musical sensibilities. She learned to listen and revere. An early predeliction for music decided her future work. After some study with local teachers, she came under the musical guidance of Mrs. C. S. P. Cary, a noted teacher of Rochester, N. Y. At 21 Miss Graves accepted a position as teacher of music at Ingham University, LeRoy, N. Y., continuing her studies while there with Prof. Claude Crittenden, a pupil of Kiel, Kullak and Liszt. Her marriage shortly after to Crosby Adams, a gentleman of rare musical taste, a fine singer and a most appreciative admirer of his wife's musical talents, resulted in their removal to Buffalo, where they became identified with the musical interests of the city, Mrs. Adams continuing her favorite occupation of teaching music. Later they

removed to Kansas City, Mo., where Mrs. Adams' work found recognition, both in her classes and in her position as organist of one of the largest churches of the city.

All these years of teaching had suggested to Mrs. Adams methods of developing the artistic side of music teaching from the very start, and with her youngest pupils. They had also revealed the need of a musical literature for children for which there was no adequate supply. It was in Kansas City that Mrs. Adams began writing for little people the compositions which have made her name familiar to conscientious and progressive music teachers all over the country. Her wide experience in musical work, as organist, lecturer, ensemble player and musical critic for some of the best musical publications, prepared her for entrance upon her work in the wider field of Chicago, to which city Mr. and Mrs. Adams removed in 1892. She was soon immersed in the musical activities of the city, quickly securing the recognition of which she was so worthy. Her work here is not only with pupils, but with teachers, large numbers of whom come to her for instruction in her methods of development. She has devoted much effort to enabling her pupils to produce a fine and artistic quality of tone in their playing, and she has proven that even very young children can play with beautiful tone quality and illustrate artistic playing at a very early age. To that end she believes the training of the ear to perceive tones unrelated and related, and a fine perception of intervals should precede the first work at any instrument, and the unfolding of this faculty be carried along all the time with expression on the chosen instrument.

class of seniors in one of the leading kindergarten schools of the city.

To her friends Mrs. Adams is the embodiment of the music she teaches and composes. She seems a living illustration of the harmonious mental and spiritual development which we should expect as a result of a cultivated musical nature. The home of Mr. and Mrs. Adams is the center of

MRS. CROSBY ADAMS

Mrs. Adams' musical compositions have been graded to suit the needs of pupils in the early stages of work. The children themselves have pronounced favorably upon these pieces, a tribute which Mrs. Adams values more highly even than the many letters from teachers, attesting their usefulness. She is especially interested in the relation of music to kindergarten work. having charge of a large

delightful gatherings of musical and literary people. The recitals given by her pupils are events looked forward to with eager interest both by pupils and friends, and an invitation to these musicales is a much-prized honor. These programs represent a very discriminating touch in the selection of material suited to each stage of the child's development.

LOUIS AMATO

'Cellist of the Chicago Orchestra, there is no man in Chicago held in higher consideration than Louis Amato. He was born in Paris, which city he left when 6 years old for Madrid, Spain, where he began the study of the 'cello at the conservatory there under the care of Victor de Mirecki, the premier prize winner of the Paris Conservatory, and a pupil of the great Franchomme. Mr. Amato obtained second prize at the conservatory in 1883 and the first in 1884. He then left for Paris, where he entered the conservatory, and in 1885 after the first year took second prize and gained the first in 1886. After serving five years in the army as a clarinetist he decided in 1891 to come to the United States, and obtained a position with the Chicago Orchestra. Two years afterward he was soloist with the orchestra playing Caprice Hongrois, G. Delsart, and again in 1893 when he played Raff Concerto. Mr. Amato has made himself very popular and is in strong request for private engagements as well as for tuition.

WILLIAM ARMSTRONG

William Armstrong is a native of Frederick county, Maryland. The founder of the family in this country was the Rev. John Armstrong, of the Established Church, Yorkshire, England, who came to America shortly after the Revolution. The present is the third generation on his mother's side in this country, the founder being John Channing Mossie, a professor in the University of London, who came to America on a lecture tour, remaining permanently. Both sides of the family intermarried with families prominent in Colonial and Revolutionary history; in the instance of the Armstrongs with the Johnsons of Maryland, six brothers of whom were officers in the Revolution; one Thomas Johnson, nominated George

Washington as commander in chief of the Colonial armies, and afterward first governor of Maryland; another, Joshua Johnson, the father of Mrs. John Quincy Adams, being the first American consul at London. Mr. Armstrong studied at Stuttgart and Vienna, and was for five years music critic of the Chicago Tribune, subsequently devoting himself to lecturing.

He has lectured in England and America, making his first London appearance at Queen's Hall June 18, 1897, and later before the Royal Academy of Music. In addition to magazine work he is the author of two books—"Thekla; a Story of Viennese Musical Life," and "An American Nobleman."

MAURICE ARONSON

Taking rank among the most successful younger artists of Chicago is Mr. Maurice Aronson. As pianist, instructor, lecturer and critic he has gained an insight in the art of music, such as few possess. For the past three years Mr. Aronson has been a member of the piano faculty of the Chicago Conservatory, where his success as pianist and instructor has been of a rarely pronounced character, his piano recitals and lectures having been enjoyed by large and appreciative audiences.

Mr. Aronson was born in Mitan, near the Baltic coast. In early youth he showed a decided talent for music. Together with a thorough musical instruction he received a far-reaching academical education in the Gymnasium, from which institution he graduated at the unusual age of 16 years. He then sojourned in St. Petersburg, Berlin and other continental cities for the purpose of making musical studies. In 1888 Mr. Aronson came to America, locating in the South, and enjoying the reputation of being one of the best known musicians of the South. In 1896 Mr. Aronson came to Chicago in search of a wider field of activity. After studying for some time with Leopold Godowsky, the distinguished pianist and composer, the latter recommended Mr. Aronson for the piano faculty of Chicago Conservatory.

As a pianist Mr. Aronson possesses sound artistic qualities and a repertory covering a wide range. On October 17, 1899, Mr. Aronson gave a very suc-cessful Chopin recital, in commemoration of the fiftieth anniversary of Chopin's death, presenting a program of representative and rarely played works by the Polish master, preceded by a lecture on "The Unknown Chopin." Outside of his pianistic and theoretical studies, Mr. Aronson has made extensive researches in the history and literature of music and has given strong evidences of ability as a musical writer.

THE AMATEUR MUSICAL CLUB

The constitution of this very influential organization in Chicago musical life tersely sets forth in its first article that "The Amateur Musical Club is an association of ladies, formed for the purpose of stimulating musical interest in Chicago and of developing the musical talent of its members." The club was a growth from beginnings which had no pre-vision of the scope and usefulness later to be attained.

During the year 1877 four Chicago ladies met together at each others' houses for the purpose of practicing piano quartets. These ladies were Mrs. Charles J. Haines, Mrs. Frank Gorton, Mrs. William Warren and Mrs. Nettie R. Jones. Mrs. Robert Clarke also frequently met with them. The meetings were often held at the residence of General Stager, the father of Mrs. Frank Gorton. New and standard works for two and four performers were obtained from a musical library in New York and read at sight at the semi-weekly meetings, which steadily increased in popularity with the invited audiences. The idea of a club suggested itself a year or two later. Twelve or fifteen women responded to the call and meetings were held in a small room in one of the music stores. Half the program at each concert was devoted to the works of one composer, whose portrait was placed on an easel and a paper was read by one of the members. Each member sang or played whenever invited and occasionally pro-fessional musicians were engaged when stringed instruments were needed. The second season twenty-five "associate" members, not essentially musicians, were admitted.

The first preserved records of the club are the secretary's report for the season of 1881-82. The highest office of the club was then chairman of the committee, "president" being a later introduction. In 1882 the active membership was fifty-eight, associate membership sixty-seven. In 1884 the associate membership was 240 and later it was limited to 500. In 1882 at the date of the earliest records Mrs. John M. Clark was chairman and Miss Rose Fay (Mrs. Theodore Thomas) secretary. The office of the president was instituted in 1890. In that year Mrs. James S. Gibbs was elected president. Her successors have been Mrs. Theodore Thomas, Mrs. George Benedict Carpenter, Mrs. Frederic Ullmann, Mrs. William S. Warren and Mrs. Edwin N. Lapham.

In 1898 the club took possession of new quarters in the Fine Arts building, consisting of a large hall of 700 seating capacity, a smaller hall on an upper floor for active membership concerts and a studio for practice work. Active membership tests are severe and only a small percentage of applicants are admitted. Many benefactions have been bestowed upon students of promising talents and the omnipresent aim of the club is its promotion of proficiency in the musical art.

SOME PERSONAL RECOLLECTIONS OF CARL TAUSIG

A short, youthful, but compact figure, clad in black velvet, with low shirt collar and loose tie, all this crowned by a most intelligent head, with small, deep-set, keen penetrating eyes, behind a gold pincenez; quick, nervous movements, and an almost military conciseness of speech—such was the impression I received of the great Carl Tausig at my first interview with him.

It was by appointment, for I had made an application for lessons, and was now asked an avalanche of questions; "When, what and with whom?" After that had been satisfactorily disposed of I was told to play. In those days the word nervousness had no place in my vocabulary, and while I was taking off my gloves, he mentioned incidentally that the class he probably would wish me to enter met Tuesdays and Fridays. "But," I interrupted, "I have no intention of joining a class; I prefer private instructions!" "Very sorry, indeed; this is impossible, as I do not give any private instruction, it is all done in class. However, as it is not at all certain that I can accept you, even in class, it may be useless to remove your gloves."

The tone, the attitude, and such total indifference, made my youthful blood tingle, and from a feeling of sheer opposition I was determined to play. And so I quietly continued to take off my gloves, and said, as I had come across the ocean to study with him, I felt naturally, that I must accept all conditions. He then led the way into a very small music room, and evidently remembering the things I had spoken of as having studied, began by asking me for the first movement of the D minor Sonata of Beethoven, then a page or so of a Bach Fugue, a Chopin study, part of the slow movement of the Chopin F minor concerto, and then for a finish he gave me some manuscript to read. During the ordeal, he not only watched the musical rendering, but,

as my aunt, who had accompanied me, told me afterward, position of hand and arm, the manner of sitting; stood first at my side, then at the back and seemed satisfied. Evidently I had found favor, for I was given my hour, and a list of music which to prepare for my first lesson. After that my misery began. He was a quick reader of human nature, and that short interview had disclosed to him the fact that my little head was brimful of conceit, which was only too true. I was so convinced of my superiority, that in my estimation, a teacher should consider himself fortunate, who could secure me as a student. It took Tausig just two weeks to take the nonsense out of me, and he did it so effectually that I was like wax in his hands, and never suffered a relapse after that. The scales fell from my eyes, and I saw myself as I really was; with much talent, but immature, and given to extreme exaggeration in sentiment, all of which was an abomination in his eyes. His teaching was a revelation, but it was fully two months before I had fallen thoroughly into line. The attention to detail was immense; the slightest and seemingly most unimportant indication of the composer had to be religiously carried out. The touch had to have characteristic precision, and tone-quality was made a constant study of; the utmost regard for fine articulation, and sharp sense of rhythm was insisted upon. His teaching of phrasing was most artistic, every smallest phrase had to have a plastic outline, and he used, according to the stronger or lesser degree of shortening a phrase, the word "Schneide" or "Abesetzen." Nothing arbitrary in the way of interpretation was ever permitted; the attitude was always one of deepest respect for the composer, and each and every student could not fail to be imbued in the end, with the utmost reverence and admiration for such teaching.

Tausig was not fond of giving lessons, and reduced rather than increased, the number of his pupils each year, so that, to have studied with Tausig, meant much. It was simply a case of "noblesse oblige" with him, and in that light he gave of himself to his pupils with full hands. To those in whom he took particular interest, he would, from time to time, give an hour or so of private instruction at his own apartment, and these occasions remain forever a most precious, cherished memory. While Tausig hardly ever inspired a warm personal affection, for his was too repressed and consequently undemonstrative a nature, yet his strong mental qualities, added to his wonderful musical genius, made willing slaves of most of his pupils. They came to him from all parts of the world; those from America were, beside myself, Max Pinner, of New York, and Joseph Trenkel, of San Francisco, both now dead. Rafael Joseffy, the great master's greatest pupil, is Hungarian, and came to America several years after Tausig's death. We were fellow students at the same time, and so was the Russian, Vera Timaroff; the Roumanian, Annette Barozzi; the Finn, Aline Lindberg, all artistic to their finger tips, and all enthusiastic in 'their chosen profession. I returned home a year before his death; during that year Sofie Menter became his pupil, and was so highly regarded by him, that they had actually planned a trip to this country together, when the great master was suddenly carried off by typhoid fever, while attending a performance of Liszt's "Saint Eliza-beth," at Leipzic. Liszt was with him to the last, and closed his eyes; that pupil, who was probably the best beloved of all the hundreds who had sat at Liszt's feet.

Tausig had a strong philosophic mind, and was a close student of Schopenhauer, who at that time was the ideal and idol of the entire artistic world. He also had strong leanings toward the natural sciences, and often expressed a desire, that he might be able to devote all of his time to a study of them. The truth is, that

Tausig, although at his death, only 29 years old, had climbed the heights far beyond all other artists, and stood alone and solitary; only a few superlatively endowed people were able to follow him, and this led to frequent misunderstandings even with friends, which increased the natural pessimism of his nature to an almost morbid state. His childhood was passed under sad and unfortunate circumstances, the mother having left husband and children in order to follow and marry another man. Tausig tasted this same bitter cup in his own married relation, so that there seemed little left in life, except his art. He reduced his playing at Berlin to one, or at most, two concerts a year, but they were occasions of the highest importance. Weeks before every seat in the old Singacademie was sold out, and the stage itself had to be utilized, the entire space, except where the piano stood, being filled with chairs.

Tausig's face, when he appeared before an audience usually looked as if hewn out of marble, so white and set. The emotions lying back of that mask must have been something terrific in their intensity, but everything was in such iron-like control, that only those who knew him well, surmised the tumult within. No one ever saw him after a concert, there was no conviviality, no late suppers, no adulation by admiring worshipers; he went straight to bed with a novel, which was his pet remedy for a disturbed nervous condition. In all my experience with him, as a listener, in the classroom or on the concert stage, I have never, to my knowledge, heard him strike a false or even doubtful note. His technique was absolutely infallible, and the most daring feats were accomplished with an altogether classical repose. Such clarity and beauty of tone, such sparkle and brilliancy, such massive force without the element of noise, such spontaneous virtuosity combined with such plastic beauty and objectivity of interpretation, have never been heard since. It was indeed a rare privilége to hear such playing, and the audience never failed to demonstrate their rapturous delight in the most enthusiastic manner. I witnessed the simultaneous rising of an entire audience once, when he was playing the A flat Polonaise of Chopin. As he came to the middle episode in E Major, and the tone masses in those octaves began to rise higher and higher, it seemed as if an electric current had passed through that entire audience, as they arose of one accord, amid the ever-swelling flood of tone from the master fingers, until every corner of that big hall fairly vibrated. And still those crescendos were mounting, until your very heart throbs almost suffocated you, and you seemed swallowed up in the intensity of that memorable performance. Ever since that night I have endeavored not to hear that Polonaise played, have fled wherever there was danger of it appearing, have vigorously denied myself many musical pleasures, when that number happened to be on the concert program, until I heard, years ago, Teresa Carreno play it. She has the same majestic splendor of opening, the same stately tread, in place of the usual virtuoso style of tearing through it; and what shall I say of her octaves? Their dazzling brilliancy, dropped from her wrists of steel, make her performance of it, as of equal rank with that greatest of masters, Carl Tausig.

REGINA WATSON.

FRANK T. BAIRD

Frank T. Baird is one of the most prominent as well as the most popular teachers in the United States, having gained a reputation both in England and America.

He was born at Worcester, Mass., but the greater portion of his boyhood was passed at Bellows Falls, Vt. It was in his native city, where he studied with Benjamin D. Allen, that he first took up the organ, and he was only 17 when he came to Chicago, where he obtained his first engagement at St. John's Episcopal Church. A short time afterward he accepted a position as organist at the Third Presbyterian Church. Here he remained for twenty-three years, twenty-two of which years he was director. During much of this time he studied the organ and harmony with Clarence Eddy and Dudley Buck and the piano with Emil Liebling.

Mr. Baird's abilities brought him into notice, and he was soon able to supplement his duties as organist with considerable accompanying work. His appointment with the Apollo Club gave him an opportunity which his energetic disposition quickly embraced. He made the acquaintance of America's great contralto, Annie Louise Cary. He became her favorite accompanist and with her made a number of tours. It was owing to her advice also which induced him to study the art of singing with a view of becoming a teacher.

He placed himself under the direction of Sbriglia, in Paris; Shakespeare and Henschel, in London, and Lamperti, in Dresden. The result of such training became quickly apparent. As a teacher his success was immediate, and a number of his pupils who had acquired instruction from him gained considerable public favor. Among these may be mentioned Miss Helen Buckley, who studied with Mr. Baird for five years; George Hamlin, who studied four years with him and was two years tenor in Mr. Baird's choir;

S. Fisher Miller, with the same choir for five years, and who is now occupying a high-salaried position in a church in New York.

Mr. Baird made tours with Miss Cary, Clara Louise Kellogg, Emma Thursby, Myron Whitney, Anna Drasdil and a number of others at the time prominent before the public. He freely acknowledges the benefits received from the association with such artists, and also more particularly from his playing under the direction of Mr. Tomlins with the Apollo Club.

That he might keep himself in touch with the great European teachers Mr. Baird's trips abroad during his summer vacations have been frequent. He numbers among his close and intimate friends many prominent artists, among whom are Ben Davies and David Bispham.

Honored and respected he enjoys the esteem of his musical associates as well as all with whom he is brought into contact. Mr. Baird's studio is one of the finest in the city and his teaching hours are always full. At the present time he has under his charge a number of excellent voices from whom he expects great results.

GENEVRA JOHNSTONE BISHOP

Chicago takes just pride in having possessed the residence of this famous artist, who has contributed to the world's knowledge and inspirations of music so generously and who is considered one of the leading oratorio singers in America. Her voice, a pure mezzo-soprano, of wonderful range, and full of distinct carrying power, raises her to the rank of a thorough artist. She has done much toward elevating the musical standard of this city, and possesses, in addition to her wonderful artistic attainments, a charm of personality and grace of manner that serve to heighten the esteem in which she is universally held.

She was born at Marion, Ohio, the daughter of Hon. J. C. Johnstone, one

of the leading lawyers of that state. To the excellent musical education received at home she added several years' study abroad, during which time she was a pupil of Mme. Anna de La Grange, of Paris, Randegger and Frederick Walker, of London. In her earlier professional career Mme. Bishop sang for two years in the Congregational Church at Toledo. She has commanded the second highest church salary in America, it being exceeded only by that of Clementine De Vere. She possesses an immense repertoire, including, besides the principal oratorios and operatic airs, several interesting programs for recital work.

Personally, Mme. Bishop is tall, magnetic, of fine figure and carriage,

GENEVRA JOHNSTONE BISHOP

and dressing with charming taste. She possesses a wide musical acquaintanceship and in 1892 was the guest of Mme. Patti at Craig-y-Nos, Wales, and the same year she was entertained by Wagner in Beyreuth, during the Wagnerian Festival. Her nature is most kindly, and to every young artist she is sympathetic and inspiriting.

During the past season Mme. Bishop has been singing on the Pacific coast, opening a studio at Los Angeles on account of the climate. In June she will go to Europe.

HELEN BUCKLEY

It illustrates one of the most lovable qualities of this gifted young singer of Chicago, that after winning great success abroad, and with a splendid career there awaiting her, she preferred to return to the scenes of her old home. She possesses a sincere love of her art, but side by side with

don the pupil of Signor Randegger, her progress was steadily onward. Talent, energy, devotion and sincerity won quickly for her a recognition of artistic worth.

Her successes at the English capital were many and complete. She was a favorite singer at the musicales

it runs her deep devotion to friends, whom she wishes to share equally in all her triumphs.

The foundation of her artistic success she attributes to Mr. Frank Baird, her first vocal teacher. The unfortunate necessity which comes to many students, of unlearning and eradicating earlier musical culture was not her lot. When in 1896 she bade farewell to friends to become at Lon-

given by Jacques Blumenthal, the well-known composer. One of her most enjoyable engagements in England was her selection as the only vocalist for the reception of the Duke of Genoa and his Italian fleet at Portsmouth. While in London she made drawing-room recitals a specialty. Among other well-known people for whom she sang may be mentioned the Duke of Wellington, Duchess of

Manchester, Countess of Dundonald, Lady Abinger, Countess of Normanton, Countess of Dunmore, Viscountess Somerton, Countess of Fingal, Lady Hardman, Baron d'Erlanger and Sir William Robinson.

Upon her return to America Miss Buckley made her first appearance in 1897 at a vocal recital, scoring a great ovation. She was the soprano with a quartet of which Mary Louise Clary was alto, William Rieger, tenor, and Arthur Beresford bass, which on tour gave 102 concerts. She has sung four times in a season with the Apollo Club and also for the Mendelssohn Club.

Among other important engagements was her appearance in the first production of a German work with David Bispham in Milwaukee. Her courage was admirably shown on one occasion when she secured an engagement in New York by singing in a long distance telephone from Chicago. She has met and vanquished the numerous difficulties which confront all musical careers with a readiness as striking and effective as in the above instance, and all true musicians will join in congratulations upon her success. Miss Buckley is soprano at the Fourth Presbyterian Church.

WILLIAM NELSON BURRITT

William Nelson Burritt, one of the best known and ablest vocal teachers in the country, was born in Michigan in 1852. He has reached his present position through force of character and conscientious study. With Emerson, Mr. Burritt holds that "the sole inlet of the so to know, is the so to be," and he has given his life to the acquiring of knowledge that he may be able to give the result of that knowledge to others. Educated by the best teachers of his own country, as well as those of Europe, he has carried his work steadily forward year after year. He visits the old world almost yearly in search of progressive thought, that he may add later developments to his own accumulation of knowledge. Believing that honest work and that alone wins, he has never sought to advance himself by extraneous methods. The excellence of his work and that alone, has brought him the appreciation which is doubly valuable since it comes unsought.

GRACE BUCK

Miss Grace Buck is a native of Chicago, being of English parentage. For some years she sang as an amateur, being a member of several musical clubs. Her first instruction was received from Miss Lillian G. Smyth. Miss Buck was then taken to Europe, where her education was completed, and she studied under some prominent teachers in Paris and London. Her voice was put in the care of Madame Anna de la Granges, with whom she remained some two years. Three years ago Miss Buck went abroad, and worked for a year under Madame Marchisi. Upon her return she made a successful debut. Miss Buck at present is working most satisfactorily under M. W. F. Neidlinger, and will in future devote her time to concert and recital work, and also to teaching. In teaching Miss Buck takes a great interest, and looks forward to her work with untold pleasure. She has ambition, energy, and determination—her tastes have always leaned toward the artistic—her voice is a pure mezzo soprano—of delightfully sweet quality and very extensive range. Miss Buck sings French and German with an excellent accent, and is equally at home in lyric or dramatic music. Undoubtedly she is one of the most popular singers of the West.

SYDNEY PRESTON BIDEN

Of those taking a foremost place among the younger artists of Chicago, Sydney P. Biden, the baritone, certainly needs special mention. He was born in St. Louis, Mo., and having discovered he was gifted exceptionally as regards voice, worked seriously and assiduously. He is now in Europe, and will spend the next two years in Berlin and London in vocal studies. Especially has he devoted himself to oratorio, and in his repertory are embraced twenty oratorios, but he has also made a special study of the German Lieder. His appearances in Chicago were so successful that he received engagements all over the country, public and press uniting in his praise. In the result of his studies abroad much interest is of course manifested, and if the promise of his former work be fulfilled Mr. Biden will return to Chicago a finished artist to whose limit of success no measure is possible.

MRS. JOHANNA HESS BURR

Mrs. Hess Burr is so well known throughout the American musical world that it seems almost a superfluity to speak of what she has been able to do. In the wide circle of vocal instructors of today hers is one of the foremost names. This enviable reputation has not been easily obtained. It is the result of work unceasing, of energy never failing, of artistic resources absolutely unbounded. Not in Chicago nor in the cities of its immediate vicinity alone is Mrs. Hess Burr known, esteemed and honored. From the East, and even from abroad, have come pupils to a trainer and teacher of whom those who had met her knew no words of praise too profuse, no recommendations over strong.

Known for a number of years as one of the most proficient accompanists in this country, that was the branch of her profession which first made her name prominent. To be able to satisfy the fastidious tastes and the high requirements of Madame

Melba, of Mr. Bispham, and indeed of all the greatest artists of the day, to be able when accompanying to act as

the co-worker, sinking entirely her own identity in the desire to do the artist justice—this is the great gift that has brought Mrs. Hess Burr into such prominence and into such constant request.

A large number of those best known in the city's musical circles, whose reputations are already established on a firm footing, or who are now winning reputation, owe their successful training to her painstaking and most earnest work. Her school in Chicago is one of the best known in the West, and the pronounced success attained led her a couple of years ago to found a branch school in Milwaukee, which has also in every sense of the word proven itself a success and well worthy of Mrs. Hess Burr's reputation.

In ' speaking of this admirable woman, in whom the true artistic instinct is a second nature, a visit to the charming studio on the fifth floor of the Fine Arts Building gives striking testimonial to the estimation in which she is held by those whose names are written in the largest type on the firmament of music.

Tasteful little gifts, daintily inscribed photographs from the leading artists of the time, all speak in no uncertain terms of good service given. Amid these memorials, which necessarily must arouse the artist's truest pride, special attention will be directed to the splendid tribute paid her by Theodore Thomas. His gift of a portrait is inscribed: "To one of those rare persons who not only do good work but always their best." These words of Chicago's great director tell indeed the secret of Mrs. Hess Burr's success.

To each and every one of her pupils the best work in her power has been given; their interests have been at all times near to her heart; their good has been studied far more than her own. The furtherance of art, and more particularly such branches as she has made her own, has at all times been her greatest aid, and neither her labor nor her purse has ever been found lacking where the cause was deserving.

MAX BENDIX

In the history of music in Chicago, among those standing well to the fore, mention is made of an artist who at the time of the World's Exposition, when heavy storms had forced the retirement of the director, Theodore Thomas, ably and satisfactorily took up his arduous duties, gaining for that never-to-be-forgotten occasion all the musical laurels it was able to obtain.

But Max Bendix needed no such introduction to the people of the United States; already his reputation as a musician, violinist and concertmaster had been powerfully established. In either one of these capacities he had appeared in every city of importance in the Union, and his career has established him before the public as not only an able but a remarkably brilliant addition to the ranks of musical notables.

It was in New York in 1885 that Mr. Bendix first came to prominence as concertmaster of Van der Stucken's orchestra; later he was offered and accepted a similar position with the German opera. The character of his work while occupying the last mentioned was brought before Mr. Theodore Thomas (Max Bendix was then 20 years old), but his exceptional abilities and really remarkable talents as an orchestral violinist and soloist had attracted the attention of the leading orchestral musicians of the United States. For the Thomas Orchestra a concertmaster was needed, and Mr. Thomas, after giving Bendix an opportunity of playing for him, at once offered him the responsible and exalted appointment as concertmaster of the Theodore Thomas Orchestra, as the Chicago Orchestra was then known. This appointment Mr. Bendix held from 1886 to 1896, during the last five years of which he also served as assistant conductor.

A series of concerts was organized during the summer of 1892, the conductorship of which was given to Mr. Bendix. They continued for six weeks, with successful results of a most artistic and gratifying character.

In the Exposition orchestra of the World's Fair, during the following year, Mr. Thomas retained Mr. Bendix as assistant conductor of the orchestra of one hundred and fourteen artists, being selected from the leading orchestral players of the world. As

musicians everywhere acknowledge him to stand at the front of our American violinists.

It is, of course, as a violinist that Max Bendix has made his name most chiefly known, and in this regard wherever music in its truest and highest sense is appreciated his name is held in the greatest honor and esteem. His repertory is unusually large and covers all the standard compositions to be found in violin literature.

Mr. Bendix added to his orchestral

MAX BENDIX

has been mentioned before, the resignation of Theodore Thomas in August found Mr. Bendix chosen unanimously as sole conductor.

He continued with the orchestra for two years longer, and in 1896 decided to devote his talents to teaching, and since his severance from the Chicago organization Mr. Bendix has given his time exclusively to his work as a soloist and as a teacher. In the latter he has won an enviable reputation for remarkable results, while, as a soloist

work by organizing and directing the fine string quartet which bore his name and which appeared with the greatest possible success in every city of any consequence in the West.

The following is a partial list of compositions played by Mr. Bendix with the Thomas orchestra:

Moligne, Concerto in A minor—Brooklyn Philharmonic.
Schumann, Santasse in A minor (1888)— Chickering Hall, New York.
Brahms, Concerto in E minor (1889)—Chicago, Ill., Orange, N. J., Rochester, N. Y.

Beethoven, Concerto in D (1890)—Philadelphia, Pa., Chicago (2).

Moszkowski, Concerto in C (1891)—Lenox Lyceum, New York, Philadelphia, Pa.

Lalo, Spanish Symphonies—Lenox Lyceum, New York, Philadelphia, Pa., Chicago, Ill.

Paganini, Variations; "I Palpiti" (1891)— Lenox Lyceum, New York.

Dvorak, Concerto A minor (1891)—Chicago.

Wieniawski, Variations, Op. 15 (1891)— Chicago, St. Louis.

Godard, Concerto No. 2 (1892)—Chicago.

Vieuxtemps, Concerto E major (1893)— Chicago.

Saint-Saens, Concerto No. 3 (1894)—Chicago.

Brahms, Concerto, Op. 77 (1895)—New York, Philadelphia.

MacKenzie, Pibroch (1895).

Saint-Saens, Havanaise.

Wieniawski, Faust—Toledo, Cleveland, O.

Since 1895 Mr. Max Bendix has been touring all over America and has now opened a violin school, which has the indorsement of Ysaye, Sauret, Thomson and Halir, in Carnegie Music Hall, New York.

MR. AND MRS. T. S. BERGEY

As a director of singing societies and musical clubs Mr. T. S. Bergey has made for himself in Chicago a most enviable place. He now directs a large choir at St. John's M. E. Church and also very ably directs the Jane Addams Choral Society at Hull House. A native of Cass City, Mich., Mr. Bergey received his musical education at Chicago, at first with Fraulein Ella Dahl, a graduate of Leipsic Conservatory and a grand opera singer of recognized merit. Encouraged by his success as an amateur, he chose music as his life work and completed a thorough course in voice production and singing with Frederick W. Root and later with George Ellsworth Holmes, also studying oratorios and English ballad singing with Whitney Mockridge. His splendid baritone voice has gained for him an excellent position in the Chicago musical world.

Ellen Sutterlin Bergey, his accomplished assistant, began her musical career at eight years of age as piano soloist with a large orchestra. Born in Greencastle, Ind., she graduated from both the literary and musical departments of DePauw University. Her first teacher was Walter Howe, now director of the Symphony Orchestra, San Francisco. Later she studied several years with William Sherwood. Mrs. Bergey, as an accompanist has been associated with some of the most celebrated local and visiting artists at Chicago. As a thorough pianiste and accompanist she is now an able assistant in the musical work of her husband.

BIRDICE BLYE

Miss Birdice Blye, one of the most distinguished American pianistes, though not a Chicago musician, is well known here, and this winter is making Chicago the center of her concert work. Few musicians have had such a beautiful career, so full of interesting triumphs and successes from her first appearance at five years of age up to the present. At ten years she made a sensation in London and the continental cities by her extraordinary playing and won the praise of the severest critics in London, Paris, Dresden, Berlin, Vienna and other great musical centers of the old world. Oliver Wendell Holmes wrote of her: "Miss Blye is the most fascinating child I ever met. She is phenomenal in beauty, talent and charming manners." We can imagine a child of such rare personal charms and musical genius would naturally win all hearts, and she was received in the most aristocratic circles. She played before several of the courts of Europe, the principal nobility and most distinguished people, social and artistic, in every city visited. She has twice been a guest at the White House in Washington. On her father's side Miss Blye is related to one of the most illustrious American patriots, John Hancock, one of the signers of the Declaration of Independence, and to the Lees of Virginia. Her mother is a woman of literary taste and musical ability, whose forefathers were of the English nobility. Miss Blye studied at the Academy in London, winning the medals, and in New York with Rafael Joseffy and Edmund Neupert, who dedicated to her one of his compositions, his masterpiece.

After a series of concerts in the principal Eastern cities, where she was received with perfect ovations and where she played with Anton Seidl's orchestra, Mr. Seidl and Mr. William Steinway were so impressed with her wonderful talent that they urged her to go to Germany. Later she entered the Royal Hoch Schule in Berlin for a thorough course, taking piano with the director, Professor Rudorff, voice with Adolf Schulze, counterpoint and ensemble with Waldemar Bargiel and musical form with Dr. Phillipp Spitta. Miss Blye had a great love and reverence for Beethoven, and Dr. Hans von Bulow, the great Beethoven interpreter, became very much interested in her interpretation of Beethoven's works. Miss Blye completed her

studies with the incomparable Rubinstein, who was enthusiastic in praise of her many musical qualities and introduced her to the prominent musicians of Germany as "the great American pianiste." Miss Blye wrote her reminiscences of the great master for the Musical Courier and afterwards revised to read before the Authors' Association and prominent clubs. This and other articles were extensively copied by the press and show Miss Blye has also talent with the pen. Miss Blye has used the Steinway piano from the very beginning of her career, and the two names of artist and piano have become so inseparably connected that one scarcely thinks of Miss Blye without also thinking of the Steinway.

Possibly no American ever enjoyed the friendship of so many distinguished people at home and abroad, and Miss Blye has so many souvenirs of appreciation, gifts from almost every place she has been, from rich and poor, high and low, and the unique and interesting collection shows she knows how to value them, for the humblest objects are as carefully preserved as the most valuable. Among her hundreds of autograph photographs is one of Longfellow, who named her "the little golden-haired princess." Bancroft, the historian, sent her baskets of roses from his famous rose gardens, saying: "Even the roses bloomed brighter in her presence." There is also a picture of the gallant General Sherman, who gave her a letter to the Ambassador at the Court of St. James, James Russell Lowell, the poet, which read: "I send with this the sweetest poem in the English language, entitled Birdie Blye." A little tribute from Manuel Garcia of London, not long ago, says: "I do myself the honor of sending you my photograph, with every good wish for the new year." So many delightful incidents have occurred, so many charming acquaintances have been made, that Miss Blye's life is an unusually happy and beautiful one.

Music is not Miss Blye's only gift. She has been thoroughly educated in the English branches under private tutors. She is a fine linguist, speaking several languages fluently, and paints like an artist in oil and water colors. She studied painting at the Grosvenor Art Gallery in London, and several of her pictures were on exhibition, attracting much favorable comment. Miss Blye had advantages of study in the principal capitals of Europe, where the whole atmosphere is musical, and one has opportunities of studying the sister arts, which are absolutely necessary for the broadening of the intellect and developing all the faculties of a true musician. Courted, admired and surrounded, as she has always been, by every thing to mar girlish simplicity, Miss Blye is charmingly modest, and lives up to her ideals of all that is sweet and good in woman.

Miss Blye has played in several hundred concerts in Europe and the Eastern cities, and the brilliant success which she has achieved forms a faithful fulfillment of the prophecy of that greatest among authorities, Anton Rubinstein.

MRS. ANNA GROFF BRYANT

A true artist, a born teacher—both are successfully shown in the life of Mrs. Anna Groff Bryant. There are few vocal teachers having the qualities necessary to make a perfect instructor. Mrs. Bryant, being a gifted musician, careful and painstaking and possessing unusual knowledge of tone production, is in some respects unsurpassed, as the results obtained in the voices she has trained bear credible witness. Mrs. Bryant works from a legitimate basis. She always seeks to advance the artistic side of a pupil's nature. Her entire life is devoted to her work of making artists, not singers who can only sing a few songs, but artists, whose work, from beginning to end, will bear investigation. Mrs. Bryant works for beautiful tone as well as the perfect art of singing. In her studio are heard some excellent voices, most of whom are beginners and trained entirely by her. Some few have studied with other teachers and have come to Mrs. Bryant for her method of tone production, as she has made this a great specialty.

Mrs. Bryant graduated from the Northwestern University in 1888, and since that time has devoted herself to the study of voice and music. The first five years of her study she was trained as soprano and then later it was finally discovered that her voice was a contralto. Because of that experience of wrong training in her own voice she was led to investigate the physiology, the anatomy and the acoustics of the voice. In that way she discovered all about the defects of speech, such as stuttering, stammering, lisping, as ent vocal conditions Mrs. Bryant has thoroughly mastered and now stands as one of the most accomplished throat and vocal specialists in the city, and all this in addition to her remarkable method of interpretation. In the ex-

MRS. ANNA GROFF BRYANT

well as the defects of the voice, palatal tones, nasal tones, guttural tones, throaty tones, from which come the shrill, sharp tones which we so frequently hear in public performances. The larynx, the diseases of the vocal chords, then the study of the management of the breath—all these differ- amination for actual training of voice Mrs. Bryant obtained medals and diploma at the World's Fair. Mrs. Bryant will return to concert work next year, and, in conjunction with her husband, who has an exceedingly good tenor voice, she will give some recitals and also make an extended tour.

MRS. CARRIE R. BEAUMONT

Among the pianists of the city taking high place this talented lady must not be omitted. Her training has been unusually complete, and she very excellently utilized her opportunities. In her early days she studied with Madame Rounseville and Mr. Whitely and later with August Hyllested at the time connected with the Gottschalk School faculty. Having taken a teacher's certificate and graduated, Mrs. Beaumont took the post-graduate course of the Gottschalk School. There, in the annual contest, she won the Hallet & Davis piano and possesses another tribute to her good work in the diploma and medal for playing at the World's Fair. Now for eight years she has been teaching music in the city, for the last four years as accompanist to many of the most prominent musicians, who are ever ready to seek t' aid of such an excellent and enthusiastic artist. She is the accompanist of the Gottschalk School and teaches piano and sight reading. She has met with far above the ordinary measure of success and, as has been said before, has assured herself a high position among the musicians of Chicago.

CHARLES C. CURTISS AND THE FINE ARTS BUILDING

Close friends for many years, as young men engaged in the strenuous life of the marvelous Western metropolis, the career of the late George Benedict Carpenter, the proprietor and achiever of the Central Music Hall building and that of Charles C. Curtiss, the "inventor" as he is wont facetiously to speak, of the Fine Arts Building, present a singular and startling coincidence. Both battled manfully for high ideals against obstacles and discouragements apparently insurmountable, and both, with an indomitable fortitude and persistency conquered by sheer force of true grit and gave to the world a new illustration of the power of an idea. To each honorable struggling resulted in the creation of innumerable friends, honoring alike for noble endeavor and successful accomplishment through means not to be questioned by the most exacting. Of Mr. Carpenter's work and death, the treasured and sincerely mourned by all Chicago, the story is elsewhere very fully told. Easier in many ways is it to speak of him whose work is finished than the one who is still with us. To Mr. Carpenter the Central Music Hall building is the most fitting of monuments, and with it his memory is inseparably identified. In the Fine Arts building, with its several auditoriums, "the Studebaker," the home of English opera, the most handsome, elaborately appointed, and, in all ways, richest in the city; University Hall, where are given all the events of the miniature musical season, our song and piano and musical recitals, the Amateur Musical Club concerts, etc., etc., and with its Assembly Room, the theater of so much of the social life of the smart side of Chicago—in the Fine Arts building Mr. Curtiss is secure of a no less imperishable fame.

What the Central Music Hall building was to its day and generation, so

is the Fine Arts building to the Chicago of the present, which owns a vastly more complete and rounded civilization. Besides its auditoriums already referred to, which, it will be seen, provide for so many varied interests, the building has taken a most important part in the new activities of our modern life, as evidenced by the many social organizations now housed therein, comprising clubs for both men and women, having a "raison d'etre" in literary and artistic aims— of these it may be said that almost every one in the city, including the

FINE ARTS BUILDING

Caxton, the counterpart of New York's "Grolier Club" for men, the Woman's Club, the Fortnightly, the Amateur Musical, the Wednesday Club, the Daughters of the American Revolution, the Young Fortnightly, the Thursday and the Friday Clubs and yet others either have rooms in the building or meet within its hospitable precincts. Besides these there is the University of Chicago College Teachers' and Trustees' room, no less than three art rooms for the sale of the choicest paintings and engravings, the unequaled collection of Japanese and Chinese art objects of Henry Deakin and the art furniture emporium of W. K. Cowan & Co., the group of music and dramatic workers, which includes such celebrities as Sherwood, Spiering, Neidlinger, Frank King Clark, Seeboeck, Mrs. John Vance Cheney, Mme. Hess Burr, Dr. Robert Goldbeck, Mrs. Milward Adams, Mme. Anna Morgan,

that distinctive character which has make it known everywhere where beautiful rooms and miniature theaters elicit universal admiration, are such publishers as West, Harper & Brothers, D. Appleton & Co., Maynard, Merrill & Co., the Barry Educational Company, The Dial, Chicago's foremost literary journal, and one of which the whole country is proud, etc., etc.

While, as Mr. Curtiss is wont to emphasize, it is this distinguished constituency which has given the building its tremendous prestige; it is, no doubt equally true that the building, planned as it was for just such occupancy, and

THE STUDEBAKER

and others, who completely fill three floors of the mammoth structure. Perhaps even more highly prized is its artist colony on the uppermost floor, which comprises such men and women as Lorado Taft, Ralph Clarkson, Oliver Dennett Grover, E. J. Dressler, Charles Francis Brown, Joseph C. and Frank X. Leyendecker, W. J. Reynolds, Mrs. Virginia Reynolds, Bertha Menzler, Marguerite West, Mrs. S. W. Moore, names synonymous with the advancement of art in Chicago, the very cream of its artistic world.

Others on the literary and educational side who help to give to the building

inviting, as it was made in all its appointments, was primarily the means through which has been assembled under its roof practically all that is best of the best side of Chicago life.

Entering the building one is at once impressed by its broad groined corridor that this is no commercial edifice, and throughout the decorations and the furnishings, the presence of cozy corners and convenient benches artistically shaped and of waving palms, suggests and confirms the character of the building and gives it, as has been said of it, an atmosphere of its own.

At the outset and before the building

had established itself, it required a nice discrimination and no little of what is known as nerve when the long and spacious corridors were empty to "turn down" good responsible tenants whose business did not fit with the ordained uses of the building, but Mr. Curtiss was unfaltering in his faith in the issue and turned a deafly inflexible ear to the whispering of the merely sordid sort, and to-day enjoys the privilege of laughing at those who then shook their heads and now unanimously agree that the enterprise has been superbly managed and, as one often hears, "as only Mr. Curtiss could have done it."

the music house of Lyon & Healy, which he left to accept the position of manager of the Root & Sons Music Company, from which he resigned to go abroad in 1881. Upon his return he became identified with the management of the Chicago branch of the Weber Piano business which remained under his direction until 1895, when he disposed of his holdings in the Manufacturers' Piano Company, of which he had been the president, and retired to devote himself to this great undertaking.

It was during the period referred to that Mr. Curtiss had built for his busi-

UNIVERSITY HALL.

Born in Chicago July 31, 1847, all Mr. Curtiss' liftime has been passed amid its rapid development. His father, coming from New England in 1833, found but a straggling village, where now more than 2,000,000 of people claim residence. He plunged actively and prominently into the life of that formative period and was an important figure in it, as every "old settler" of the city well knows; before he died, in 1859, he had twice been honored with the chief magistracy.

Charles Curtiss was twelve years old at his father's death. Before he was seventeen he was in the army and saw service during the civil war.

It was quite by accident, he tells us, that he became bookkeeper in 1869 for

ness in Chicago the building known as Weber Music Hall—the first of its kind ever constructed, and it was this undertaking that first directed his attention to the value of the idea when fully ultimated. He had in this preliminary enterprise tested the possibilities of the plan and proven practically that the idea of centralizing the artistic and literary concerns of the city was something more than a Utopian dream, and, his mind being of an artistic and literary order, became enamored with the undertaking. In him the artistic instinct found the rare combination of a splendid business capacity—and to think was to act. For almost fifteen years, he tells us, this idea engrossed his most profound attention and before finally devoting to it his entire time he had canvassed the whole field exhaustively on its practical as well as its ideal side. Every important building in the country of an approximate character was visited and thoroughly inspected preliminary to drawing the plans in which the most approved points of each were incorporated, thereby resulting in the production of a building, as is universally admitted, with many novel features never before attempted. There is, it may reasonably be asserted, no building, public or private, in Chicago in which its citizens have so much pride as the Fine Arts Building.

The Messrs. Studebaker Brothers, large owners of Chicago property, broad-minded and public-spirited men and much devoted to artistic and educational concerns, impressed in the first instance by Mr. Curtiss' evident sincerity, by his high personal character and his recognized ability, became finally interested in the project and it was through their munificence that the idea now rapidly crystallized into a fact.

The location chosen—facing the Lake Front Park on Michigan Boulevard and adjoining the Auditorium Hotel, with which it is connected, on the one hand, and the Chicago Club, on the other, is admittedly quite the most superb in the whole of Chicago, and the three buildings occupying it make perhaps the finest and most imposing block anywhere in the world.

Notable indeed was the assemblage which on Oct. 5 and 6, 1898, gathered here upon the occasion of the formal opening of the building and its real dedication to the high purposes for which it had been prepared. An occasion which was made the occasion of general and lavish hospitality by all those who had been so fortunate as to secure studios in the rooms of the different clubs and associations. Praise was everywhere and amazement with those who had not enjoyed a previous glimpse of the many peculiar features of the building. There was no dissonant voice in the universal acclaim that here was an ideal building created for an ideal purpose.

A function of the building which could not well have been anticipated, but is one of the most beneficent features has been the establishment of English opera by the Castle Square Opera Company, of which Henry W. Savage of New York is the proprietor, at popular prices—through which hundreds of thousands of people who heretofore probably have never enjoyed the privilege may now hear all the standard operas capably rendered at an expense of from 25 cents to $1. These performances have been attended by prodigious audiences, and their educational value can hardly be overestimated.

Although a gentleman of quiet tastes, Mr. Curtiss is very well known in the highest social circles of the city and enjoys the personal esteem and friendship of many of its most prominent citizens. He is a member of the Loyal Legion and of the Chicago Literary Club and the Caxton Club.

MRS. CARRIE JACOBS–BOND

One of Wisconsin's most talented daughters is Mrs. Carrie Jacobs-Bond, A native of Janesville, Wis., Mrs. Bond began making songs when she was only four years of age. She has accomplished a vast amount of work, having written no less than sixty-five songs, and of all of these, with but two or three exceptions, has composed not only the music but the words also.

She is a most versatile composer, and she has also a fine, clear mezzo-soprano voice of sweetness and depth. The Chicago Tribune says of her: "Mrs. Bond's talent as a composer, performer or vocalist would secure for her an enviable reputation in the world of music for her excellence in each branch is phenomenal."

Mrs. Bond is kept busy giving recitals made up entirely of her own compositions, both instrumental and vocal. Recitals and entertainments for children, with children's songs, form a particularly interesting portion of her work.

As a writer of children's music, Mrs. Bond has scored a great success and a collection of four songs just published and which she sang in a recital of her own compositions, recently given at Kimball Hall, Chicago, have proved to be especial favorites with the music-loving people of that city. "A Little Shoe," "A Lullaby," "Have You Seen My Kittie," and "When My Ships Come Home," compose this quartet of childhood's airs, which are of much delicacy and pathos.

MARGARET CAMERON

Not long since a young lady pupil studying with Margaret Cameron made the remark, "I never knew what it was *to be taught* until under Miss

Cameron's instructions, and I have taken lessons from several others." This very broad praise is assented to by many, and if pure musical taste, joined to intelligent application form a basis for the giving of instruction Miss Cameron well deserves the encomium of her pupil. In her early girlhood Miss Cameron resolved to devote herself to music and after a few years of desultory study in Canada she entered the Chicago Musical College as a pupil of Mr. Hyllested. For sometime she remained under his painstaking care, making the progress an industrious scholar is sure to do with an able teacher. Then came the thought of study abroad and the decision to go to Vienna—for the height of Miss Cameron's ambition was to study with Leschetizky, and to this incomparable master Miss Cameron feels she owes more than she can in words express.

On returning to Chicago Miss Cameron taught for a few years in the Gottschalk Lyric School. In 1899 she opened a studio of her own in the Fine Arts Building where in addition to receiving their lessons her pupils meet occasionally "en classe," and it is indeed remarkable how speedily the young people lose all amateurish characteristics and enter on the path that leads to professional finish.

Miss Cameron has before her the prospect of a successful and busy life in her chosen vocation and already has been successful in gathering around her hosts of friends and admirers, every one of whom wishes her Godspeed.

FRANK KING CLARK

One of the most successful bassos to-day is Frank King Clark. Mr. Clark was born in the State of Washington and before coming to Chicago made his home in Tacoma, Washington. Although educated in Columbia College, New York, for the profession of law, he gave up the hope of a business

press everywhere has been unanimous in his praise.

Mr. Clark's rapid rise is one more evidence of the power over audiences of a big, hearty, manly voice pleasantly produced and intelligently delivered. Repeated overtures from operatic organizations have not moved Mr. Clark

career to devote himself to the study of music. Since a very early age he has evinced unusual musical talent and since entering the profession his rise in the artistic world has been phenomenal.

His first appearance was made a little less than three years ago and in that short space of time he has become one of the leading singers and has appeared with many of the famous organizations of America. His singing, as well as his voice, is exceptional and the

from his determination to devote himself for the present to the field of oratorio and concert. His ambition, however, is for the grand opera stage and in another year or two at the latest he will go to Europe to pursue his studies there in preparation for an operatic career.

He is to-day one of the best of American bassos and ranks with the leaders in his profession. The newspaper criticisms everywhere teem with expressions of praise for his work.

MARY WOOD CHASE

This talented musical artist of Chicago is a native of Brooklyn, N. Y. Her girlhood was spent at Ithaca, N. Y., and immediately following her graduation from the high school at the age of sixteen she completed a three years' course at the New England Conservatory, Boston, Mass., devoting also some attention to literary culture. After teaching in the West and South at the head of the musical department of a prominent college, she studied for nearly four years with Oscar Raif of Berlin. Called suddenly home, she was obliged to cancel five engagements in as many European cities. Locating at Chicago, she has taught with brilliant success and has given numerous recitals in Western cities, receiving the most generous praise wherever she appeared. The dean of music of one of the Western universities said that in ten years the university had never listened to an artist whose entire program was so thoroughly satisfactory.

FREDERICK CARBERRY

A prominent artist in writing of this popular young tenor says:

"Mr. Carberry possesses a sympathetic, velvety tenor voice of marvelous sweetness and magnetic charm, smooth and even through its large compass, rich and effective on the upper register, a healthy, resonant voice which at once fills the hearer with a comfortable confidence in its natural resources of reach and power. And the truth is that Mr. Carberry sings as summer songsters do, because it is second nature with him, because he must sing.

Besides an excellent voice, which Schumann considered the greatest of all gifts, Mr. Carberry displays in his singing a manly idea, a fervor and energy that would hardly be expected from his slight and slender physique. Thrilling in tender passages, his voice is broad and his style authoritative in compositions of a forcible character. One wonders at the perception of fitness and fine feeling of truth which

FREDERICK CARBERRY

can draw from that apparently delicate organization the powerful accents of intense power.

The wonder ceases, however, when it is known that, besides voice and talent, Mr. Carberry has the advantage of a serious and well-cultivated

intellect, and scholarly habits of research and observation. All the critics are struck with the admirable intelligence that characterizes his interpretations. The rendering of his selections, they say, is always tempered with heart and brain. Every word, every phrase, is full of meaning, because he means all that he sings.

Frederick Carberry is a singer to whom can be applied the much abused expression of 'artistic temperament' —a perfect proportion between the various gifts in a singer that go to make the complete artist and harmonious *modus vivendi* in the use of those gifts. This explains why Mr. Carberry is always re-engaged wherever he has once sung; why he shares equally the honors with his more famous seniors, particularly in large works demanding the exercise of the highest artistic faculties; why it can be safely predicted that, with his youth and ambition, he is on the threshold of a most brilliant lyric career."

To Mr. Carberry's credit it should be stated, as a lady was heard to say of him, that he has a "normal head." Sensible, unassuming, unspoiled by praise, he offers to psychologists and physiologists the phenomenal instance of a modest tenor. This should certainly be reckoned as the most significant earnest of his future career.

Recently Mr. Carberry has toured the country with the Bendix Grand Concert Company, where his success has been very decided.

MRS. GEORGE BENEDICT CARPENTER

By birth a Chicagoan, it is but natural in accordance with the traditions of the city that Mrs. Carpenter should possess business as well as artistic merits. Widowed years ago, she became the lessee of Central Music Hall and managed the building most successfully, making the acquaintance in the pre-Auditorium years, of all the principal singers and musicians who visited Chicago. Retiring from business a few years ago with an ample

fortune, founded by her husband's bequest, increased by her clever management and administration of Central Music Hall, she went abroad with her son and daughters for the benefit of the latter's musical education, an education which has made Miss Marian Carpenter one of the delightful violinists of the day.

While abroad the entire fortune of Mrs. Carpenter was swept away. Returning to Chicago, she adopted a unique and successful business. As musical director she supplied clubs in all parts of the country with musical

der. That Mrs. Carpenter has this combination of qualities her signal success amply testified. She is one of

MRS. GEORGE BENEDICT CARPENTER

talent, and found engagements for many artists. The position was one of extreme delicacy, and required both executive and artistic ability of a high or-

the conspicuous successes among women who have ventured into business.

MARIAN CARPENTER

Miss Marian Carpenter, a resident of Chicago from her birth, is the daughter of Mr. and Mrs George Benedict Carpenter, thus inheriting from both parents her exceptional musical talent. This evincing itself at a very early age in the perception of "absolute pitch" and a peculiar sensitiveness to music in all forms was early directed to the study of the violin under Edward Heimendahl, and since pursued under the finest masters both at home and abroad. Among the latter are included

Professor Jacobsohn, Max Bendix, and Professor Emanuel Wirth, the latter the colleague of Joachim, with whom Miss Carpenter spent two years in Berlin, returning to continue her studies with Max Bendix, though with no intention of leading a professional life. Later the necessity for taking such a position found Miss Carpenter prepared for the debut she made two years ago, which has been followed with success in the most marked degree. Not only has Miss Carpenter been in demand in the most exclusive social circles of Chicago, but her public appearances in recitals and concerts in Chicago, Detroit, Bloomington, Cincinnati, etc., have been a series of tri-

this season has appeared in connection with the readings of Mr. George Riddle, engagements being filled for the Art Institute of Chicago, the Pittsburg Art Society and the Minneapolis

MARIAN CARPENTER

umphs exceedingly flattering to so young an artist. Miss Carpenter is the violinist of the "Studio Trio," which

Institute of Arts and Letters, besides quite a number of clubs.

JULIA L. CARRUTHERS

Whether as composer, teacher or pianiste there might be some difficulty in ranking this representative of Chicago's music. She has accomplished so much in all branches of the art as a teacher of children that her place is assured; while as the teacher for teachers who undertake the training of children she is known all over the country. Normal work has always appealed most strongly to Miss Carruthers and it was the special gifts evinced in this direction that caused her to be offered charge of the normal department of the

Chicago Conservatory. Entirely in favor of sound elementary instruction for the young, her method of imparting that training so peculiar to herself, but so satisfactory and in its results so great a success, has procured her a large class of pupils, among whom are numbered well-known teachers and the children of several of the leading musicians of the city—a strong testimonial to her remakable powers. That music should be recognized as an expression of the highest in the human nature has been her constant contention, and this she considers the logical sequence to the development of the musical perceptions and faculties. What she seeks to impart are musical thought and musical comprehension, not mere mechanical execution. To many music is second nature. Miss Carruthers is evidently one of these so favored. Bounteous fortune has blessed her, her ways are songs with tuneful melodies easily understood her reputation was quickly established. She lectured and was given frequent opportunity of exhibiting the work she could do—practical work as opposed to the numberless theories in vogue with children. At the World's Fair, and having organized a number of children's recital pro-

JULIA L. CARRUTHERS

winning, her personality most magnetic. Although still young, for ten years she controlled the largest children's class in Chicago. Before the number of pupils so entirely occupied her hours Miss Carruthers played much in public and was made an honorary member of the Amateur Musical Club when such an honor was rarely bestowed. As a writer of children's grams, she founded later a *kinder* symphony orchestra, an institution unique in the musical history of the city and whose concert she has since made an annual event. After her resignation from the Chicago Conservatory Miss Carruthers received a most flattering offer from the Sherwood School of Music, with which institution she became identified last year.

If ever there was a specialist in the teaching of music it is Julia Carruthers, as her method of children's musical training and normal work with teachers (who com⌐ from all parts of the country to study with her) are individual to her. Her inspiration and equipment for this work have been derived considerably from Calvin B. Cady. Wherever Miss Carruthers may be it is certain her work in the field of music· will be sound, satisfactory and alike honorable to herself and to the city with which she is associated.

EDMUND W. CHAFFEE

In addition to extended instruction in America this well-known teacher of harmony, counterpoint and composition, whose studio is 58 Kimball Hall, completed a four years' musical course

in Berlin. He was born in Paw Paw, Ill., and when a child began his musical education with a local teacher. Coming to Chicago in 1880 he studied the piano successively with W. S. B., Mathews, F. G. Gleason and Emil Liebling. For four years he taught piano at Mendota, Ill., then in 1887 went to Europe and remained three years in Berlin. Entering Stearn's Conservatory in that city, he completed a full course—piano with Professor Heinrich Ehrlich; voice with Fraulein Jenny Meyers; harmony, counterpoint and composition with Ludwig Bussler. During the last year Mr. Chaffee was appointed assistant teacher of harmony. His work in the conservatory was supplemented by private lessons in musical theory from Professor Heinrich Urban, a most excellent teacher.

Returning to America in 1891, Mr. Chaffee became a resident of Chicago, and a member of the faculty of the Gottschalk Lyric School. He is yet a member of the faculty and also one of the directors. His time not thus employed is absorbed by the demands of his private studio.

D. ALVA CLIPPINGER

The fame of D. A. Clippinger as a teacher and conductor of music extends far and wide and brings to his studio at 40 Kimball Hall many pupils from all parts of the country. The door stands open to him for a public career, but Mr. Clippinger gives preference in his artistic career to the art of teaching, though yielding to some degree to his equally marked talent as a musical director and conductor.

A native of Ohio, he began his musical studies at the Fort Wayne conservatory, where he completed a course in composition, singing and piano. As director at musical conventions and at musical departments of summer assemblies and Chautauquas he laid the foundation for his subsequent success as director of large choruses and choirs. For two years he had charge of the musical department of the Fort Wayne College, then in 1887 came to the broader field in Chicago. By hard work he has won a foremost place as teacher and conductor. Though winning immediate success of the most substantial character, Mr. Clippinger was impelled by his true artistic spirit to acquire in Europe the broadest musical instruction. In 1890 he became

studying oratorio and German Lieder, singing under Georg Henschel. In America he has achieved high distinc-

D. ALVA CLIPPINGER

a pupil in voice production under Herr Julius Hey of Berlin and the following year studied under William Shakespeare. Again in 1897 he went abroad,

tion. In addition to studio work he directs the musical department of the Lewis Institute and has charge of the music at the First Baptist Church.

MR. HOLMES COWPER

Mr. Holmes Cowper, the tenor, whose voice delighted the vast audiences at the Omaha Exposition, where he made his first appearance in America, is a native of Canada, having been born in the town of Dundas, Ontario. He was educated at the grammar school there, and after spending some years at the Hamilton Collegiate, passed thence to Pickering College, previous to engaging in banking in the employ of the Imperial Bank of Canada. The growing demands upon his time which the proper cultivation

of his voice called for necessitated the relinquishing of his business career, and he devoted himself assiduously thenceforward to the pursuit of his art under the tutelage first of Miss Jean Forsyth of Winnipeg. Afterward he spent two years in London, receiving instruction from Frederick Walker, member of the Royal Academy of Music, and while there in addition to the many concert engagements which were pressed upon him, he filled the position most satisfactorily of tenor soloist at the St. James Church, Pic-

MR. HOLMES COWPER

cadilly. Much of the rare beauty of Mr. Cowper's tones is due to the great assistance of his wife, herself a most accomplished organist and accompanist, Mrs. Cowper having studied harmony and organ with the best teachers in America and England.

The peculiar richness of Mr. Cowper's voice at once marked him for a high place in the ranks of modern singers, a place which he will always hold if the advancing power and extended range of vocalization be any criterion of success. It is at this day a voice of singular sweetness and delicacy of tone, and the possession of a dramatic instinct which accompanies it, form a combination which will lead the owner, still a young man, to the very summit of the ladder of artistic fame.

MABELLE CRAWFORD

Mabelle Crawford is a singer whose natural gifts and thorough training entitle her to a foremost place among Chicago's prominent artists. Miss Crawford made her debut eight years ago, at the age of 16, and since that time has continuously occupied a lucrative church position. For the past four years she has been contralto soloist at St. Paul's Church, and also of the

Kehilath Anshe Mayno Synagogue, and has delighted audiences throughout the United States with her splendid voice in opera, concert and oratorio. Miss Crawford's work is always characterized by great intellectuality and artistic refinement, and she has concertized with some of the greatest artists, among whom are Mr. William Sherwood and Mr. Max Bendix. Miss Crawford's two appearances at the International Exposition brought her fresh laurels, and she has been contralto soloist at the great New York Chautauqua for the past three years. Since Miss Crawford's return home she has received letters from members of the faculty saying: "No singer has ever achieved greater success upon the Chautauqua platform, or given better satisfaction than she." Her career will be carefully watched by music-loving people.

CENTRAL MUSIC HALL AND THE LATE GEORGE BENEDICT CARPENTER

For many years the Central Music Hall was the largest audience room in Chicago, and as such its place in the musical history will always remain firm and steadfast. As its name implies, it is central. From west, from north, from south, its facilities for transportation cannot be excelled. It is the starting point for many suburban services, and is in close connection with every railroad line out of the city. Within the last two years even greater improvement has been made in this direction, for the erection of the elevated road—fortunately a block away and consequently working no detriment to the musical properties of the hall—and the completion of the

Union Loop, have enormously increased its accessibility.

It was in 1879 that the rapidly increasing musical necessities of our great city were grasped by a number of leading capitalists and influential citizens, and a stock company formed to erect the Central Music Hall block and utilize to the best possible service. The outcome was the happy fulfillment of many cherished ideas of the late George B. Carpenter, who became its

it became the recognized musical center and from that time to the present it has been the home of some of the chief musical organizations of the city, among which may be readily recalled the Chicago Musical College, the Apollo Club, the Mendelssohn Club and the Tamaso Mandolin Orchestra. The tenants of the offices are not confined to the musical profession, but doctors, artists and others have always been eager to avail themselves of the

APOLLO HALL.

first manager and whose untimely death deprived the literary and musical circles of Chicago of one of its brightest lights.

The Central Music Hall Company performed its task well. In addition to the large auditorium, from which its name is derived, the building comprises a smaller hall known as the Apollo, seating 200 people, and suitable for rehearsals and receptions, twelve stores and about seventy offices. No sooner was it completed than

accommodation offered. The management has at all times been most liberal in its policy, and as improvement after improvement has been brought forward in this most progressive age, immediate advantage has been taken. Through its spacious entrance thousands of people pass daily, but so excellently is the building constructed that possibly the strongest impression which a visitor receives is the atmosphere of quiet refinement everywhere prevailing and which is so necessary to those who have need of studios, and is so usually foreign to buildings possessed of the distinct advantage of being centrally located.

Twenty years have elapsed since the Central Music Hall was formally opened to the public, who united with the local press and with all visiting artists in enthusiastic praise for the manner in which the comfort and well-being of both artist and audience had been considered. This, too,

plete with earnest thought and the truest piety, but at the same time so fancifully and delightfully poetic.

In the direction of furnishings and decorations, the Central Music Hall management has been liberal and indeed lavish. The entrance and foyer have been redecorated in new designs and colorings, thereby making this audience-room, where the public has so long been accustomed to feel at home, still more attractive.

RECEPTION PARLOR OF APOLLO HALL.

had been done without the slightest loss to the necessities of acoustic principles and properties. The galleries are so splendidly constructed that there is not a seat in the house but gives a view of the stage. The organ is one of the finest in the country and is heard to excellent advantage at the services every Sunday which have been for many years a feature of the city. Here it was that Prof. David Swing, now with the majority, was accustomed to deliver his eloquent discourses so re-

On its platform there are few artists of world-wide fame who have not, at some time or another, appeared, and the roll of distinguished men and women contains a great number, "familiar to our lips as household words:" Henry Ward Beecher, Hon. Schuyler Colfax, Hon. Daniel Dougherty, Thomas B. Reed, Phillips Brooks, Mrs. Livermore, Mrs. Elizabeth Cady Stanton, Mme. Besant, Matthew Arnold, Edwin Arnold, Conan Doyle, Mark Twain, George Cable, F. Hopkinson Smith, Thomas Nelson Page, John W. Stoddard, Ian Maclaren, James Whitcomb Riley, Opie Reid, Marion Crawford and Anthony Hope.

Lyric Artists.—Mme. Adelina Patti, Carlotta Patti, Christine Nilsson, Mme. Gerster, Mme. Albani, Mme. Nordica, Clara Louise Kellogg, Mme. Scalchi, Annie Louise Cary, Miss Emma Thursby, Signor Campanini, Signor bourg, Scharwenka.

Violinists—Ole Bull—his last pub-

lic appearance, May 22, 1880—Remenyi, Musin, Wieniawski, Camilla Urso, Cesar Thomson and the 'cellist, Gerardy.

Pianists—Paderewski, Mme. Carreno, Fannie Bloomfield-Zeisler, Joseffy, De Pachmann, Sherwood, Hambourg, Scharwenka.

Musical Organizations—Theodore Thomas' Orchestra, Boston Philharmonic Society, Gilmore's Band and all local societies of any repute.

A NOTE ON OPERATIC CONDITIONS AND INTERNATIONAL POSSIBILITIES

It has been claimed that American men have not equally good voices with American women. I deny that claim. It is the lack of opportunity and merit that conveys the impression of this falsely assumed situation.

The American man does not regard too fixedly the necessity of an active business career to make it secondary to a career in art. In a majority of cases inquiry will prove that the American man has others depending upon him either through choice or obligation. As direct consequence no matter how good the voice may be, there will be hesitancy on the part of the man to enter upon a career with such prescribed limitations as America now offers to him as a singer.

There is the church choir, which only in exceptional instances means entire support; there is light opera work, and there is teaching. Concert work is seriously interfered with by foreign artists, who, firmly established in public favor, through frequent appearances in opera, are more desirable from a financial point of view to concert promoters and managers.

It is true that the best prima donnas coming to us are American; it is also true that we hear men singers in every cast in the Grau performances who could be put to shame by singers resident among us but never given opportunity. Mr. Damrosch and Mr. Ellis on the other hand did evince a

desire to aid the American men singers. Again, there are American women singing in opera in nearly every one of the principal cities of Europe and who have small hopes of being brought to their own country by similar engagements.

Simply because opera is an exotic with us and we can never hope for anything else until we have opera in English established on the broadest lines and with a dignity commensurate with our national importance. In Boston, in New York, and latterly in Chicago continuous opera in English along modest lines has received generous recognition. MacDowell once said to me that he would not write an opera for performance by the Abbey-Grau company, but that he would consider writing one for the Castle Square organization because it stood for something American, which the other did not. San Francisco has, for twenty years, claimed a securely founded opera in English. The list of works produced at the Tivoli during the course of its existence shows runs for Gounod's. "Faust" of thirty-seven nights; Verdi's "Trovatore" thirty-two nights; Weber's "Der Freischutz" twenty-eight nights and the same composer's "Oberon" for an equal number. That proves at least the appreciation of the people in this direction. It also proves the incomprehensibility of the situation that we, who as a people, are so self-reliant in all else, should in this one branch of musical art, the opera, be so dependent. Assuredly emancipation has come in a measure and must grow with the growth of time. The immediate and generous recognition of the public and helpfulness of the press in the case of the Castle Square venture have proved how eagerly a change of conditions is awaited. There is another phase of the situation which is of interest to us, and that is the movement actively urged by Mr. Fuller Maitland and Sir Alexander Mackenzie looking to the establishment of a national opera in London.

With the nearer relations existing between our own country and England, with a common language, with a literature appealing equally to each people, a reciprocal relationship in this branch of musical art would seem but a natural consequence. It would mean a strengthening of musical conditions in both countries, it would mean an extended field and hopefulness not alone for our singers, but for our composers. We are in America and England struggling under many conditions that are identical. We need to think of the future more than of the present. And after all the future of today welcomes the presence of tomorrow. It has been perpetually held aloft that we have no composers capable of writing acceptable opera either in America or in England. If such is the case, why does this condition exist, even granting such an assertion to be fact. It exists because musically, we have persisted in speaking a foreign language to the exclusion of our own.

If conditions had gagged our literature to the extent that they have gagged our art we should today be in a fair way of forgetting our own tongue. How do we know until we have properly encouraged our com-

posers and given them full opportunity what they can or cannot do. English speaking peoples have not yet brought forth a Verdi or a Gounod. A goodly share of the fault as far as this condition goes is our own. If art will starve through discouragement there is small doubt that a certain camp of our critics will give our composers every opportunity.

To listen to such writers is to give our individual aid in killing off all hopeful self-assertion in our composers. We cannot spring into completion in a day nor has another nation furnished any such precedent. But we can, by working together, bring that day nearer. If we loyally support the good we have, yet better will follow. A pessimistic general at the head of pessimistic troops never yet placed a battle to the credit of his country.

Our strength lies in optimism and not in pessimism and our strength lies together. It is to the one nation or the other that we must look for librettos in English and on themes that appeal directly and pre-eminently to us. It is to the one nation or the other that we must look for the truest musical reflection of those themes.

The sooner we recognize these facts and that as Americans and Englishmen we should stand together in a common musical cause the better. Advance in the one country means for the other enlarged opportunity in this field. Our singers as well as our own composers are vitally concerned. In England there is a movement to further opera along national lines. In America the demand for opera in English has made itself splendidly apparent. There is no better time to combine in formulating practical plans for mutual musical strength and advance than the present.

WILLIAM ARMSTRONG.

.CHARLES W. CLARK

Charles W. Clark is of the highest type of the American artist and an exemplification of his courage, determination and success in music. A native of Northwestern Ohio, Mr. Clark first came to Chicago in 1888 and seriously devoted himself to music. In this ing the grand opera field. Mr. de Reszke was seconded by Mr. Grau of the Metropolitan Opera House, who made the Chicago singer an immediate offer to assume important roles in the repertory of his company, both in this country and at Convent Garden.

brief space of eleven years he has attained his present notable position and won for himself distinction in concert and oratorio work throughout this country. More recently, through the personal request of Mr. Edouard de Reszke and at his strongly expressed desire, Mr. Clark contemplated enter- His large clientage and the long list of his concert and oratorio engagements caused Mr. Clark to refuse this offer, which, however, is still held open, Mr. Grau and the distinguished Polish basso, both being firmly convinced of the success awaiting him in the operatic field.

Mr. Clark's first engagement in Chicago was as a member of the quartet choir of the First Centennial Baptist Church. Subsequently he signed to sing in the choir of the First Presbyterian Church, Evanston, of which the Rev. Dr. Hillis was pastor. When Dr. Hillis accepted a call to the Central Church in Chicago to succeed Dr. Swing, the new incumbent prevailed upon Mr. Clark, of whom he has for years been a stanch friend and firm admirer, to follow him. As a result Mr. Clark has been soloist in the Central Church from that time until the present, excepting the period of his study and concert work in London and the English provinces. This course was undertaken on the advice of Mr. Georg Henschel, whose enthusiasm for Mr. Clark's voice and attainments prompted the offer of important concert engagements under his direction as inducements for Mr. Clark to take up his residence in the English metropolis. Mr. Clark's London debut was made as soloist in a Wagner concert under Mr. Henschel's conductor-ship, February 18, 1897, and was followed ten days later by a second concert appearance in Bach's Passion Music, "St. Matthew." Succeeding these engagements Mr. Clark sang in important concerts in London, Manchester, Liverpool, and other cities with the foremost organizations, taking part in miscellaneous programs, and as soloist in cantatas and oratorios.

Returning to America two seasons ago, he immediately fulfilled engagements with the Handel and Haydn Society of Boston, with which organization he was heard twice in brief succession; with the Oratorio Society of New York; the Oratorio Society of Baltimore; in a Wagner concert and in the Brahms "Requiem" with the Chicago Orchestra, under direction of Mr. Theodore Thomas, at the Auditorium, Chicago. During the past season he has sung all over the country besides filling engagements with all the local organizations, including two appearances with the Apollo Club.

MRS. GEORGE A. COE

Whether as pianiste, instructor or lecturer on musical subjects, this distinguished member of the faculty of the Northwestern University School of Music takes a foremost place among those who are laboring forcefully and zealously for educational progress.

Born in California, her first musical instruction was obtained from Ernst Hartmann, a well known follower of the Kullak School. Then she went to Boston, taking up piano with Carl Baermann, and musical theory under John W. Tufts. So marked were her abilities that the position was offered her of head of the piano department of the University of Southern California, at Los Angeles, where remarkable success attended her efforts.

She sought, however, the highest in her art, and going to Berlin spent three years in that city in musical training. At the completion she took the admission examination for the *Konigliche Hochschule fur Musick.* In this so high is the standard set that very few Americans essay, and of all applicants, including the Germans, but one-third are successful. Mrs. Coe was of the latter, and for her instructors were assigned, piano, Heinrich Barth; ensemble playing, Waldemar Bargiel; theory and composition, Reinhold Succo. During her last year in Berlin she devoted herself to private study under Moritz Moskowski, and returned to this country with testimonials of the most enthusiastic character from her various teachers.

Mrs. Coe made Evanston her home, and her talents and exceptional attainments won immediate recognition, and for the past six years she has been connected with the University School of Music in that town. Beyond these responsible duties, however, her engagements by various clubs and societies have been many. A notable course on "Wagner and the Wagnerian Music

opera, the sonata and nocturne, was equally successful. Mrs. Coe is evidently a born lecturer; she possesses the faculty of entertaining while imparting instruction, has a large range of subjects, and it is good to know is about to broaden her sphere and be

MRS. GEORGE A. COE

Dramas," before the Evanston Orchestral Club, a season or two ago, made a great impression, while another course of lectures on "Primitive Music," which covered the history of notation, the Chinese and other systems, as well as the little known music of the American Indians, oratorio,

heard more continually in public. Remarkable favor was shown by her audience to her latest recital in Evanston, where she gave a program of modern compositions. In addition to solo performances, she has played with the strings the great quintets of Brahms and Goldmark, as well as the

B flat trio of Schubert and the trio opus 97 of Beethoven. Next season it is probable she will be heard more frequently in such ensemble work in which she has shown particular ex-

cellence, and her many musical admirers are looking forward to such events with much pleasurable anticipation.

MARIE CARTER

Miss Carter began her musical career as a singer in Minneapolis, the city of her girlhood. At the age of sixteen years she began singing in the Franklin Avenue Methodist Episcopal Church of that city, leaving it for a position in the First Presbyterian Church choir, whence she went to the Wesley Church, one of the best in that city. Her musical education at Minneapolis was commenced with George W. Ferguson.

Three years ago Miss Carter resigned her church work at Minneapolis to come to Chicago, here to con-

tinue her musical education. She has sung in the Englewood Baptist Church and at present is a member of the South Congregational Church choir.

Her voice is a dramatic soprano. She is devoted to her choir work, but is preparing for the concert and recital field. Since her advent in Chicago she has been studying with Mrs Genevieve Clark Wilson. Recently she sang the "Shakespeare songs" at the Art Institute and has fulfilled recently many concert engagements and private recitals, besides being engaged for some important Chautauqua work.

JEANNETTE DURNO

Miss Jeannette Durno early showed the possession of great musical talent, and commenced the systematic study of the piano before the age of 6. She was placed under competent instruction in Rockford, Ill., a city justly famed for its high standard of musical culture. Phenomenal progress was made, and she soon became known as "Rockford's Musical Prodigy." Her public appearances were always hailed with delight, and called forth the highest encomiums both of public and press.

Miss Durno graduated with highest honors from the Conservatory of the Rockford Ladies' College. She then studied under J. J. Hattstaedt, director of the American Conservatory, Chicago, and graduated in June, 1893, with highest honors and first gold medal.

She went to Vienna in 1894, and studied under Theodore Leschetizky for three years, returning to America in 1897.

Miss Durno appeared in concert in Vienna with Ben Davies, Adolf Peschier and other artists, and since her return to America has achieved notable successes.

A SHORT REVIEW OF THE CHICAGO ORCHESTRA'S CAREER

The benefits which Chicago derived from the World's Fair are manifold. Science received that priceless heritage, the Columbian Museum, while art— the divine art—was endowed by the establishment of a permanent orchestra—one of the greatest grand orchestras ever built on a permanent foundation.

The idea of a permanent orchestra for Chicago was conceived by a number of its public-spirited as well as wealthy citizens, who pledged their financial support to the then prospective institution for a term of three years in the sum of $1,000 each year. The fund thus created was known as the guarantee fund. The result of this step was that the Orchestral Association was incorporated under the laws of Illinois, and this association supports the Chicago Orchestra, whose conductor is also one of the most prominent orchestral conductors in the world—Theodore Thomas.

The object of the orchestra's organization was first of all to educate the people of Chicago in the musical field by affording them an opportunity to hear the standard works of the classicists, and also to give them the newest creations of the recognized composers of the present day. That the educational effects have been realized in a very high degree can be seen by a comparison of the "request" programs of the past season with those of the first year or two of the orchestra's existence. There is a dignity and high standard about the present request programs which were totally absent in the earlier. This is doubtless due in great measure to the fact that Mr. Thomas has adhered strictly to his own ideas, something which has often called forth some very severe criticisms. But Mr. Thomas has always had a definite purpose in view, and all things considered, he seems to know better than his patrons what they ought to have.

Then, too, it was also the desire to offer to our sister cities the benefits and pleasures which orchestral music afford, as well as to give the very best to those who come to the concerts at first merely for the rest and immediate pleasure received, but who later on become, by reason of the merits of the work, actively interested in its support.

The work of the orchestra has, one might say, covered the entire catalogue of musical literature. Each season has given the patrons of these concerts the very best solo talent obtainable, and the list of soloists who will appear this season is undoubtedly the most brilliant ever offered. The one idea—to give the very best— seems constantly to predominate, and when it is deemed necessary to obtain an artist directly from abroad it has been done.

The outlook for the future is most gratifying. There is a greater interest in the work, and consequently a greater attendance, and naturally the receipts are swelled.

ELAINE DE SELLEM

Modern English and French songs are the specialty of this contralto, who has filled many important church positions and has engaged successfully and extensively in oratorio and song recital work throughout the West. Her musical education was commenced at the age of 15, with Madame Feilbergl-Lassen, of Copenhagen. At the age of 18, after two years with Madame Linne at the American Conservatory, she took the first prize at graduation, being the youngest pupil who had ever been awarded that honor. Among church positions she has filled have been the Jefferson Park Presbyterian, Memorial Baptist, Central Church of Christ, and Emanuel Methodist of Evanston. For two years she has taught in the American Conservatory. Her range is low D to high C, and her most excellent work has met with high appreciation. The past season Miss De Sellem has been

on tour with the Bendix Grand Concert Company. The critics have predicted for her a splendid career.

EARL R. DRAKE

Earl R. Drake, the well-known violin virtuoso, received his musical education under Schradieck, of Cincinnati, and Carl Hild, of New York. He also attended the Hoch Schule in Berlin, Germany, during the summer of 1892, where at the invitation of

He recently purchased from a Chicago collector a beautiful "Stradivarius" valued at $5,000. Mr. Drake's three recitals in Chicago last year, at which he brought out three new concertos—the Bruch, Saint Saens and Euna—proved to be notable events.

Joachim, he accompanied both the master and his pupils on piano, gaining an experience which he values very highly. Mr. Drake has written a number of compositions, one of which, "A Polish Dance," has been received with special favor, being used in concerts by nearly all the leading violinists in this country.

Mr. Hannah, manager, has engaged the Earl Drake Concert Company for thirty nights this season. This, in addition to teaching his large class and directing the meetings of the Drake Violin Club, composed of twenty-five of his pupils, for the purpose of the study of chamber music, makes this artist a very busy man indeed.

ARTHUR DUNHAM

One of the younger organists of Chicago, whose abilities have been quickly recognized, is the subject of this sketch. At the age of 14, in 1889, he became organist at the Second Presbyterian Church of Bloomington, Ill., in which city he was born, March 8,

he still holds. Mr. Dunham has been an earnest and faithful student of music and was for five and a half years under the instruction of Clarence Eddy, and until the latter went abroad. He is the accompanist for the Apollo Club of Chicago, and at the anniver-

1875. At the age of 13 years he devoted himself seriously to the study of the piano and organ, and in October, 1893, at the age of 18, he sought the wider field for his musical talents in Chicago, taking charge of the organ at the Leavitt Street Congregational Church. In 1895 he became organist at Sinai congregation, which position

sary concerts of the Chicago Orchestra, December 8 and 9, he was organ soloist, winning immense success. Mr. Dunham's playing is remarkable for splendid technic. He enjoys one of the best church organs in the city, and his repertoire embraces a wide range from Bach to the modern style of English and French organ music.

THOMAS TAYLOR DRILL

Thomas Taylor Drill was born in Birmingham, England, and comes of a musical family. His father was for many years organist of the famous St. Patrick's Cathedral in Dublin. Mr. Drill first commenced singing as a boy in the great choirs of New York City, viz., Old Trinity Church and St. John's Chapel, where he was leading soprano boy for several years. When his voice changed and he became a basso he

filled the position of solo basso in the following well-known Protestant Episcopal churches: St. Ann's, Grace, St. Luke's, Church of the Redeemer and Christ, all of Brooklyn. During Mr. Drill's engagement in the choir of the Church of the Holy Spirit he sang the solo bass parts in most of the principal oratorios.

Choral services were given every Sunday afternoon, under the direction of George Le Jeune, the famous writer of hymn music and organist and choirmaster of St. John's Chapel and became so popular that the crowds filled the church edifice to overflowing.

Mr. Drill has had the finest possible advantages in the study of the development of the voice, and the proper rendition of songs, ballads, oratorio and operatic music. As a boy soprano he was under the constant care and tuition of Dr. A. H. Messiter (who for the past thirty years has been choir-

York he was chosen by Dudley Buck, the well-known composer, to create the very important and trying role of "Christopher Columbus" in his dramatic cantata of that name, and was highly complimented by Mr. Buck for his artistic work.

Upon Mr. Buck learning of Mr. Drill's intention of leaving New York, he wrote him a letter from which we quote the following: "I learn that you have finally decided to go West. You will be a musical loss to us, but

THOMAS TAYLOR DRILL.

master of Old Trinity Church, New York) and also of George F. Le Jeune. When he atained his bass voice he continued his vocal studies with Ivan Morowski, and also with Mr. William Courtney. During the visit to this country of the great baritone and famous teacher, M. Jacques Bouhy (the original "Torreador" in Bizet's opera, "Carmen,") Mr. Drill had the advantage of a thorough course of voice culture and dramatic singing.

During Mr. Drill's residence in New

a gain wherever you may locate. You will doubtless soon find your musical affinities and make the mark your voice and art well deserve."

Mr. Drill's voice is a basso cantate of large range and power; sympathetic and dramatic. He makes a specialty of enunciation and pronunciation, as those who have heard him can testify. In addition to his ability as vocalist Mr. Drill has been more especially successful as a choir director and a teacher of artistic singing and the proper development of the voice.

EDYTH EVELYN EVANS

Miss Edyth Evelyn Evans is without question one of the leading contraltos of the West today. Her voice is rich and mellow, with a range that is truly phenomenal. She sings equally well such roles as the contralto parts in "The Messiah" and "Elijah" and the splendid music allotted to Delilah in "Samson and Delilah." In the presentation of these works she has been associated with such artists as Genevieve Clark-Wilson, Jenny Osborn, Evan Williams, Glenn Hall, Frank King Clark and Charles Clark. Everywhere that Miss Evans has sung the press has been unanimous in her praise. Her repertoire is extensive and embraces all the best known oratorios and a large number of arias and songs. Every season she is coming into greater request, and the present season has witnessed a number of successes that establish her position among the leading contraltos of the country.

GEORGE EAGER

All the world loves a man of warm, generous impulses. Those qualities, united with artistic talents, give the possessor a magnetic influence upon his human environment. Yet George Eager, one of Chicago's most popular pianists, whole-souled and devoted to his work and to his pupils, prefers the retirement of a teacher's life to the publicity of a concert artist.

the piano. For general excellence he was awarded the Heilbig prize.

Returning to America in 1891, Mr. Eager opened a studio in Steinway Hall, New York, and became a member of the Mozart Club of that city. In 1892 he was induced by George W. Lyon to come to Chicago as director of the piano department at Ferry Hall Seminary, Lake Forest. In this work

He was born at Enfield, Mass., the son of parents both of whom excelled as amateur musicians. Inheriting their taste for music he began at New Haven, Conn., while pursuing his literary education, the study of the piano under Samuel S. Sanford, now in charge of the musical department of Yale University. He subsequently took a course of four years at the Leipsic Conservatory of Music, Germany, the pupil of Jadasson and Schreck in harmony and theory and of Dr. Bruno Zwintscher and Dr. Carl Reinecke on

he is still engaged, devoting some time also to teaching in Chicago.

Paderewski, listening to Rubenstein Demorest, the remarkable child pianist, and a pupil of Mr. Eager, remarked: "You have great talent and have been well taught. You should thank God and your teacher." Mr. Eager possesses that rare quality of transmitting his musical ideas to his pupils, without destroying the proper equilibrium of component forces. The success of his efforts is beyond praise.

HENRY PURMORT EAMES

Henry Purmort Eames, although a young man, having been born in Chicago in 1872, is already acknowledged as one of the leading pianists in the country. He has been but six years before the public, and in that time has established himself in the West and Northwest. In addition to the long studies in music in this country under eled after that of Ann Arbor. This year such inducements were offered that he has signed a two-years' contract, and it is encouraging that he is able to see his way clear to go so far away from a great musical center. Mr. Eames is most attractive personally, and has no eccentricities of manner, items which go a great distance toward

W. S. B. Mathews and William Sherwood, and in Europe under the late Madame Clara Wieck Schumann and the Dutch virtuoso, James Kwast, Mr. Eames enjoys also the advantage of university training. He went still further embracing the law, but the work of his heart was music, so in the fall of 1893 he left the law office and entered the concert field.

Last year he accepted for one year the directorship of the pianoforte department in the Nebraska State University School of Music, which is modgaining favor for any artist, instrumental or vocal. To show with what esteem he is held in his new field the following quotation is made from one of the Nebraska papers of recent date:

"Mr. Eames, director of the pianoforte department, and who is an enthusiastic believer in the value of chamber music, was heard in two numbers of that character. Mr. Eames demonstrated again the range of his attainment and the depth of his scholarship. His own performance can be counted upon to express technically and artistically whatever the composer demands, and his readings are moreover enriched by a personal subjective faculty of interpretation in the highest degree delightful. Mr. Eames has proved in the last year the breadth of his musical culture, as well as his skill in teaching, and in public performances. He is to be congratulated upon his success, and upon the influence he exerts for musical righteousness in Lincoln."

In the lecture-recital field he has done excellent work, for it needs just the combination of musical and intellectual knowledge which he possesses. He has been most successful in this line for so young a man.

MRS. LUELLA CLARK EMERY

Mrs. Luella Clark Emery has been one of those fortunate people who succeed as they deserve. Mrs. Emery, after being engaged six consecutive seasons at Spirit Lake Chautauqua, has signed for next season. She has also been engaged for other Chautauquas and during her short residence in Chicago has been accompanist for Madame Ragna Linne and Mrs. Genevieve Clark Wilson, Miss Sibyl Sammis and several other well-known local artists. But her accompaniments have not been confined solely to our singers and violinists, as she has been frequently in request for visiting artists.

Mrs. Emery is not only a remarkably good accompanist, but also an organist of exceptional ability. She is organist at the Fifth Presbyterian Church, where she gives a recital every Sunday. Her concert engagements have been very numerous and very favorably spoken of, both the city and out of town critics making admirable mention of her work.

She also played in the May Festival chorus in the Chicago Auditorium. Mrs. Emery has a large class of organ and piano pupils.

H. W. FAIRBANK

The subject of this sketch is a native of Michigan. He was born in Grand Blanc, Genessee County, near the flourishing city of Flint. His musical propensities were inherited from his parents, both of whom played an important part in the musical life of the locality in which they lived. As early as 8 years of age he played the melodeon in church and Sunday-school, having taken a term of music lessons from Miss Huldah Johnson of Flint. About that time his father gave a home to a poor German refugee, Henry Schaefer by name, who was a fine musician. This association was an important factor in the creation and development of a correct musical taste in the mind of the young student. At the age of 12 his family moved to Flint, Mich., and young Fairbank soon became a member of the famous Gardner's band and Orchestra. He also was enabled to practice occasionally on the pipe organ of St. Paul's Church. At 17 he entered the University of Michigan, graduating four years later with the degree of B. A. While at Ann Arbor he was organist at the St. Andrew's Church, and on leaving college he be-

came teacher of music in the public schools of Flint, where he remained five years. Then he entered the public schools, and for several years has had charge of the music in Hyde Park, Englewood, Lake and South Chicago High Schools. He has been organist of the Oakland Methodist Episcopal, Christ Methodist Episcopal and Englewood Baptist Churches, being at the last mentioned organist and director for nine years. He has published considerable church and school music, and has written one opera and several songs. He was recently nominated by Dr. Andrews for the position of supervisor in chief of the Chicago schools. He resides at the Julien Hotel in Englewood, and has a summer residence at Bay View, Mich. He is the director of the great May festivals, held each year at the Auditorium, having a chorus of 1,200 ladies' voices, while for several years he has been musical director of the Spirit Lake, Ia., and Marinette, Wis., Chautauqua assemblies. Mr. Fairbank is a member of the Chicago Manuscript Society, of the Englewood Club and also of the Monticello Club.

KATHARINE FISK

Most interesting is the personality of this great contralto, charming as a woman, and world renowned as an artist, whose international reputation necessitates the division of her time from the end of November to the mid-

Madame Fisk, western born, we are proud to say, has sung considerably throughout the United States and in Great Britain, with the London Philharmonic Society, Richter, Colonne, Crystal Palace, London Symphony,

dle of February in Great Britain and the balance of the year in the United States. A beautiful woman, her wondrous art, cultivated alike in its vocal and dramatic powers, her delivery eminently dramatic and her voice pure, noble and vibrant, nothing is left wanting to stamp her as one of the greatest contraltos of the day. What a list of appearances has been made, and each of these has been a veritable triumph!

Sir Charles Halle and Scottish orchestral concerts. She has also taken leading parts with the Gloucester and Norwich festivals, Royal Choral Society, Queen's Hall Choral Society, Liverpool Philharmonic Society, the London Ballad Concerts, Patti concerts and any number of others. In her debut at the Gloucester Festival, in 1895, the London *Daily Telegraph* said: "The festival debut of Mrs.

Katharine Fisk was another noteworthy event. Those who heard her recognized an artist of no common order, one richly endowed with natural advantages, and the result of patient study."

Honored and respected by her fellow-professionals, eagerly welcomed by the people wherever she appears, lovable as a friend and most charming under all circumstances, America has every reason to be proud of its gifted daughter, who is unquestionably one of the finest of contemporary musical artists.

Mrs. Fisk's American successes have been no less great than her European triumphs. She has enjoyed some of the most important engagements of the country for the past three years, and this season is in great demand for the artistic events both in the East and West.

MRS. O. L. FOX

This prominent local Western teacher who for the past fifteen years has been an honor reflecting member of the Chicago Musical College, is a native of Boston. The study of music was begun at the early age of seven, and ten years later not merely was she a most successful choir singer, but she had also made for herself a high place as a solo artist at musical conventions in all parts of New England. Mrs. J. H. Long, the celebrated Boston teacher, with whom Mrs. Fox studied considerably, was asked in June, 1869, to select a soprano for the second Presbyterian Church of Chicago and she recommended Mrs. Fox for the position. The following year the latter made her debut with the Chicago Orpheus Society in Hadyn's "Creation." The appointment with the Second Presbyterian Church was held until the great fire of 1871, when she returned to Boston and for twelve months studied hard. At the end of that time an appointment was offered her at the Fourth Presbyterian Church, Chicago, then in charge of Professor Swing.

It is, however, as a teacher that Mrs. Fox is best known, and a large number of the most prominent of the singers who graduated from the Chicago Musical College owe their training to her patient, earnest work and sterling abilities. In this regard she has received a very powerful indorsement, from Delle Sedie, the eminent French master, commending the thoroughness of her instruction, and laying special stress on the accurate placement of the voices which came to him after they had passed under the care of Mrs. Fox.

The subject of this sketch is a woman of considerable literary ability, and was five years musical critic on the *Indicator*. She has also contributed largely on musical matters to other periodicals. The writing of words for songs is another accomplishment of Mrs. Fox, and Chicago musicians often avail themselves of the opportunity to obtain good verses. In this last achievement she has become widely known, as several of the songs for which Mrs. Fox has written the words have had remarkably successful sales.

From one end of the country to the other this gifted lady is known for her great talent in training for concert or operatic work.

MRS. O. L. FOX

ORGAN STUDY

"Plenty of room at the top," and situations for all who arrive there. No truer thing was ever said. It should be the constant support and reward of the earnest, untiring student.

Organ study in America was never in more peculiar condition. Out of every fifty pupils but one studies for the love of it, or ever expects to scale the heights. About twenty of these fifty will have come into the city from cities and towns anywhere within 3,000 miles, to take a few hurried half-hours in preparation for the playing of the new organ "now being set up in our church." Fifteen will be those holding situations, $2 to $5 per week, who can never spare the time for serious study, but must be put through a certain amount of simple work which will fill their Sunday service lists. A dozen will take from one to two terms of solid work each year for three or four years, and then "rest upon their laurels," such as they are. A couple will study faithfully for a year or two and then conclude they have gone far enough. The remaining one will go on year after year, study hard, think, hustle, fight his way inch by inch, and come out winner and master. The forty-nine will say of him, excusing themselves, "Lucky fellow! He had time, talent and money!" A more pathetic case does not exist than that of the student, who, having time, money and talent, stops study just at the most critical period, because the parents argue: "You now have the best organ in town and the best salary ($3 to $5 per Sunday), will, with further study, be no more appreciated, and, from a business point of view, are wasting both time and money." Confronted with such argument, one becomes dumb. How many are today traveling along the old and sure highway of Rick, or Lemmens, or Best, or Archer, or Stainer, Bach, Merkel, Rheinberger, Thiele, Guilmant, Widor & Co.?

There are those who say: "Why don't you compel pupils to go that road or turn them away?"

I will answer with the following little anecdote: As I was leaving my home one morning I said to my youngest son: "Papa is going down to earn some bread and butter for you." As quick as a wink he retorted, "And some cakes, too!"

There came to me once, from one of the famous organists of the country, a pupil who ought to have been feeding on solid musical food; he had compelled that artist to finger, arrange and registrate the most trivial compositions extant. I could only blame the conditions in the country which would permit of such a pupil gaining a livelihood. All success to the Guild of Organists which hopes to see the day when only those who have taken examination and passed into the ranks will be eligible for position. And just here allow me to add that every organist who has the interest of his profession at heart should put his shoulder to this wheel—I do not mean the "cold shoulder." There are men and women in this town drawing good salaries who butcher services, who never make preparation, and who take no pride in good playing. I make this statement on actual hearing.

If one is going into organ study with a purely commercial end in view, I trust such a one will bear in mind that before a merchant can sell his goods he must rent a store, purchase fixtures and a stock and advertise. And just as he uses his capital for his stock so must the organist look upon his outlay for knowledge. Time and money are necessary for a good equipment, and nothing short of that should be recognized. If music committees of churches would trust to a committee of organists for selection of organists, just as in foreign countries, organ study would flourish "like a green-bay tree," and be serious and earnest enough to delight the soul of the strictest purist. HARRISON M. WILD.

LEOPOLD GODOWSKY

That so consummate an artist as Leopold Godowsky, the renowned pianist, should have chosen Chicago for the continuance of his ripe and

devoted to it his life. Leopold Godowsky is not yet twenty-eight.

He was but three years old when remarkable musical talent was shown,

brilliant life work is a significant indication of the present rank of the city as a musical center. Music never found a truer servant or a nobler, abler or more enthusiastic devotee than when in his very early years this brilliantly talented young Russian pianist nurtured and nourished on its beauties,

and at seven he had composed some piano pieces so filled with melodies, original and yet so musically mature, that in the later compositions of this master some of these have been reproduced. His debut was made at nine, and subsequently he played with thorough success through a portion of

Germany and through Poland. Then resuming his studies at the Royal Conservatory, Berlin, he there remained until he was fourteen.

At this time he made his first visit to the United States, playing in many of the principal cities in association with several great artists, among whom was the violinist Ovide Musin. His success was very pronounced, but returning to Europe he continued his studies. To study with the great French master, Saint-Saens, had become the ambition of his life, but he was a boy of sixteen, and having been overreached in the business matters of his recent tour he was practically without resources. Saint-Saens, too, was known to refuse to accept pupils. A happy opportunity, however, arose and at a "Reunion des Artists" weekly meeting, an organization of which Saint-Saens was honorary president, Godowsky was given an opportunity to play. Having heard the young artist play and examined several of his compositions Saint-Saens invited him to play at the "Trompette," a well-known art club. So good was his performance, that, following the concert, he was requested to play a composition of his own. He gave the "Don Quixote" poem symphonique, arousing such enthusiastic praise from Saint-Saens that he was embraced on the stage before an audience of the elite of the Parisian artistic world. Shortly after this Saint-Saens agreed to accept him as a pupil, and there he remained until 1890.

In the latter year he went to London to play in a series of concerts, achieving the most marked and distinguished success. He became in great demand for concerts and recitals, and in all the most important cities of Europe proved that not only had he benefited by the training of a great master, to whom his gratitude was at all times acknowledged, but that he was himself the possessor of great natural gifts, which, increased by his sound training and earnest study, made him one of the greatest piano virtuosos of the day.

Having decided on another American tour he returned to the United States in the fall of 1890, and, after some decided Eastern concert successes, in which his marvelous command of difficulties and splendidly broad, yet eminently educated, interpretation gained him triumphal appreciation, he accepted a position with the Broad Street Conservatory of Music, at Philadelphia.

In 1895 he was induced to come West and identify himself with the interests of Chicago's music. For that coming the city is markedly benefited, and our musicians are proud to acknowledge among them this pianist whose absolute individuality is almost disguised in his lack of self-assertiveness and remarkable unpretentiousness. Every appearance is the occasion of new laurels; great before, year after year his greatness becomes the more pronounced. His repertory is enormous, covering every composition of note in piano literature, and difficulty is a word unfound in his lexicon, and one translated by him into an opportunity to display ability. He is the composer of over one hundred pieces, all distinguished by splendid musicianship and some of which are placed on the favorite programs of the greatest living artists of the day.

L. G. GOTTSCHALK

This noted operatic singer and teacher, of Chicago, was born in New Orleans, and when an infant removed with his parents to Paris, where his oldest brother, L. Moreau, the celebrated pianist, was then receiving his musical education. Our subject developed a voice, studied at Paris under Ronconi, Rizzo, Lamperti and others, and soon after gave a successful series of concerts through America. Returning to Europe he began a brilliant career as an opera singer. He sang in Gounod's "Faust," the role of

I. GASTON GOTTSCHALK

Mephisto about 200 times, and that of Valentine nearly 100 times. During a five years' engagement with Max Strakosch he sang with Gerster, Cary, Kellogg, Rose, Tietjens, Belocca and Campanini. Later he was with Minnie Hauk and with Kellogg and Brignoli during their American tour. He appeared with Pauline Lucca in Convent Garden, London, and in Paris he won great distinction, where he engaged in both singing and teaching, among his pupils being the nieces of the King of Servia.

In 1886 he became vocal director of the Chicago Musical College, retiring a few years later and establishing his own school, which he now maintains. In Chicago Mr. Gottschalk's work has been mainly that of a teacher. He numbers among his pupils many prominent singers who in several cases hold lucrative operatic or choir engagements. Mr. Gottschalk's latest addition to the music of Chicago is his operatic club, which is formed for the purpose of bringing young singers before the public.

MRS. A. J. GOODRICH

It is rather unusual for a lady to choose and successfully follow the theoretical side of music, but that is what Mrs. Goodrich has done. Undoubtedly she was influenced by her constant association with a noted theorist, yet the fact remains that Mrs. Goodrich is an expert practical musician, not of the mechanical, but of the poetic, spiritual type. She is a fair pianist and organist, a rapid sight-reader, well versed in the history and literature of her art and an accomplished vocalist, having sung in concert, opera and oratorio. Perhaps on account of these earlier accomplishments she has been enabled to win the most complete success in a department which is almost universally considered as a bugbear—to be talked about but not understood. Mrs. Goodrich does not content herself with good results among talented pupils only, but with those who seem to possess no aptitude for harmony she particularly concerns herself, and may claim the unusual dis-

MRS. A. J. GOODRICH

tinction of having been universally successful. Mr. Goodrich (whose wife is his best pupil) admits that neither himself nor any one else has yet developed his system of harmony as completely and practically as she has done. Since the organization of the Sherwood Piano School Mrs. Goodrich has directed the Harmony department.

FREDERIC GRANT GLEASON

He was born in 1848 in Middletown, Conn., where his father was a banker. Both Mr. Gleason's parents were enthusiastic amateurs, and did much to encourage the love of music so evidently part of the young Gleason's nature. While he was still a boy he was placed under the care of Dudley Buck, after he had showed his talent by composing an oratorio or two and several cantatas without receiving any instruction.

In 1865 a fragment of "Tannhauser" fell into his hands, and at once made him an ardent admirer of the great composer, whose name was then scarcely known in this country. From that time Gleason became a Wagnerite, and upon going to Europe became an active partisan of the master. In 1869 he entered the Leipsic Conservatoire, where he remained with Moscheles, Plaidy, Lobe, Richter, Papperitz and Dr. Oscar Paul until the death of Moscheles, when Mr. Gleason went to Berlin to continue his studies and became a member of the Wagner Verein, which was laboring to raise funds for the production of the "Ring of the Nibelungen" at Bayreuth.

After this he studied with A. Loeschhorn, Oscar Raif, August

Haupt, and while in Berlin enjoyed opportunities of meeting Richard Wagner and heard him drill and conduct a picked orchestra for several concerts in Berlin, among them that notable gathering at which the "Kaiser-marsch" was first performed soon after the return from Paris, in the presence of the Emperor William, Prince Bismarck and all the kings and dignitaries of the new German Empire.

Frederic Grant Gleason returned to the United States in 1875 and accepted a choir appointment at one of the prin-

"Otho Visconti," which was given in the old Gewandhaus in 1892, and afterward in other European cities. In 1883 Mr. Gleason received a medal of honor from the Associazione dei Benemerite of Palermo, Sicily, for "distinguished services in the cause of art." Frederic Grant Gleason was elected president of the Chicago Manuscript Society in 1896 and president-general of the American Patriotic Musical League in 1897. He was selected to compose the "Auditorium Festival Ode," a symphonic cantata for the dedication of the Chicago

FREDERIC GRANT GLEASON

cipal churches in Hartford. Later he accepted a call to New Britain to a still larger organ, and in 1877 he removed to Chicago, where he has lived and labored for twenty years.

At the foundation of the American College of Musicians he was made a Fellow of the College, a member of the board of directors, and after several re-elections resigned both offices owing to press of other work. He was then invited to become a member of the New York Manuscript Society soon after its foundation, and made an honorary vice-president. His first orchestral work to be produced in Germany was the Vorspiel to his opera,

Auditorium, which was produced with a chorus of 500 voices, solo and orchestra, on that occasion.

Selections from "Otho Visconti" and from each act of "Montezuma" have been in the repertory of the Thomas Orchestra, and have been frequently played for years past. Mr. Gleason's works were represented in the orchestral concerts of the Columbian Exposition, and his orchestral writings have been heard from Boston to San Francisco, as well as in Europe. Some of Chicago's prominent composers and pianists have been pupils of Mr. Gleason.

A. J. GOODRICH

Few musicians have had such varied experiences as have fallen to the lot of A. J. Goodrich. He has conducted choral societies, operas and orchestras; given instruction in piano playing, singing, harmony, counterpoint, composition, orchestration and analysis; lectured on history, musical form, analysis, etc.; served as reporter, staff correspondent, sub-editor and chief editor of several music journals; contributed largely to the musical and newspaper press, written several original text books and composed volumes of music, from a song to a symphony.

Mr. Goodrich's principal works are text books, to-wit: "Complete Musical Analysis" and Goodrich's "Analytical Harmony," with supplement, published by the John Church Company; "Music as a Language," a small reference book, published by G. Schirmer; "The Art of Song," illustrated lecture, published serially in Werner's Magazine, and the new text book now ready for the press, "A Theory of Interpretation."

His contributions to The Musical Courier have also been more or less important. A few of these may be mentioned, "Evolution of the Dance Form," "Personal and National Characteristics in Music," "The Harmonic Basis of Wagner's Operas and Music-Dramas," "Character and Development of the Leading Motives in Wagner's Music Dramas," etc.

EDITH GRAMM

Edith Gramm, daughter of Otto Gramm, Esq., of Laramie, Wyoming, was born in Laramie and began the

study of elocution with the intention of making that art her life work. After discovering through her study of elocution that she possessed some histrionic ability, Miss Gramm decided to cultivate her singing voice and enter the light opera field if time should warrant her in so doing.

Miss Gramm went to Philadelphia to the Ogontz school and studied instrumental music, with Michael J. Kegrize, as a foundation for her proposed work. Mr. Kegrize was then and is now the leading piano teacher there.

Miss Gramm then applied to Mr. W. H. Neidlinger, the well known composer and voice builder, for vocal lessons. Not being able to enter Mr. Neidlinger's class, she was placed with his assistant, Mr. E. K. Towns. With Mr. Towns she remained until he followed Mr. Neidlinger (who in the meantime had gone to Paris to teach) to Europe.

After some other desultory and unsatisfactory study, Miss Gramm was taken by her father to Paris and placed directly under Mr. Neidlinger.

A year ago she returned to America and continued her studies with Mr. Neidlinger in Chicago, with whom she is completing her musical education. She has a charming voice—soprano—and has been received in many song recitals and concerts this last year with great success. It is probable that Miss Gramm in the course of the coming year will enter her chosen field of light opera, having already received much encouragement from several managers and conductors.

MRS. JANE GRAY HAWKES

Mrs. Jane Gray Hawkes, one of our most popular young sopranos, is a native of Pittsburg, Pa. Mrs. Hawkes, then Miss Gray, made her first public appearance with Hope Glenn and Emma Juch in her native city when but a young girl. Since coming to Chicago she has studied with Mme. Sara Hershey-Eddy and Noyes B. Miner, of this city. Mrs. Hawkes has a very high soprano voice of excellent quality, and sings with feeling and in a most artistic manner. Jane Gray Hawkes was the soloist who accompanied the Chicago Southern States Association south during the Atlanta Exposition, receiving an unprecedented ovation in all the southern cities where they stopped. She also sang at the sixth anniversary of the Auditorium in this city with great success.

Mrs. Hawkes was one of the faculty of the American Conservatory for several years, but since her marriage she has taken up her residence in California, where social engagements alone have the benefit of her beautiful voice and very exceptional training.

MABEL GOODWIN

The subject of this sketch was born and educated in New England. At sixteen years of age she became a church singer, obtaining a soprano position. She then connected herself with a ladies' quartet and a mixed quartet, after which she studied two seasons with Mme. Hall in Boston. Seven years ago Miss Goodwin came to Chicago and commenced studying with Mr. Karleton Hackett. From the time of her arrival she has had invariable success, being engaged in many important social functions and also at the Sixth Presbyterian Church, where she has been soprano soloist three years. During the season 1896-1897 Miss Goodwin went on a concert tour with the Slayton Company, and from her performance at a concert given during this trip at Galesburg, she was secured as head of the vocal department at Knox Conservatory. Since resigning her position at this institution Miss Goodwin has been connected with the American Conservatory. She is soprano at the North Side synagogue as well as at the church before referred to. Her voice is of wide range, sympathetic quality, and in oratorio or concert work she is a most delightful artist. Miss Goodwin was a member of the Matinee Musicale at Woodlawn until she went to Galesburg, and has frequently been chosen to sing at the annual concert program of this club.

MINNIE FISH-GRIFFIN

To have enjoyed the distinction of appearing twenty-one times as soloist with the Chicago Orchestra under Theodore Thomas during the past few years might, were it needed, be the fitting introduction of Mrs. Minnie Fish-Griffin to the charmed circles of musical celebrities. These repeated appearances, however, may properly be considered as incidents merely to a career that has been wide and conquering.

Gustav Engel, Heinrich Ehrlich, Otto Lessman and others, spoke in highest terms of her work. In the Vossische Zeitung of Berlin Gustav Engel said: "In the concert given in the Sing-Academie last evening by Minnie Fish-Griffin we learned to know a singer whose voice not only shows rare cultivation and fine musical training, but possesses the true quality which nature alone can bestow."

Mrs. Griffin's voice is a high so-

Mrs. Fish-Griffin is one of the few vocal artists who are first musicians and secondly singers. Her father was a musician of high order, with a beautiful tenor, and the voice of his gifted child received from him the utmost care from her earliest childhood. Besides the instruction she received from her father she was the pupil of Sig. Agusto Rotoli of Boston, Ernst Catenhusen, formerly of Milwaukee, and of Felix Schmidt of Berlin, Germany. While studying in Germany she appeared in oratorio and concert in many of the large cities, and before leaving Berlin gave a concert at the Sing-Academie. Berlin critics,

prano of purest quality, and she is an artist in all phases of vocalization. Besides her work with the Chicago Orchestra she has appeared frequently with the Apollo Club of Chicago and other prominent organizations, and she ranks with the foremost oratorio singers. Last season she sang in more than fifty cities in the middle and western states. She has an unusually large repertoire of oratorios, concert arias and songs in English, French, German and Italian. Her concert numbers are invariably given from memory, which adds a pleasing spontaneity and naturalness to her singing.

VICTOR GARWOOD

Mr. Victor Garwood may be written down as one who loves his vocation as teacher of piano. He is organist at a large church, where his musical efforts are thoroughly appreciated, but in his affections it must give way to the piano, the instrument for which he was specially trained and which as time passed on absorbed his interest more and more. His gifts and scholarship would have justified him in adopting a public career, but he relinquished such an ambition and became instead a most finished teacher. He is connected with one of the local conservatories of music, but his devotion to his pupils is his self-sufficing life work. Musicians of his temperament and capacity for work are they upon whose shoulders rest the labor of perfecting native musical talent. He has many pupils and their progress is his definition of success. The pupil himself of Oscar Raif of Berlin and many other eminent teachers, the methods of Mr. Garwood may be regarded as his own, developed by his own conscientious and intelligent experience.

MRS. JESSIE L. GAYNOR

Jessie L. Gaynor was born in St. Louis in 1863, where her father, Capt. Henry W. Smith, was for years a prominent business man. Her parents both possessed artistic talent in a marked degree. Her mother, Susan Fennimore Taylor, had a genuine appreciation of art and music. From her earliest childhood Mrs. Gaynor looked forward to a career as a musician. The piano was her chosen instrument, although she spent some time under the best voice teachers and acquired some knowledge of the violin.

The study of composition was carried on through her years of prepara-

MRS. JESSIE L. GAYNOR

tion, but her actual writing began in the year 1890. The first published work was an album including seven songs. This little book, sent out with great hesitation, has proved a success for both composer and publisher, and has been followed by the "Rose Songs," "Songs for Little Folks," "Songs of the Child World" and "Five Songs." Besides these collections, she has published a number of songs separately, among which the "Spring Song" and "Das Rathsel" stand as most characteristic.

Mrs. Gaynor's songs have met with cordial appreciation from singers and have received kind treatment at the hands of the critics.

MRS. EMMA WILKINS GUTMANN

Mrs. Emma Wilkins Gutmann has been connected for a number of years with the most prominent musical institutions in Chicago as a teacher of

piano, and is classed with the successful educators.

She has had the advantage of study with some of the best teachers in this country and spent considerable time under the famous masters, Raif and Leschetizky, in Europe. Mrs. Gutmann devotes a great deal of time to study and to investigating different methods, not merely theoretically but practically. By so doing, she is able to judge of their value, using the best ideas and discarding the rest.

Her little book, "Talks with Piano Teachers," is a reference book for young teachers and advanced pupils, and is full of suggestions that will lead teachers and students to think for themselves and to devise ways of their own.

Mrs. Gutmann is a member of the faculty of the American Conservatory of Music. Progressive in her ideas, thorough in her methods, a woman of strong personality, she has made for herself a decided place in the community, a position which becomes year after year more pronounced.

MRS. SARA SAYLES GILPIN

Mrs. Sara Sayles Gilpin, a pupil of Mme. Zeisler, began the study of

music at an early age, and at nineteen was graduated from the American Conservatory of Music in Chicago with the highest honors, having thoroughly studied harmony and vocal as well as instrumental music. For piano playing, Mrs. Gilpin received the gold medal the first year, and the second year the conservatory's free scholarship.

After graduating and determining to continue her studies, she chose for her teacher Mme. Fannie Bloomfield Zeisler, unquestionably one of the most accomplished pianistes and teachers in America, and one of the world's great artistes. After six years of hard study under the influence of this wonderful woman, Mrs. Gilpin has herself become a perfect mistress of her art. She has the artistic temperament of her great teacher; always plays exquisitely whether in the realm of the romantic or the classical, and is more and more successful as a teacher. She lives in touch with the great world of music, and her enthusiasm in the good work knows no bounds.

THE POINT OF VIEW

America is musically under the domination of Europe. Europe is its schoolhouse and law-giver in artistic matters. We look to Europe for our standards and send our talent there for instruction and approval. In a certain sense, music is cosmopolitan and knows no nationality. The best there is in the art is sought for and adopted by the best taste in all countries; but the average of musical activity in each of the four great European countries, Germany, Italy, France and England, is what a student has to consider when he goes from this country to one of them to absorb the theory and practice of the art of music. This average might be illustrated thus:

In England, music is a retainer. There social eminence is the most desirable and the most honored thing there is. Everything is subservient to it and music is made to walk humbly in the train of society. There is a great deal of activity in the lower grades of musical effort which does not come under this classification.

School music and choral singing, including church music, flourish independently and admirably in England, but taking London to represent that country, the success of a musician seems to be measured by the social eminence which his art can aid him to attain. The Queen and the Prince of Wales can make, even if they cannot unmake, the career of a musician with very secondary reference to musical excellence.

Artists must, indeed, be the demigods of the musical world to feel that they can achieve success independently of the great ones of society. Concerts to be really first-class must be under the patronage of Lord This, my Lady That and Sir The Other. The feeling of exalted importance which takes possession of the English musician who has obtained a title is something which an American must come in contact with to fully realize. An American musician, returning recently from a residence of several years in London, and speaking of some musicians of that city, who, judged at this distance by their artistic productions only, seem like ordinary mortals, said, lowering his voice in a sort of awe, "They are great people over there." It is probable that social distinction is valued in other countries, but in no other does society, however exalted, succeed in chaining music to its triumphal chariot.

In France, music is royalty. Probably in no other country is musical talent honored in so distinguished a manner. The most eminent musicians of Paris are often men of slender means, but the esteem in which they are held by their countrymen might be indicated by a paraphrase of the old saying, "To be a Roman was greater than to be a king"—substituting the word Musician for "Roman." The great musicians there can confer distinction and need not give solicitous care to obtaining it for themselves.

In Italy, music is an innamorata. It is a goddess to which human adoration is paid. It receives the intense, passionate, exaggerated, overwrought treatment of the lover to the one he idealizes. The exaggeration which one witnesses in musical performance in Italy is carried to grotesque extremes and appears to outside observers in the same category with the hyperbole, superlatives and heated protestations of one who is very much in love.

In Germany, music is a Divinity. It is reverently esteemed by the Germans. Exaggeration is not countenanced. Society has no influence whatever in determining its status. Indeed, at least two of the prominent German musicians have taken the position that their art rendered them superior to the behests of royalty. An audience of Germans, listening to the classics, reminds one of an audience of devout worshipers in church. One who comes in late, making a disturbance, to the solemn rites of a German classical concert is regarded with withering indignation. One might as well interpolate slang in the Scriptures as to interpret the acknowledged masters flippantly to German connoisseurs.

Music students, returning to this country from a considerable sojourn in any one of these countries, generally bear the impress of the prevailing ideals which have just been indicated.

One returning from France, if he has received anything more than could have been gotten at home, will manifest in his treatment of the art something of the finish and refinement which suggests the consummation of human luxury—the purple and fine linen of kings' palaces. These have an element in their musical attainments which is highly prized by the daintiest taste of our communities on this side —a certain genuine flavor of aristocracy.

Those who return from Italy are likely to bring too many exaggerations to find favor. They invariably have the tremolo in a highly developed state. They place great dependence on a very high note at the end of a song, for instance, and their repertoires always have the biggest concert numbers which the operatic library can afford. Their former friends usually disown them in the remark that their style is "too operatic" for church music, or any of the ordinary uses to which singers hereabouts are put.

Those who have had a considerable residence in England generally show that they have been under influences which were not purely musical. Their expenses in London have been so great that business considerations, including the patronage of the mighty, have outweighed or suffocated their artistic endeavors.

From Germany one is likely to return in pretty good order. They have worked toward as pure an art ideal as can be found anywhere upon the globe and they show the effects of few or no distractions from a course of earnest work. Their wardrobe may be scant, but their repertoire is rich. Their social triumphs may be few, but their artistic attainments are apt to amount to something. They have not been patronized, nor bullied, nor fleeced unduly, and they are usually in pretty good condition for musical use. In every other department than in voice, the German ideal is quite irreproachable; but their standards of vocal tone are often poor, for they are in the habit of exalting the thought and the inspiration of music to such an extent that the tone which conveys this thought to the ear becomes in their estimation comparatively insignificant.

So it seems that when we speak of the influence of Europe upon this country or of adopting European ideals, or of European training for students, we need to know which country we are talking about. We need to get a point of view which takes in the whole horizon.

Frederic W. Root.

KARLETON HACKETT

Mr. Karleton Hackett is a native of Boston, and from his earliest years has been a musician. As a boy his instrument was the violin, but as soon as his voice changed he began the study of singing, and to that fascinating pursuit he has devoted his life. He studied the voice in Boston for five years, also entering Harvard College and taking the Theory of Music with John

K. Paine. Completing this course Mr. Hackett went to Florence to study with Vincenzo Vannini, with whom he spent more than three years fitting himself for the opera. Later he studied the oratorio and German songs with Henschel in London. On returning from Europe Mr. Hackett settled down in Chicago, where the success of his teaching has been such that he has been obliged to devote all his time to his pupils and to give up everything else. A director of the Voice Department of the American Conservatory, Mr. Hackett is also an extensive writer on musical and vocal matter, being a regular contributor to the principal music magazines of the day.

JOHN J. HATTSTAEDT

John J. Hattstaedt, director of the American Conservatory, is an American of German descent, having been born at Monroe, Michigan. He was fortunate in enjoying a first-class general education, including a collegiate course at a German gymnasium, and also very excellent musical instruction. With characteristic independence and energy, he entered into professional life when comparatively young, being actively engaged in teaching at Detroit, Michigan, and afterwards at St. Louis, Mo.

In 1875 Mr. Hattstaedt came to Chicago, having accepted an engagement as teacher of the piano at the Chicago Musical College. This position he held for ten years, being at the same time lecturer on Musical History. After an extended European tour he formulated his plans for a music school according to his own ideals, and accordingly founded in 1886 the American Conservatory of Music, which, under his excellent management, from a modest beginning has grown to be one of the largest conservatories in the United States.

Mr. Hattstaedt is a musician of solid attainments, a scholar and thinker. He is undoubtedly in the front rank of piano teachers in the country, his pupils being represented in all parts of the United States, while many occupy prominent positions either as teachers or concert artists. His lectures, which cover almost all phases of musical art, are always attended by teachers and students, and his writings bear the stamp of originality as well as solidity.

GEORGE HAMLIN

One of the genuinely novel and artistic events of the musical season of 1898-99 was the first recital in America of Richard Strauss' charming Lieder by George Hamlin. The unanimous opinion of the press at this initial recital at Chicago was highly laudatory. Mr. Hamlin has continued during the past season these difficult recitals, so admirably adapted to his voice, though many of the leading churches of Chicago and his concert debut was made only four years ago. Since then he has appeared with all the leading oratorio societies of the West and many of the East. Among these may be mentioned the Cincinnati May Festival, New York Oratorio Society, and the Liederkranz Society, the Chicago Orchestral concerts under direction of

not to the extent of overshadowing his extended repertoire of oratorio and recital work. Praise has been unstinted in his behalf as a leading and classic tenor of America.

Mr. Hamlin has the distinction of being an American singer in every sense of the word. He is a native of Illinois and his entire musical education has been received in America and from American teachers. Here, too, have been his successes, until he now holds one of the foremost places among concert tenors. For eleven years he has sung continuously in Theodore Thomas, Chicago, Cincinnati, Des Moines and Toledo Apollo Clubs, Providence, R. I., and Milwaukee Arion Clubs, Pittsburg Mozart Club, Louisville and St. Paul Musical Clubs, St. Louis Choral Symphony Society, Handel and Haydn Society of Boston, Minneapolis Philharmonic Club, Buffalo Orpheus Club, Ann Arbor May Festival and Cincinnati Sangerfest. His recent engagements as leading tenor for musical festivals and choral concerts have been many. His repertoire contains several very interesting programs for recital work, as well as the principal oratorios, cantatas, etc.

Mr. Krehbiel, musical critic of the New York *Tribune,* says of him: "Mr. Hamlin has a voice of fine, manly timber, which he uses with good taste, and his musical instincts are evidently of the best. One of the most delightful features of his singing is the unvarying purity of his intonation." A few excerpts from a multitude of friendly criticisms may be added: "Extremely pleasing and a master of vocal art."—*Musical Cour-ier.* "At the head of American tenors."—*Louisville Commercial.* "An exceptionally strong Samson."—The *U. of M. Daily.* "The most satisfactory tenor ever heard here."—*Minneapolis Times.* "Has a true lyric tenor of high range and of excellent quality."—*Pittsburg Times.* "Mr. Hamlin has a tenor voice of sweet and sympathetic quality and he is evidently a conscientious student."—*Boston Herald.*

Mr. Hamlin's successes in the East recently have gone far to place him in the lead as American tenor.

MRS. ROSE CASE HAYWOOD

No teacher in the musical circles of Chicago has met with more decided and rapid success than Mrs. Rose Case Haywood, who has been for two years an assistant of Leopold Godowsky in the Chicago Conservatory.

She entered the field as the pupil of Leopold Godowsky, Moritz Moszkowski and Bruno Zwintscher, and her work has proved her to have been a worthy disciple of these great masters.

In addition to her musical training she has received college advantages in America and Europe such as few women ever enjoy. Mrs. Haywood's ability as a writer has been shown by the success of her little book, "Musical Sketches," and by the publication of her articles in such papers as the Chicago *Tribune,* the *Times-Herald,* Milwaukee *Sentinel* and the New York *Musical Courier.*

Her series of lectures, "Beethoven and the Sonata," "The Piano and Its Abuses," "American Music," "Woman as a Composer," "Woman as an Interpreter," have been highly commended for originality of thought and literary excellence.

VICTOR HEINZE

Mr. Victor Heinze is one of the most finished and artistic pianists, as well as one of the most scholarly teachers of this country. He has won his way into prominence by the breadth and versatility of his accomplishments equally as artist and educator. From his father, Leopold Heinze, the author of several standard theoretical and didactical works in use throughout the German, French, Austrian and Russian conservatories, Mr. Heinze inherited a powerful mentality; the tireless energy, thoroughness, sagacity and keen perceptions of the student. From his mother, a lady of Polish birth, the sensitiveness and dreamy melancholy which characterize that gifted and unfortunate race. Within himself he happily combines the essential qualities of the artist, trained mental force with tenderness and delicacy of feeling.

The German government recognized his unusual capability by entrusting to him the position of director of the Musical Department of the Royal School of Schweidnitz when he was but twenty-one years of age, a distinction which will be correctly estimated by those who know the exceptionally high character of these governmental schools. Added to his musical proficiency, it was his rare faculty of imparting instruction which conferred upon him so eminent a position. Many instructors of standing now teaching in the Old World are indebted to him for their thorough musical education. After four years of exacting labor, he resigned this position, thereafter devoting his entire attention to the piano forte.

His collegiate and musical education were acquired in Breslau and Berlin, but when Professor Leschetizky's celebrity became world-wide owing to the remarkable achievements of a brilliant galaxy of his pupils—Paderewski, Slivinski, Hopekirk, Essipoff and Madame Bloomfield-Zeisler—he placed himself under that master, becoming a pupil and most ardent admirer of his system of piano playing.

After having acquired this thorough, clear, yet simple method of teaching, Mr. Heinze, although one of the fine performers of this country, makes teaching his life-work. His undeniable efficiency as an eminently capable musical educator makes the training of independent, developed musicians his highest ambition. He teaches privately, believing that in such instruction alone can the best possible results be obtained in the case of each individual student. As a performer his varied style is marked by a brilliancy rarely evinced, and the breadth and resonance of his massive tone in heavy compositions are remarkable. In interpretation he is invariably scholarly and well balanced, and his playing demonstrates the thinker as well as the artist. He evinces passion and warmth without undue sentimentality.

Mr. Heinze is today one of the best equipped exponents in America of Leschetizky's incomparable method of the art of piano playing, and is in possession of testimonials of unstinted praise from teachers of acknowledged standing in this and other cities as to the value of his instruction, after having studied under his tuition. As a many-sided musician he is conspicuous for the breadth and completeness of his culture.

VICTOR HEINZE

AUGUST HYLLESTED

This gifted and richly endowed pianist has contributed generously to the elevation of musical standards, especially in the art of piano playing. He was born in Stockholm, Sweden, in June, 1858, the son of a prominent musician, who gave him the best possible educational advantages. At the age of six years he began a five years' tutelage under Holger Dahl, of Copenhagen, and at eleven went on a concert tour throughout Scandinavia. Then entering the Royal Conservatory at Copenhagen, he studied every branch of music except singing, remaining until nineteen years old, when his services were engaged as pianist and musical director of the Ferdinand Strakosch Italian Opera Company. A year later he became organist in Hykjobrix Cathedral, and director of its musical society. After two years of successful work he studied piano in Germany with Theodore Kullak, and counterpoint with Ferd Kiel. He was then for three years, at Weimar, the pupil of Liszt, who in a private letter said of him: "Among the many pianists I have had the opportunity to hear, I find only few who are really talented artists; but among these few is particularly the Scandinavian pianist, August Hyllested."

A concert tour through Europe was

a series of artistic triumphs to Mr. Hyllested. He appeared before most of the reigning families of Europe, received from the Italian government the gold medal of the order of "Per Merito Artistico Musicale." In London he appeared at the Crystal Palace and throughout Great Britain received the patronage and attention of royalty and the nobility. He received the diploma of the order of "Cavaliers of Honor," and was appointed court pianist to the Princess Louise of Denmark, a position which he still retains.

In 1886 occurred his first American appearance, in a series of concerts in Steinway Hall, New York, with Ovide Musin, followed by an extended tour. In 1894 Mr. Hyllested returned to Europe, remaining there four years, meeting with remarkable success as virtuoso and gaining high praise from the world's greatest critics. In 1898 Mr. Hyllested returned to America, and resumed teaching at Chicago. He has since then given an extended series of recitals throughout the Eastern States and Canada, has appeared with the New York Philharmonic Orchestra, arousing the greatest enthusiasm among musicians and critics.

GLENN HALL

Mr. Glenn Hall, while not a native of Chicago, came here at an early age and received all of his literary and the greater part of his musical education in this city.

His father, Dr. Randolph N. Hall (president of the Illinois Medical College), himself a singer of more than ordinary talent, recognized his son's vocal abilities while he was still a small boy. This led to special training under Mr. Frank Baird and Mr. Frederick Root, with the result of many successful engagements as "Boy Soprano."

During the period following Mr. Hall's change of voice, in addition to preparing for college, much attention was given to the study of piano and musical theory under the direction of Mr. Allen Spencer. After an absolute rest of three years, he sought the opinion of vocal authorities, who immediately pronounced his voice a tenor of rare beauty. Serious study was at once commenced and was pursued for four years under Mr. Wm. Nelson Burritt, with constant gain in voice and style. A year's study under Mme. Hess-Burr followed, with gratifying results, while another teacher to whom he acknowledges much indebtedness is Mr. Karleton Hackett. Mr. Hall spent the past summer with Mr. Georg Henschel in London, who speaks enthusiastically of Mr. Hall's voice and musicianship.

As a church singer Mr. Hall was first engaged by the Forty-first St. Presbyterian Church, and later, with an increase of salary at each change, at the South Congregational Church, the First Baptist and the First Presbyterian, where he still sings.

Mr. Hall's voice is a robust tenor of wide range and beautiful quality. Each succeeding year seems to add to its strength and attractiveness. His musical intelligence and broad general culture seem to fit him peculiarly for oratorio and song recitals. Mr. Hall's repertoire includes all the standard oratorios and songs in French, German, Italian and English.

His recent public successes have been chronicled in the musical and daily press, and need not be re-enumerated here further than to say that Mr. Hall has sung with the Apollo Club of Chicago and many of the important choral societies at all times with most gratifying results.

MRS. ANNETTE R. JONES

The successful musical career of Mrs. Annette R. Jones may be ascribed to many causes. Aside from her sterling musical ability, she has always enjoyed an exceptional social position and represents a unique feature of the artistic life in Chicago. Our city has particular cause to be proud of her, as she owes her entire advancement to home study, never having cared to avail herself of foreign travel or research. Mrs. Annette Jones is one of the founders and charter members of the Chicago Amateur Club, whose program she has often graced with her artistic performances. As a teacher she possesses that rare quality, a delightful personality, which attaches pupils strongly; her pianism is distinguished by lucidity of perception and brilliant execution; she is a phenomenal sight reader, and artists consider themselves fortunate when enjoying the rare privilege of her accompaniment. Take it all in all, Mrs. Jones has won her laurels fairly and is an honor to the musical profession.

NELLIE GERTRUDE JUDD

Since she came to Chicago, Miss Nellie Gertrude Judd has scored a phenomenal success. Perhaps no singer is more popular for "at homes" and similar engagements. She is gifted with a sweet, clear soprano voice, remarkably sympathetic and of unusual carrying power, while her manner is most unaffected and charming.

For four years she was the pupil of

repertoire includes the best known operas and oratorios, and as a song singer she is particularly pleasing, as she is equally at home in German, French and English songs.

"No arrival in recent years has awakened more interest in the musical profession than Miss Nellie Gertrude Judd, the young soprano. The fresh young voice, the

ROGERS & SMITH CO.

Fraulein Schoen-Rene, an opera singer of note and an exponent of the pure "Bel Canto." Going abroad with her teacher, Miss Judd was enabled, through her, to study in Paris with Mme. Viardot Garcia, of whom it has been said, "To be received by her as a pupil stamps one as an artist." Of her singing in London the papers of that city speak with enthusiasm, praising both her voice and method. Returning to America, Miss Judd embarked upon a musical career that has commenced most auspiciously. Her

admirable method, diction, enunciation, almost perfect French and German accent are a few of the attributes. The *tout ensemble* of the singer tells of culture and taste without any extravagances and exaggerations, than which nothing could be more pleasing."—*Musical Courier.*

Miss Judd's recent successes in Chicago are too well in the public mind to need chronicling. She has just been engaged for the Union Park Congregational Church.

MRS. HELEN LESTER JORDAN

In the training of voices this well known artist of Chicago has met with conspicuous success. The testimonials of her pupils have in them the ring of sincerity and gratitude and afford many striking instances of the efficacy of her instruction. In her studio she does not make the common boast that her method is entirely her own, but prominent masters of the country, including Mme. Fursch-Madi, and has sung under such noted directors as Seidl, De Novelles, and Janotti, director of Carl Rosa Company, of Great Britain. She has received very flattering press criticisms from the foremost critics of the leading cities of America.

says she teaches the methods so successfully adopted by Lamperti, and Marchesi, his great pupil—the method that has developed the voices of Melba, Calve, Emma Eames, Sybil Sanderson, Sigrid Arnoldson, Campanini, Plancon and others.

On her mother's side Mrs. Jordan comes from a distinguished Southern family. Her father was born in the old Lester home in Connecticut, which was founded in 1630. She has had many years of preparation for her work and has studied with the most

Mrs. Jordan is a constant and conscientious student of the leading writers on voice culture. She is, moreover, an unusually enthusiastic worker and possesses the happy faculty of imparting her enthusiasm to her pupils.

In her work she individualizes, giving to each voice its own proper course to pursue in order to attain the best results.

Mrs. Jordan has had the experience of a series of very successful seasons on the stage in both comic and grand opera. Concerning her voice, a well known musician says: "She has a fine voice, with a range from A flat below the staff to F in alt under perfect control, the three registers being remarkable for their smoothness. The quality of her voice is warm, rich and full; the tone color excellent; her phrasing is flawless. There are many people who feel very deeply, but have not the power to express it. Mrs. Jordan is particularly gifted that way.

Every emotion, humor, pathos, strong dramatic situation—she feels it all, and in her voice and facial expression expresses clearly the nature of the music."

It is, however, as a teacher, and not as a singer, that Mrs. Jordan is applying her gifted talents, and her success is the best testimonial of her splendid ability.

GEORGE H. KELLAND

Mr. George H. Kelland, basso, one of Chicago's well known singers, is another product of the English church choirs. Born in Lancashire, England, he first attracted attention when boy soloist in one of the leading Episcopal churches of that celebrated county. On leaving England he first located in Winnipeg, Canada, where he soon became prominent in musical circles and is still remembered in connection with the Choral Society and also the Amateur Theatrical Society—in both of which he occupied a conspicuous position. Since residing in Chicago

he has been connected, as soloist, with some of the leading churches of the city, notably the First Baptist, Trinity Episcopal, etc., and is at present engaged as bass soloist at the Cathedral of the Holy Name.

Mr. Kelland is pre-eminently an oratorio singer, his capabilities in that line, notably in connection with the "Messiah," "Creation," "Elijah," etc., entitling him to a prominent place among the leading exponents of that class of music, while his talents as a concert singer are also well known.

WALTER KNUPFER

PIANIST

J. H. KOWALSKI

Musical talent, even of a high order, counts but little in the making of a great educator unless accompanied by professional enthusiasm and a genuine interest in the welfare of the student. It has been the merited fortune of J. H. Kowalski to be classed as one of the leading vocal teachers in Chicago. His personality, his devotion, unusual musical ability. At five Mr. Kowalski began a nine years' course of piano instruction with Pechowski. At the age of seven he became leading boy soprano at St. George's Episcopal Church, New York.

Adopting music as his life-work, he studied voice production and singing four years under Errani, at that time

his success have brought him many pupils from all parts of the United States and Canada. Mr. Kowalski also possesses in wonderful measure the faculty of training children's voices for solo work. Many of his pupils now fill important positions as teachers and singers.

Born in Poland in 1855, Mr. Kowalski was brought by his parents to America when three years old. His father was a distinguished Russian officer, but neither parent possessed a leading vocal artist in New York. For three years he was musical director of an opera company; then for a year as pianist and accompanist toured with Ole Bull. Coming to Chicago, he was for two years assistant to George Sweet, then most worthily succeeded that great teacher, meeting with the most pronounced success. He is popular and his attractive studios in Kimball Hall are the inspiration and haunts of many music loving people.

EMIL LIEBLING

It might be difficult to decide in what this eminent musician of Chicago most, excelled, whether as lecturer, teacher, composer or pianist. He has created for himself in the art circles of his adopted city a field peculiarly and pre-eminently his own. His association with the musical growth of the

ing and is consulted by leading teachers who travel long distances to coach up in their repertoire. His activity and influence thus extends into many communities where his name and personality are comparatively unknown to the average musical amateur.

Besides piano recitals Mr. Liebling

city has been more decided than that of any other individual. As concert pianist Mr. Liebling represents the best modern school. He has played in public perhaps 400 different compositions, the vast majority of which he would be able to play offhand at any moment asked for. In that respect he stands almost alone among artists.

As piano teacher he stands at the head of one of the largest and most active musical clientelles possessed in America. He is an authority on teach-

gives lectures with practical demonstrations on piano playing and teaching. He is a ready talker, *au courant* with musical personality and history, and his wonderful mastery of the compositions of all the great writers gives him unequaled facility and amplitude of illustration.

Mr. Liebling has composed many works of high merit, among which are notable the Concert Romances, opus 20 and 21; a charming gavotte moderne, opus 11, and the brilliant Florence Concert Valse. He has also edited a special edition of the Heller and Loeschhorn etudes. He has achieved renown as a writer upon musical subjects, always with something to say and always saying it in a direct and suggestive manner.

His musical career extends over a period of twenty-five years, a period teeming with activity and most gratifying success. In personality Mr. Liebling is agreeable, with the incisive and potent manner of the master artist. In his many incursions throughout the country he has invariably charmed. By his happy and forceful methods he has frequently condensed into a single evening's talk and recital a generous and sustaining musical inspiration to communities to whom artistic advantages had been few and very incomplete. In this educational work he has highly excelled.

When in the spring of the present year (1900) the Mendelssohn Club was seeking a foremost attraction, Mr. Liebling was invited to play Moskowski's new concerto for the first time in this country. His thoroughly conscientious work, his brilliant pianism and student interpretation roused an enthusiasm the Central Music Hall has seldom witnessed, and gained him a deserved appreciation from press and public of which any artist might be proud.

MENDELSSOHN CLUB

The Mendelssohn Club of Chicago, a male choir of sixty voices, was founded some ten years ago with the avowed object of sociability among musicians. While within its ranks today sociability and general good-fellowship are recognized and felt by even the public, the members of the past five years are such by reason of superior vocal ability. To be indorsed by two members, to pass an examination before the music committee, to sing three consecutive rehearsals with the club and then to be balloted for by the entire membership is the test of every applicant.

The first concert given by the mannerchor was in Steinway Hall, June 11, 1895, under the direction of Mr. Frederic W. Root. The following year Mr. Harrison M. Wild was elected conductor, and he has remained at the post ever since.

During the short life of the club as a singing body it has sung some ninety different numbers, nothing but that which is best being given a hearing, and has been assisted by some of the greatest vocal and instrumental artists of the world. It has been called upon by Mr. Theodore Thomas to assist in a Parsifal excerpt and in Liszt's Faust Symphony. The greater portion of its work is done a capella, but last season, its second concert, with the assistance of the Thomas Orchestra, it produced Max Bruch's Fritjof.

Out of the twenty-three compositions given a hearing in the season of 1899-1900 by the club, twenty were new to Chicago.

The concerts of the club are given upon a somewhat unique plan. A subscription to the three concerts is issued, no seats are reserved, all subscribers have the same privileges, and single tickets are sold to no one. There is but one honorary member, the founder of the club, Mr. D. A. Clippinger. The president from the society's inception to 1896 was Mr. J. A. Cameron. The present officers and active members are as follows:

Musical Director — Harrison M. Wild.

Officers—George H. Iott, president; George J. Pope, vice-president; W. C. Boorn, secretary; C. H. Strawbridge, treasurer; E. J. Strawbridge, librarian.

Directors—Walter R. Root, W. S. Hine, Henry W. Newton, W. G. E. Peirce, Louis Spahn.

Membership Committee — Harrison M. Wild, musical director; F. S. Russell, first tenor; G. M. Hobbs, second tenor; C. B. Kimball, first bass; Wyatt McGaffey, second bass.

Honorary Member—D. A. Clippinger.

Active Members—Geo. H. Baber, F. M. Bogle, W. C. Boorn, A. McN. Campbell, H. C. Cassidy, Chas. N. Chambers, W. H. Cork, Jr., Ernest E. Eversz, J. S. Fearis, H. F. Grabo, Wm. Hearn, G. Heathcote Hills, W. S. Hine, H. E. Hitchcock, Glen M. Hobbs, Barron S. Hobbs, W. F. Holcombe, F. A. Howard, H. D. Fletcher, F. W. Maynard, Geo. H. Iott, Lester B. Jones, C. B. Kimball, J. Herbert King, Karl Knorr, J. H. Kurtz, Wyatt McGaffey, C. A. McKeand, Wm. T. McLain, S. W. Mountz, H. R. Moyer, Louis Nahm, H. W. Newton, Edward H. Niese, D. A. Noyes, John H. Noyes, W. G. E. Peirce, C. H. Phelps, Arthur V. Vogelsang, Ashton D. Goodrich, G. J. Pope, W. H. Pratt, A. E. Remick, Frank K. Root, Walter R. Root, F. S. Russell, Chas. H. Seamans, H. J. Siebold, Louis Spahn, Percy R. Stephens, C. H. Strawbridge, E. J. Strawbridge, Justin M. Thatcher, E. F. Waite, John D. Walker, G. F. Wessels, W. C. Williams, H. W. Wollin, Wm. Henry Thompson.

WILLIAM LEWIS

(See Page 24)

BERNHARD LISTEMANN

With musical triumphs won abroad, in many of the most critical centers of Europe, Bernhard Listemann, while yet early in his musical career, came to America and here as violin virtuoso and as instructor he has made a lasting impression. He was born at Schlotheim, in Thuringia, in 1841. As a child he evinced a passion for the violin and so great was his talent that a public career speedily opened to him. When a small boy he appeared in public, playing the Adagio of Spohr's Ninth Concerto. He became the pupil of David at Leipsic, and there his work attracted wide attention. The position of court violinist to the reigning prince at Rudalstadt was offered him, and that position he continued to fill for nine years, in the meantime continuing his studies at Leipsic under Joachim and Vieuxtemps.

In 1867 he came to America and began a series of concert tours. Theodore Thomas, in 1871, tendered him an engagement as soloist with his orchestra, and later he filled the same position with the Harvard Musical Association. The Boston Philharmonic Society inaugurated its famous history under his initial directorship, and later he was a leading member of the Boston Symphony Orchestra. Recognizing the future of Chicago, he located in this city and today no artist in Chicago ranks higher.

MARIE COBB LAMSON

By her recent marriage to Mr. Lamson, of Washington, D. C., Miss Marie L. Cobb gives to that city a portion of

the time which Chicago had previously monopolized. She will be much heard in concert, and, as her many friends here rejoice to know, Mrs. Lamson promises that Chicago shall have frequent visits.

As a pianist of brilliant attainments Mrs. Lamson has won enviable distinction. She is a native of New Orleans, and, after a preliminary education in this country, she completed her artistic studies abroad. She was placed under the direction of Herr Von Wieck, Clara Schumann's brother, and later was a student of Hans Von Bulow, who took a great personal interest in the talent she displayed. Her education abroad was completed with Sgambati as her instructor. "It follows," remarks the *Musical Courier*, "that, with natural ability, Miss Cobb is an artist of brilliant accomplishment and it is positively refreshing to hear her interpretations. She is a charming woman, of fine presence and a splendid linguist." She has made a decided conquest in the concert field, winning at every hand high encomiums by the brilliancy and masterfulness of her interpretations.

FRANCES CAREY-LIBBE

Frances Carey-Libbe, the bright and popular contralto whose picture appears in this work, undoubtedly possesses one of the most remarkable and purely contralto voices in the city. Though still quite young in years, her success has been remarkable, some of the best critics predicting for her a brilliant future.

Frances Carey-Libbe was born in Oswego, N. Y., August 31, 1874, and from childhood has attracted attention of musicians by her voice and talent, for she possesses far more than ordinary dramatic ability.

Coming to Chicago when quite young, she has been a careful and constant student at her art. She has held many responsible church positions in the city, among them being solo contralto in Sinai Temple for two years.

Her voice is beautifully rich and full throughout, her low tones being especially noticeable for their depth and volume. Her upper register has all the brightness and resonance of a dramatic soprano, possessing a range which is truly wonderful.

Mrs. Carey-Libbe sang her first oratorio at the age of nineteen, and treasures some very flattering testimonials regarding her work.

She has been singing in concert oratorio and opera since that time, and has a repertoire of nearly all of the oratorios and a number of operas.

Mrs. Carey-Libbe is a thorough musician and can at all times be relied upon to give a conscientious, well studied and finished performance.

MME. RAGNA LINNE

Was born in Christiana, Norway, and is a descendant of Karl V. Linne (Charles Linnæus). Her extraordinary voice, a magnificent dramatic soprano, was carefully trained by eminent vocal teachers, notably by the renowned Mme. Marchesi, at Paris, who has ever cherished for Mme. Linne the warmest regard.

After appearing with distinguished success in concert and opera at some of the principal European centers, Mme. Linne came to Chicago, where she has ever since occupied a foremost position as a concert singer and teacher.

Mme. Marchesi writes that Mme. Linne is an authorized interpreter of her method. Mme. Linne has also been the recipient of strong indorsements from Mr. Georg Henschel and Sig. Alberto Randegger, of London.

FREDERICK LILLEBRIDGE

Leo Koflen, the celebrated organist at St. Paul's, New York, said: "In a competition at this church last year among a great number of organists—about a hundred, including some of the best of New York—Mr. Lillebridge was selected as the one who showed the greatest knowledge of the science of music and most ability as an organist."

As composer and pianist Mr. Lillebridge is one of the brilliant musical characters of Chicago. As a teacher he follows the method of Tausig, but modified by his own experience as a guide. He has systematized technic so as to save the pupil much time and devoted much of his attention to tone production and expression.

The technic of Mr. Lillebridge has been pronounced faultless. His phrasing is most excellent, his execution brilliant and his interpretation impressive. The St. John *Sun* says: "The gem of the evening was a composition by Mr. Lillebridge for voice, organ, violin and piano. It was most noticeable for beautiful harmony, its melody, and for that nameless something that is invariably added to the music of artists." Similar testimonials are almost legion in number.

CHARLOTTE LACHS LILLEBRIDGE

man-Swedish parentage, she became the protege of Niels W. Gade, the great Danish composer, who was enthusiastic over her voice. At the age of sixteen she was admitted as a pupil in the Royal Conservatory of Music at Munich, and became a favorite pupil of the eminent teacher, Hans Hasselbeck, brother and teacher of Rosa Sucher. She continued her musical studies at the conservatory five years, and has since sung in concerts in Germany, Sweden and America. As a teacher she has been very successful. She teaches the Italian method, making a specialty of a broad and noble style of delivery, developing voices at times from very unpromising material. She has many pupils occupying positions as teachers and church singers.

Both as soprano and as teacher this talented musician of Chicago has obtained excellent recognition. Of Ger-

Her voice is a rich dramatic soprano, showing magnificent compass and training and impressing one with a sense of withheld energy and reserve force.

EDWARD MEEK

Edward Meek has devoted the most of his life to the study of music as an art. His earlier years were given entirely to instrumental music and theory. When, later on, he began the study of vocal music, the cultivation of his own voice and the teaching of voice culture absorbed his attention and enthusiasm. His best work was done under the direction of one of New York's leading masters, from whom he received fresh impetus to his enthusiasm and great encouragement for future success. Mr. Meek's method, which, practically speaking, he has developed for himself, after much patient work, is singularly easy to grasp, as it is both simple and clear. Two prominent features of this method are the manner of breathing and the smoothness with which the voice is carried throughout its entire range.

To these may be added the repose of body and the entire freedom from nervous tension, upon which Mr. Meek lays great stress, believing it to be most essential to the best results. He

is most certainly an artist, conscientious, broad and of great ability, who will make his work and influence felt. He has a fine, rich baritone voice of wide range, and he has sung to large audiences in many states with flattering success. With a voice full of pathos and power, and one which appeals to the heart and mind alike, his rendition and interpretation of a great variety of songs is satisfying and pleasing, as it is sympathetic and original. His studio is No. 608 Fine Arts Building, Chicago.

MRS. GERTRUDE HOGAN MURDOUGH

As some of our sweetest singers have wrought their melodious verse inspired thereto by the beautiful lakes, hills and woodlands of Wisconsin, so some of our most gifted musicians have had the wild, free, sweeping meadows and uplands of Iowa for their native heath. Mrs. Murdough first saw the light in this land of promise, and the musical atmosphere of her native state seems to have dowered her with rich gifts.

Mrs. Murdough early manifested musical gifts of no common order, and so her musical instruction was immediately begun, and at fifteen years of age she herself became a music teacher. Even in her youthful years she possessed in a marked degree those wonderful molding powers and that striking faculty of arousing musical enthusiasm in her pupils which has since made her unsurpassed as an instructor. Feeling both quickly and profoundly, she at once establishes between herself and her pupil a tender and inspiring relation; she places herself *en rapport* with the most various natures, and to the child gifted musically she becomes an ideal, because only such a child can fully realize the strength of her musical aspirations.

When, largely through her individual efforts the musical conservatory in Tama, Iowa, of which she had been given charge, became firmly established on a thorough basis, Mrs. Murdough determined to pursue her musical studies in Chicago. Again she paid her way by dividing her time between practice and music teaching.

A period of time spent abroad in study under the best foreign masters, such as Raif of Berlin and Leschititsky of Vienna, have reinforced Mrs. Murdough's innate genius, though to Raif she traces her richest musical growth. Thus the best modern methods of musical instruction are hers, not only because of her own gifts, but also because of her large development in accordance with the best musical ideas of the age in the greatest musical centers of the world. This has resulted in such a sympathetic and feeling rendering of the works of the masters as places her far above the rank and file of accomplished musical instructors.

One of the most helpful things she ever wrote, judging from its rich results, is an essay on musical memory and the best methods of cultivating it. And it ought to be said, in justice to Mrs. Murdough, that, working along the lines it suggests, she has accomplished notable results in her teaching, developing musical memory to a power and accuracy immensely enhancing the student's musical ability both in the comprehension and the interpretation of the most difficult and beautiful classical music. This is well illustrated by the Bach Fugue work, which her pupils render so beautifully and voicefully, and which is perhaps the most perplexing music composed, both for memorizing and for large interpretation. Mrs. Murdough is still a young woman and the future must bring much to her, provided the necessary years and strength shall be allotted her. Her musical career so far has certainly been one of which any noble and ambitious woman might well be proud. She is now connected with the American Conservatory of Music as one of its most distinguished instructors.

C. E. R. MUELLER

Mr. Mueller belongs to a musical family, two brothers and two sisters having devoted themselves to music, thus following their father's example.

Born in September, 1847, in the town of Auma, in Thuringia, he came to this country in July, 1860. While he began the study of music at the age of about eleven years, it was not with the intention of making it a profession. From 1861 to 1863 Mr. Mueller attended the Concordia College, at Fort Wayne, exchanging that in 1863 for the University of Chicago.

During all this time music had not been neglected; on the contrary, he had, besides keeping up his study of the piano, studied without master the organ, and had obtained considerable proficiency in harmony. In 1871 he went to Europe to study music and to travel. At Leipsic he did not find what he expected, and in 1872 he went to the Stuttgart Conservatory, where Lebert, Speidel and Pruckner were his masters of the piano, Faisst of the organ and theory, and Koch of singing. All these facts will show that Mr. Mueller's education, both general as well as musical, rests on a broad foundation. It is certain that there are not many musicians who, besides Greek and Latin, master German, English, French and Italian.

Returning to America in 1876, he introduced himself in a concert as organist and composer. On various occasions he also appeared as pianist. Chicago had at that time not yet overcome the effects of the panic of 1873, and thus Mr. Mueller was induced to go to London, England. He stayed there nearly two years, enjoying the recommendation of Messrs. Aug. Manns and E. Pauer. Receiving a call as teacher of the Hamburg Conservatory, he went there in October, 1879, successfully holding that position until the summer of 1880, when he resigned it and came back to Chicago, thus ending his "Wanderjahre."

Elected in the fall of 1882 teacher of singing in Chicago High Schools, and assisting at numerous pupils' concerts, he showed the excellence of his method both of the piano and the voice. Ever progressive, a careful observer and student, he improved on the methods taught by his teachers.

It would be surprising if a man of his education had not written on music, and accordingly we find that he, besides acting at various times as critic for several German and American papers of this city, has contributed to them articles on musical subjects.

Aside from these, he analyzed Schumann's Mass for the program of the music festival of 1882, and for the Saengerfest of 1881 he wrote the analyses of all the works performed. These analyses have been highly spoken of by noted musicians.

Having for some time made the study of Schubert a specialty, he wrote a long essay on "Die Gesammtausgabe der Lieder Franz Schubert's." This, published originally in the *Illinois Staats-Zeitung,* appeared this year in connection with the Schubert centenary in Lessmann's "Allgemeine Musik-Zeitung." It led to an interesting correspondence with Sir George Grove, and Dr. E. Mandyczewski, the noted Schubert scholar and reviser of the "Gesammtausgabe," honored him with a letter of which he may justly be proud.

It can truly be said that in no other essay on Schubert's songs can be found so much exact and valuable information about the different settings of the same poem, the number of poems Schubert composed of the different poets, the harmonic peculiarities of the music, the embellishments used in the songs—all features which make it an essay of lasting merit.

THE NEED OF A STUDENTS' FUND

Recently a statement was published of various bequests to the Art Institute, the Chicago University and a number of other of the city's institutions, all which, with the wiping out of the debt of the Chicago Orchestra and other magnificent instances of generosity on the part of her citizens, places Chicago apparently in the very front rank for the public spirit of enlightened philanthropy of her worthy citizens. Provision is made hereby to enable the people the better to fulfill a duty in aiding the young to an education. Through such munificence the university students and the students in the Art Museum can get the best of instruction at a nominal price, besides in many cases being provided with the means of earning their own living meanwhile.

It is a duty of the parents to provide for their children while they are growing up, and equally it is a duty for an enlightened community to provide for the education of its young. But while so much has been done to make this a great center of education and art culture there has been vastly little done in the department of music. With the single exception of the provision for the Chicago Orchestra and perhaps a few scholarships for music students in some of our music schools there is nothing.

Almost daily throughout the year I am in receipt of letters from those wishing to study music and fit themselves for teachers. They are, in a majority of instances, not able to pay the expenses of the tuition from first-class music teachers and bear their other expenses as well, but are invariably asking if I can get them something to do to earn a living and help defray the cost. From an acquaintance with very many such students I am prepared to affirm that in a majority of instances they are the very ones who ought to be assisted for a few years of undisturbed study in the art. These people show talent, intelligence and character, and it is my belief that they have a right, a claim upon the community for a good musical education quite as much as the students in other branches who are more favored by these magnificent bequests. I look upon the education of young people as an important investment, and therefore I very much wish that people of wealth, who have the welfare of their fellow beings at heart, would provide a fund for cases such as have been mentioned above, this fund to be used where the recipient is found deserving and capable, and to be paid back without any or else at a low rate of interest. While it would be a positive misfortune to have any great bequest of this character unworthily bestowed or tied up to some one faction or institution, I nevertheless believe that the time is ripe for our magnificently disposed philanthropists and art patrons to look into this subject. It is a great misfortune to the entire country that there are so many incompetent music teachers, often incompetent from mere lack of funds and opportunity to study and equip themselves thoroughly for their life work. If the system of which I have spoken were in vogue to a greater degree there would be fewer incompetent instructors in music; as it is they try to rush the work of years into months of study and go out into the world as teachers before

they have fully learned the first principles of their art.

The old fashion that prevails in Europe, the apprenticeship system of seven years' service, decidedly has its merits. There the music student is required to spend many years in correct and thorough study and solid preparation for his future career; in America it is all feverish excitement and haste and a struggle for superiority in positions instead of a disposition to master one's subject. In this respect the European methods are vastly superior to our own.

It is an equally great misfortune to the community as well as to the resident musician that so much of our musical patronage is diverted to sending music students abroad instead of providing the necessary means to enable them to pursue their study in their own country, undisturbed by thoughts of expense for the same length of time that is required of them in Europe.

In the matter of students who are cramped in regard to money for their living during their pursuit of art, I consider it very commendable that they are willing to work hard and deprive themselves of many things in order to develop their talent. Many a career has been cut short or dwarfed of its possibilities by various obstacles, the first and foremost of these being the necessity of earning their daily bread.

The large centers like Chicago, where the opportunities of studying are the greatest, are unfortunately the most difficult for young students to make a living or pay their expenses in.

Our wealthy people form trusts and are wonderfully shrewd in learning how to amass a great amount of money, create colossal fortunes and make themselves the owners of the world. I read a short time ago that the United States of America was in control of the money markets of the world. But what investment in such material sources can equal an investment in the development of brain and character.

It is equally to be desired that a music lover should not allow some narrow favoritism toward this or that faction to encourage them in the habit of decrying the efforts of other artists than their particular favorites, or even of going to the length of maligning those in the same field as their particular partisans. While the people of Chicago are remarkably free from imputation of unfairness and one-sidedness toward American talent, it appears as if there were certain factions in New York where the opposite course has been a rule for many years past. It is very easy to destroy the finest work of art, which may have taken years to build up, with a single rough, indiscriminate blow. The best efforts of our cultivated musicians require such an amount of self-sacrifice and patient and intelligent development of talent that one should strive for the cause of the art to seek the good in them and bear lightly with their faults. These remarks do not apply to mediocrity. The appearance of amateurish and undeveloped persons in the concert field is certainly not to be encouraged.

WILLIAM H. SHERWOOD.

WILHELM MIDDELSCHULTE

In mentioning the prominent musicians of America the name of Wilhelm Middelschulte must always come among the first. Mr. Middelschulte entered the Royal Academy of Church Music of Berlin when very young, and at this famous school was for three years an enthusiastic student of August Haupt for organ and theory, of Albert Loeschorn for piano, and Dr. Julius Alsleben for conducting. These eminent masters, together with Franz Cammer, took great interest in their pupil, and Haupt honored Middelschulte by appointing him his assistant organist at the Royal Academy.

In a testimonial given Mr. Middelschulte by his professors they said to him: "Greatly gifted with musical talent, he has always distinguished himself in every subject by extraordinary application, so that now, at the end of his studies, we can most heartily give him a place of the highest distinction; stating at the same time that he is perfectly capable of teaching successfully any branch of music."

In 1888 Mr. Middelschulte was appointed organist and choir director at one of the principal churches in Berlin. He remained there until 1891, when he came to Chicago to accept the position of musical director and organist of the Holy Name Cathedral.

Before leaving Berlin Mr. Middelschulte played by invitation at the memorial service for Emperor Frederick III at the church in Bornstedt, near Potsdam, where the Emperor often worshiped. The day before Mr. Middelschulte departed for America occurred the funeral of his revered mas-

ter, August Haupt. At the request of the family he played on Haupt's organ the C minor Fantasie by Bach, a favorite composition of the deceased organist. Joachim and many other distinguished musicians were present.

Upon his arrival in America he at once took a prominent place among musicians. By special invitation he gave three recitals at the World's Fair. The following season he played the solo part of Alex. Guilmant's first concerto with the Chicago Orchestra, at the Auditorium, and was at once appointed organist of the orchestra, a position which he is still filling with great credit to himself. In his concert tours Mr. Middelschulte has appeared in the principal cities from the East to the West.

His extraordinary memory enables him to play all of his programs without the music, which is quite unusual in organ playing. He is equally at home in the classic or modern school.

As a composer much may be expected from his gifted pen. Bernhard Ziehn, the great authority, says of Middelschulte's "Passacaglia": "Since the Passacaglia of Bach no work of that kind has come to light which deserved comparison with Middelschulte's Passacaglia."

Mr. Middelschulte is a most excellent piano teacher and a modest and unassuming gentleman.

A proof of the high esteem in which he is held by Clarence Eddy is shown by the fact that when the latter went to Europe he entrusted all his pupils to Mr. Middelschulte's careful guidance.

W. S. B. MATHEWS

It has been said that no man in America has probably been so successfully and widely a teacher through the printing press as W. S. B. Mathews, of Chicago. As editor and author his contributions to music have been prolific and as valuable as they have been numerous. He is known to both advanced and to elementary students and everywhere throughout the country his text-books are recognized as standard.

Mr. Mathews is a native of London, N. H., where he was born May 8, 1837. A decided taste and aptitude for music displayed itself early in childhood, and the ambition of the boy from earliest recollection was to be a teacher. When about twelve years of age his musical education began. Its rapidity and thoroughness may be surmised by the fact that the following year, at the age of thirteen, he began playing the organ in church. Before he was eighteen he had become a teacher in an academy at Mount Vernon, N. H. Eager, however, to perfect himself in his chosen calling

he continued his studies. He was a pupil with Southard at Boston and later studied with Thalberg.

His tastes for the literary side of music also developed early in life. In 1859 he became a contributor to Dwight's Journal, continuing frequently through the life of that paper. He became editor of the Musical Independent in 1868, continuing four years. Mr. Mathews was for about ten years connected with the daily press of Chicago as critic on various papers.

The permanent contributions of Mr. Mathews to the literature of music embrace many valuable works, several of which are now notable text books, including "Mathews' Graded Materials for the Piano," "Mathews' Beginner in Phrasing," "A Primer of Music" (in conjunction with Dr. William Mason) and "The Pronouncing Dictionary of Musical Terms." One of his latest productions consists of two volumes of "Graded Pieces," which, with the assistance of Mr. Liebling, he has recently finished and published.

CHARLES WILBUR MACDONALD

Charles Wilbur MacDonald is a native of the state of Illinois, having been born at Lincoln in 1877. He is the son of Charles H. MacDonald, who has been connected with the music trade of Chicago for years, and is now of the house of MacDonald-Newton Company of this city. The elder MacDonald is a lover of music and has a local reputation as a singer.

and concertizing. In his teaching he has been very successful, the greater proportion of his class being composed of well known professional musicians of Chicago and surrounding cities.

In his concert work he has also been successful, having played a large repertoire, including the E minor Concerto, Chopin, and the G minor Saint-Saens. He has three other celebrated

Young Wilbur imbibed a love of music at an early age and began the study of the piano when eight years old under the tutorship of Fred L. Morey, now deceased, but well known as a musician of talent. For nine years subsequently he was with Victor Garwood as a private pupil, to whom he gives the credit of all his earlier foundation. He then went to Vienna and for two years studied under Leschetizky, the famous master of that famous old Austrian city.

Since his return to Chicago he has been principally engaged in teaching

Concertos at his fingers' ends. He has been heard in Chicago, New York, Boston and other large cities during the season of 1899-1900.

Mr. MacDonald has also composed a number of songs and piano pieces, most of them still in manuscript. Of those which have been published, favorable comments have been made.

In collaboration with V. Cassard, he has composed an extravaganza and has partially completed two light operas, which will probably be produced at an early day.

NOYES B. MINER

Noyes B. Miner was born in Norwich, Conn., where all his early life was passed. He studied the vocal art first with Mr. Charles R. Hayden, of Boston, who, thinking he recognized the teacher's faculty in his pupil, strongly advised him to prepare himself for the profession of a singing teacher. After a further course of study in Europe under the celebrated masters Vannuccini, Henschel and Rotoli and the famous prima donna, Elisa Biscaccianti, Mr. Miner settled in Chicago.

At the time when the faculty of the American Conservatory of Music was organized Mr. Miner was requested to accept the position of director of the vocal department, with which institution he remains until the present time.

EFFIE E. MURDOCK

The musical career of Miss Murdock at Chicago covers a period of more than a dozen years, during which time she has grown steadily as an artist and as a teacher of music. Her musical training has been thorough. She has studied with the best teachers in this country, both in piano and organ, and the summer of 1896 she spent in Paris as the pupil of Alex. Guilmant and Thome. For five years Miss Murdock was a member of the faculty of the Chicago Musical College. Succeeding that work she became teacher of piano and organ in the Gottschalk Lyric School, a position which she filled for six years. During the past two years she has been associated with the American Conservatory of Music.

Miss Murdock has been organist of the Sixth Presbyterian Church for twelve years, and during the past three years she has had complete charge of the choir and musical service. Under her capable direction the music of the church has acquired a high artistic standard.

As a teacher Miss Murdock has been eminently successful. Many of her pupils have engaged in educational work in various parts of the country, winning celebrity and adding to the laurels of their instructress, who is now well known throughout the West. Recently Miss Murdock has undertaken another branch of the musical work. She has prepared and delivered a number of lectures on musical subjects, which have been uniformly well received and in every sense have proved a notable success. Miss Murdock gives to her profession that devotion and earnestness which combined with her talent insures for her an enviable position in the musical world of Chicago.

CELESTE NELLIS

Miss Nellis, who was born at Fort Hays, is a daughter of Judge D. C. Nellis and granddaughter of Gen. J. B. McAfee, both now residing at Topeka, Kan.

At five years of age Miss Nellis began lessons on the piano, with her mother as teacher. When nine years old she was placed under the instruction of Mrs. Althea Z. O'Farrall-Graham, the most skillful music teacher of Topeka. In June, 1892, when fifteen years of age, she gave her first public musical recital at Topeka and received her first diploma. In September of the same year she located in Chicago, and for nearly five years received instruction from William H. Sherwood, at that time director of the piano department of Chicago Conservatory. She received her second diploma from that institution. From September, 1895, to June, 1897, she was a member of the musical department faculty of Chicago Conservatory, as assistant to Mr. Sherwood.

At the World's Columbian Exposition she represented the Philharmonic Club, of Topeka, in the National Convention of Musical Clubs, and won for Topeka a "Diploma of Honor" by her piano playing in Music Hall Building on June 23. She was heard on three separate occasions at the exposition, and won another diploma for herself and a bronze medal, which were awarded her by the "expert jury of music."

She was awarded a scholarship in the Chicago Conservatory by the Amateur Musical Club of Chicago in 1893, and was a member of that club from 1894 to 1897, during which time she appeared on the program of many of its most important concerts. Mr. Sherwood, in writing of her in 1896, said: "Miss Nellis has already a reputation for artistic qualities of interpretation, solid technic and brilliant concert work on the piano in Chicago, at the Columbian Exposition and at the Chautauqua Assembly, second to none of her age in the country. She has played the most difficult ensemble numbers with the great violinist, Bernhard Listemann, at the Chautauqua Assembly; also the difficult concerto with orchestra in Chicago, various numbers in concert for two pianos with myself, besides maintaining her brilliant record as solo pianiste in a most distinguished manner."

Miss Nellis has many flattering notices of her musical efforts from *Chautauquan Herald,* the *Musical Courier,* all the daily papers of Topeka, the *Chicago Presto, Inter Ocean, Tribune, Times-Herald* and *Graphic;* also from Davenport, Ia.; Ottawa, Ill.; Crawfordsville, Ind.; Johnstown, N. Y., and from other places where she has appeared as piano soloist.

On August 4, 1897, with her sister and mother, Miss Nellis sailed for Europe, and early in September, in a musical contest at Berlin Hochschule of Music, she won a scholarship in that institution, and was one of only two who were accepted as pupils of Prof. Barth, though nearly 200 contested. In July, 1899, she was given a public recital at the Hochschule Hall, playing in concert with the Joachim Orchestra, and then received her third diploma from Prof. Barth, and signed also by the great Joachim as director of the Hochschule.

During July, August and September she made a tour of southern Germany, Austria, the Tyrol, Italy and Switzerland, visiting Bayreuth for the season of Wagner opera. In October of last year she located in Paris as a pupil of Moszkowski, and will remain until after July 1, when she will return to the United States. During all her study in Berlin and Paris, she has been proud to still consider herself the pupil of the great American pianist, William H. Sherwood.

CELESTE NELLIS

W. H. NEIDLINGER

It is especially gratifying to hear a great musical artist, one who has breathed for years the atmosphere of his profession in the musical centers of Europe, express his confidence and belief in the future of art in America and of Chicago. Mr. W. H. Neidlinger, famous as a composer, vocalist and teacher, recently chose this city as his future home, after meeting with

his artistic intuition and his human sympathy, he has made himself one of the most popular American composers. His compositions en-gem the highest musical excellence and at the same time appeal to those sentiments of the heart which are the basis of success.

He is a native of Brooklyn, N. Y., where he was born in 1863. Beginning the study of harmony with Dudley

a flattering success. In speaking of that choice Mr. Neidlinger said: "I believe America will become the musical center of the world and that Chicago has the best chance to become the leading art center of America, as she is now the most progressive and liberal in the patronage of all arts."

Mr. Neidlinger, when he thus fixed upon Chicago as the home of his artistic career, enriched the musical talent of the city most notably, for he stands in the front rank of modern musical writers. With marked talent he combines originality, and by following those independent lines suggested by

Buck and C. C. Miller, he was later under Dannrenther in London. His first songs, published in 1889, met with the heartiest welcome. "The Serenade," "The Leaf" and "The Robin" constituted his first venture, and the sales of the first named have been exceeded by only one other song published in recent years. Mr. Neidlinger has now published upwards of eighty songs, besides about thirty compositions for choruses. One of his recent publications, "Small Songs for Small Singers," has with great success been introduced in the leading kindergarten schools of the country. In this work the gifted author performs the difficult work of combining genuine merit and that simplicity which is necessary to enlist and hold the child's attention.

Mr. Neidlinger has had a wide experience as a director of large choruses. He has directed the Amphion Society Male Chorus and Cecelia Women's Chorus of Brooklyn; the Treble Clef Women's Chorus and the Manheim Glee Club of Philadelphia; the Women's Chorus of Germantown and many other musical bodies. For three years he taught vocal music in Paris and London, a new field for an American artist. He met with flattering success, but surrendered a brilliant future there to take up his eminent work in Chicago.

H. W. NEWTON

The subject of this sketch is one of a large and growing class of our citizens—business men who are musicians.

Mr. Newton, during business hours, sells pianos and is of the firm of Mac-Donald-Newton Company. But all of his spare time he gives to music. He is the director of music at St. James' Methodist Episcopal Church, Forty-sixth and Ellis avenue, Rev. Robert McIntyre, pastor. The music here is furnished by a quartet and chorus of thirty voices. It is one of the very few good choruses in our churches. Mr. Newton seems to know how to get and hold good voices.

As one of the Board of Directors of the Chicago Mendelssohn Club, Mr. Newton is actively interested in the welfare of that organization. He was heard as a soloist with the club last

February, as well as with the Apollo Club.

Mr. Newton possesses a tenor voice, robust in character, with a very wide range. While his voice is in demand for parlor musicals, his work is in a broader field, and should he decide to study oratorio he would be at his best.

He is still studying with Frederic Root and gives his teacher credit for present successes.

Mr. Newton also finds time to compose a little. His latest offering is a "jubilate in A flat," and a duet, "A Mother's Answered Prayer."

MISS JENNY OSBORN

Miss Jenny Osborn, the young Chicago soprano who during the season of 1898-1899 rose so rapidly to fame, has probably made as much of a sensation in the artistic world as any artist during the present decade.

Miss Osborn, while quite young, is the possessor of a full dramatic soprano voice, which is under splendid control, having the full, rich quality of a mezzo, but possessing the range enabling her to do all the oratorios with ease. She has appeared with great success in most of the larger cities of the middle states and the West, always scoring an immediate success. She established a precedent by singing four times in one year with the Apollo Club of Chicago, was selected to appear at the Omaha Exposition with that club and appeared as principal soloist at the Congress of Musicians at Omaha. Miss Osborn was selected by Mr. Tomlins and the directors to sing in "Elijah" at the farewell testimonial for that popular conductor.

During the season 1898-1899 she

appeared as soloist with many of the prominent orchestras, including the Choral Symphony, of St. Louis, and the Symphony Orchestra, of Detroit, and others. She was engaged for the first production of "The Persian Garden" in Chicago, and has appeared in recital before nearly every prominent society in the West. Miss Osborn is now in Europe to have the advantage of study and appearances abroad. She will be absent from America for an indefinite time, but will return better fitted than ever to carry on the successful work she has inaugurated. She has all the qualities that command success, and is unquestionably one of the brightest of the rising musical stars in America today.

Miss Osborn for five years held one of the most lucrative positions in church work in Chicago, and last May was tendered three of the best choir positions in the city. However, she remained at St. Paul's Universalist Church until she went to Europe.

OPERA IN AMERICA

The future of opera in this country may well be a matter of deep concern to those who enjoy that form of intellectual recreation.

It cannot be denied that for many years our operatic privileges, our opportunities for hearing operatic performances, except in a very few of the largest cities—and there only for a few weeks each year—have been not worthy to be compared with those enjoyed by even the smaller cities of France, Germany and Austria, to say nothing of Italy, the birthplace of opera.

Let us for a moment "take account of stock," as it were, and after determining our assets proceed to the consideration of the means, if there be any, that may be employed to the improvement of the conditions which prevail at present.

Chicago has first and foremost in the operatic line periodical visits from the Grau Company, which spends two or three weeks here either at the opening or close of the musical season. It brings a number of stars, some new, some old, and presents a well-worn series of so-called "attractions" in its repertoire, chiefly such new and little known works as "Martha," "Lucia," "Traviata," "Huguenots," etc., depending upon the list of artists to fill the house without necessitating extra exertion and the attendant expense of staging the latest European novelties.

But in justice to Mr. Grau it must be said that he has several times made experiments in breaking away from this well-worn series, which for the most part delighted our grandfathers when America was young and to a considerable extent unsophisticated in art matters. The result was by no means encouraging. Massenet's "Werther," which achieved such a phenomenal success in Vienna and other European capitals, was accorded a single performance, and I am greatly mistaken if the receipts sufficed to pay the evening's expenses. Massenet's "La Navarraise" was the next venture, with Calve in the role which she created. Apparently taught by sad experience, the management chose this short but intensely dramatic work because, being short, it afforded an opportunity of presenting on the same bill the most interesting acts of "Il Trovatore" in the hope that the latter, being an old favorite, would draw the house. Certainly this venture was more successful than the former, yet it left much to be desired in the matter of patronage.

One would naturally suppose that the public would eagerly take advantage of an opportunity to hear what was then one of the latest operatic successes in Paris and London, but no; the house was far from full. The next year, despite the discouraging results of previous experiments, two (practical) novelties were presented: Boito's "Mefistofile," well known in

Europe for the past thirty years or more, but only heard in Chicago during a Mapleson season some twelve or fourteen years ago, and Massenet's "Le Cid," entirely unknown here.

Boito's great work, with Calve as Marguerite, and Plancon could not have paid expenses, and it is doubtful if Massenet's did much better even with Jean de Reszke in the title role. What would have been the result had each of these works been presented a number of times it is difficult to say, but a manager cannot go on repeating indefinitely works which do not cover an evening's expenses! Apparently the public can be divided into two great classes, those who are really musical and discriminating and desire new works and those who are attracted by the combination of a well-known star and familiar opera.

Of these two it must be said the latter far outnumbers the former, and is more reliable, therefore, in the matter of footing the bills. The manager thus must take his choice between new works and prospective poverty and old works with a "fighting chance" for life.

But in the past the Wagner operas have won their way into the repertoire, and nothing draws better today than the "Walkuere," "Siegfried" and "Tristan." They made their way in the first place by virtue of the astonishing amount of advertising they had received for years in the way of virulent abuse and their own inherent dramatic power, aided by the fact that for years, also, Mr. Thomas had familiarized the public with such excerpts as were fitted for concert use and thus created a desire to hear the entire work of which they formed a part.

Other attempts at producing novelties have been made by Mr. Grau, notably with "Otello" and "Falstaff," which met with fair success, largely no doubt due to the stars engaged in their production, but these do not appear to have secured a permanent place in the repertoire. Other works might be mentioned, but these will serve as

an example. During the past two years he has given no novelties, and advertised stars have sometimes failed to appear.

To turn to the German Opera Company, Mr. Damrosch, with his own company and earlier with the Metropolitan Company, has visited us frequently, presenting chiefly Wagner operas without stars other than Klafsky, Alvary, Fischer, etc., who came practically unknown to the Chicago public, but instantly won recognition. Here again the power of the Wagner operas to draw was demonstrated; the public attended and immediately recognized the three above-mentioned as unsurpassed in their respective roles.

It matters little how great the work or the cost, if the public will not attend all goes for naught, and grand opera is an expensive luxury—to none more so than the manager. The problem is not merely how to give excellent performances, but far more how to persuade the public of their excellence.

Under existing conditions it would seem vain to hope for anything more than a few weeks of grand opera on a large scale each year, for no public in this country would sustain such an expensive establishment for a long period.

To go to the other extreme, we are visited from time to time by traveling comic opera companies which appear to do a thriving business. Between works of this class, with their interpolated jests and "gags" at the sweet will of the comedians, and the seriousness and dignity of the grand opera there is a "great gulf fixed." The two publics are separate and wholly distinct. But it cannot be denied that the one form of entertainment seems to thrive while the other ekes out a precarious existence.

Yet the future of opera in America would seem likely to be in a measure influenced by comic opera, as strange as it may seem.

Comic opera, with all its grotesque absurdities, draws within its "sphere of influence" many to whom opera would otherwise forever remain a name merely.

Music of a light order is heard associated with a play of more or less (usually less) dramatic value. From this it is not so very far to a light, romantic opera, possessing some dignity with a fair share of sparkling wit and genuinely comic situation. The average *habitue* of comic opera would be as intensely bored with a performance of the "Walkuere" or "Goetterdammerung" as it is possible to conceive. I used to maintain that the man who could be drawn within the influence of the ball-room nights at the old Exposition Building would in time be educated up to where he would willingly listen to a symphony concert, but clearly his interest could not be secured as long as he would not attend either.

The same is true with respect to opera; lead him to an enjoyment of comic opera and you may reasonably hope that in time he will rise above that, eventually attending grand opera with pleasure and satisfaction.

True, 'tis a long journey, but one that can be and is made oftener perhaps than one would suspect. In Boston, New York and Philadelphia the experiment of giving a somewhat higher order of comic opera than the present prevalent comic work, which ought rightfully to be called "burlesque opera," has been tried, and with encouraging success. In fact in the two first named cities standing companies, playing genuine light opera with some heavier works at popular prices, have existed for some time past and have been well patronized, certainly sufficiently so to warrant the continuance of the undertaking and to give at least hope for the future.

In Chicago last season Mr. Henry W. Savage, who had already an opera company in New York, established a similar company in this city at the Studebaker. The chorus, recruited from the ranks of Chicago singers, was subjected to a severe course of training, and the principals were at first drawn chiefly from the New York

forces, though later local artists were cast for important roles.

Best of all the operas were presented in the vernacular and the choral portions were done by fresh young voices and with a finish and a superb volume of tone such as had not up to that time been heard in any operatic performances in this city.

Prices were reasonable, ranging from a dollar for the best seats down to twenty-five cents for the least desirable.

The repertoire embraced some well-known standard works and some of the better class of comic—not burlesque—operas, with a change of bill every week.

From the outset the venture was amply supported by the public, the houses being entirely sold out in advance of every performance. The result was gratifying not alone to the manager but to every one who had the good of opera in English at heart. It proved beyond question that the public was prepared to support opera well presented, though without great stars, and offered at reasonable prices. The success of such an undertaking will pave the way for similar ventures and ought eventually to create an opening for the American composer, not only of opera but also of grand opera.

The French company, from New Orleans, which has twice visited us of late years, was able to give opera at more reasonable prices than the Grau companies, because with excellent, sometimes really great artists, the expenses were not as heavy, and would no doubt have been far better supported had it not been that the American company at the Studebaker had already in a great measure taken possession of the field.

In Europe even the smaller cities possess each its own permanent opera company, with a public sufficiently numerous to sustain a modest establishment, while the larger establishments are forced to depend upon governmental or other subsidies to enable them to exist.

Here "the star system" has killed most save the largest ventures, and vampire-like is drawing the blood from them. The injury which that system has inflicted on musical art in this country cannot be computed. The mischief has been done; it only remains to seek a remedy, if happily such may be found.

We have in this country some of the best voices in the world, yet for years the church and the concert stage offered the only openings for their use. Fine singers are not necessarily good operatic artists. A long course of training in stage action as a preliminary to stage experience is a necessity. For this America affords but little opportunity. The finished vocalist cannot as a rule obtain an operatic engagement, because operatic companies are so few, and on account of want of stage experience, while the latter cannot be obtained without opportunity for appearance upon the stage, "and there you are !" Few have the money to secure proper dramatic training in addition to the expense of vocal culture, and still fewer the sum required to obtain experience even in small parts upon foreign stages.

The remedy for this state of affairs, and one which I confidently believe will sooner or later be found, will lie in the establishment of schools for the training of operatic artists in connection with small but excellent companies in all the larger cities, the principals recruited at first largely from the ranks of those that have had the necessary experience elsewhere, the school furnishing the requisite chorus at small expense, and giving its most talented pupils from time to time a chance to appear in small parts or as understudies, as circumstances may warrant.

FREDERIC GRANT GLEASON.

JULIA OFFICER

Miss Julia Officer has made a study of music since her early childhood. She graduated in the collegiate course at Rockford College, Illinois, where she at the same time took the musical course. Immediately afterward she went to Boston to continue her musical studies under Carlyle Petersilea, at the conservatory. Upon her return she occupied the several offices successively of treasurer, vice-president and president of the Ladies' Musical Society, of Omaha, before it was merged into the Woman's Club, and presided at the pipe organ of the First Presbyterian Church of Council Bluffs, Iowa, as choir director and organist. She then went to Chicago to continue the study of piano with Mme. Fannie Bloomfield-Zeisler.

Miss Officer has appeared as a solo pianiste in Chicago and vicinity at the leading social, literary and musical clubs. She is an active member of the principal ladies' musical club of Chicago, the Amateur Musical Club, and was a member of its program committee during the season of 1897-1898. Miss Officer is president of the North Side Musical Club, of Chicago. She is also an active member of the Apollo Club, of Chicago, as contralto, and through her efforts, while manager of artists for the musical department of the Trans-Mississippi Exposition at Omaha, 200 members of the club went to Omaha to sing the "Elijah," the "Messiah" and the "Swan and Skylark," under the direction of Mr. W. L. Tomlins, during the musical festival. The Thomas Orchestra was also secured by Miss Officer for the five weeks' musical festival at the exposition.

When the Bureau of Music of the exposition was organized it was necessary to have a musician in Chicago to attend to the business there. Miss Officer was appointed and approved by the executive committee because of her musical and executive ability, and because of her being located in Chicago as well as her wide acquaintance among the prominent musicians. At this festival the oratorio societies of Dubuque and Minneapolis also participated.

largely owing to the energetic work of Miss Officer.

Miss Officer's parents, Mr. and Mrs. Thomas Officer, reside in Council Bluffs, Iowa, where she spends several

JULIA OFFICER

Mr. Harrison Wild was engaged by Miss Officer to open the exposition pipe organ. The exposition festival was a great musical success, and it was

months every year after the close of the Chicago musical season, or, with them, seeks her favorite haunts in the mountains for the summer months.

SIGNOR AND SIGNORA DE PASQUALI

Signor de Pasquali and his gifted wife are the possessors of two such exceptionally fine voices as fate has seldom seen fit to unite in one family or under a single name. The lady is a native of Boston and a graduate of the National Conservatory of Music in New York City, at which place she studied with Oscar Saenger.

She is the possessor of a fine coloratura soprano of great range and of perfect quality. Her tone is pure, her method finished and her execution so true and artistic, even in the more difficult operatic roles, that one is surprised pleasantly and agreeably, it is true, at the fair singer's youth. To nature she owes much, for in addition to an exquisite voice she has beauty, youth and a very charming and entirely unaffected manner.

Signor de Pasquali, formerly tenor of the Royal Theater Bellini, of Paler-

mo, Italy, was brought up for the profession of civil engineer until so much attention was attracted by his voice that he decided instead to take up music. For seven years he was a close student under Bertini at the Royal Conservatory, Palermo, where during four successive seasons he obtained the highest possible honors. His debut was made in the Royal Bellini Theater of that town with the renowned Lamoreux, and his success was both immediate and decided.

Coming to the United States, his first appearance was with the Damrosch Symphony Orchestra, concerning which is the following: "On Sunday the first Damrosch concert took place. The soloists were Miss Emma Juch, Signor Mangioni de Pasquali and Emil Fischer, who sang the garden scene from "Faust." The young tenor at the side of these great artists sustained his part with honor. He has

a voice of great clearness and freshness, and a very good method, and sang with much grace and feeling."—*New York Sun.*

Notices of Signora de Pasquali have been equally flattering, as can be judged from the following paragraphs:

"In her rendition of the trying role of Marguerite, Signora de Pasquali evinced an artistic conception of the part which is sure to win her fame. When Gœthe wrote his masterpiece, and when Gounod set it to music, they must have had in their minds just such a Marguerite as Mrs. de Pasquali makes. She is young, beautiful and simple mannered; in fact, she is everything that the poet and musician

ascribed to Marguerite. Her coloratura is faultless, and she executed the most florid and difficult passages with a trueness and evenness seldom heard. She scored a genuine triumph.—*Atlanta (Ga.) Journal.*

"The event of the evening was the singing of the polonaise from 'Mignon' by Signora de Pasquali."—*Chicago Inter Ocean.*

EMILY PARSONS

Miss Emily Parsons, one of Chicago's younger pianistes, was born in Illinois, in 1877. She showed a decidedly musical temperament, but was not allowed to begin the serious study of music until her twelfth year.

When fifteen years old she became a pupil of Wilhelm Middelschulte, at that time one of the faculty of the Gottschalk Lyric School. Mr. Middelschulte soon recognized the young girl's rare talent, and to his careful

Griffin and several artists of the Thomas Orchestra.

The following two years were spent abroad, working with the celebrated German professor, Barth, in whose Berlin home she frequently appeared in soirees, always winning the approbation and encouragement of her great master.

Miss Parsons made her Chicago debut in March, 1899, the well-known tenor, Mr. Whitney Mockridge, assist-

EMILY PARSONS

guidance and constant inspiration was due her decision to make music her life work.

As a student Miss Parsons took repeated honors, winning in competition a valuable piano at her graduation and being awarded the post-graduate medal the following year. As further encouragement, in May, 1896, the young musician was tendered a testimonial concert in Steinway Hall by Mr. Middelschulte, Mrs. Minnie Fish-

ing. The event, musically of great interest, was a brilliant success. With every appearance since then her program renderings have shown marked increase in breadth and development of individuality.

For the season of 1899-1900 Miss Parsons was engaged to tour with the Max Bendix Concert Company, with which she was exceedingly successful, and the young artists' career will be followed with interest.

FRANCES CORA PERCE

One of the most promising young singers of Chicago is Miss Frances Cora Perce, daughter of Col. LeGrand W. Perce, one of the prominent members of the Chicago bar.

Miss Perce has a pure, even soprano voice, of great range, clear, sweet quality and of more than usual power. Her voice is under perfect control, her master having been Mr. A. D. Duvivier, a favorite pupil of Manuel Garcia. Miss Perce commenced her musical education by the study of the violin, her master being the well-known teacher Jacobsohn. She also studied harmony and composition under Adolf Weidig. Miss Perce's musical education has been catholic. She knows her art and appreciates its history and traditions, without which no singer can justly interpret the great musicians. She has been received with strong approval, and will have a successful career in either opera, oratorio or concert work.

WALTON PERKINS

Among the musicians of Chicago Walton Perkins, associate director of the Sherwood Music School, has a firm position. A resident of the city for thirty years, he has always been known for his excellent work in fur-

Gifted by nature, his musical talent was shown at an early age and he was given every possible advantage in its cultivation, receiving instruction from the world's great masters. Mr. Perkins is a fine pianist and a thorough

thering the cause of musical art. Mr. Perkins was born in the city of Rome, in the state of New York, in 1847. He was educated in the best schools of the country, finishing his preparation for Harvard University at Phillips' Academy at Exeter, New Hampshire. Before the close of his university course Mr. Perkins decided to make music his life work.

master of the technique of his art. He is an accomplished musician as well and has written several compositions of merit.

Although a skilled and effective performer, Mr. Perkins has for many years devoted himself almost entirely to teaching, and in that capacity has been extremely successful. He has the gift of imparting knowledge, is possessed of patience and perseverance, and by his faithful, conscientious drill his pupils are thoroughly grounded in the principles of technique. As a teacher of interpretation his long study and musicianship have admirably fitted him, and his pupils learn to apply the methods of technique to the best advantage. By his earnestness, enthusiasm and love of his work his pupils are inspired to do their best.

Until 1897 Mr. Perkins had his private studio, but in that year was honored by William H. Sherwood, America's representative pianist and teacher, who chose him as associate in the founding of the Sherwood Music School, which has already become one of the leading institutions of the country, its students being sought for by schools in different states to fill responsible positions as teachers.

Mr. Perkins has also made a fine reputation as a critic, having held the position of musical editor for some of the leading journals, among them the Chicago *Daily Times*. As a critic Mr. Perkins is just and fearless. He is quick to recognize merit and has done much for deserving artists who have come to the city at various times. His pen has ever been on the side of American artists and he has used his best efforts in their behalf.

Mr. Perkins is a member of some of the best clubs of the city and has a large circle of friends. He has two sons, one of whom is the present secretary of the Sherwood Music School.

MRS. GERTRUDE GROSSCUP PERKINS

Gertrude Grosscup Perkins is well known in the musical circles of Chicago as one of our best vocal teachers. Her education in this branch of musical art has been of the most thorough school. For six years she played accompaniments daily in the studio of one of the foremost vocal masters of the country, enjoying thereby unusual advantages. She did this for the purpose of learning to teach and to acquire the pure Italian method. In this way she heard lessons given to all kinds of voices in all kinds of conditions and had the great benefit of seeing and hearing the master's work with them.

Mrs. Perkins finished her study in London under the instruction of Whitney Mockridge, thus rounding out and perfecting her knowledge of the art.

As a teacher Mrs. Perkins has proven her excellence in many ways. Some of her pupils have obtained good positions in leading organizations, among them Mrs. Harriet Beynon Metzger, for several years first soprano of the Arion Lady Quartette; Lillith Castleberry Cooke, for several years first contralto of the same organization; Miss Mary Rhys, who has the position of soprano in one of the best-known church choirs of the city and is also making a fine reputation as a concert singer.

Mrs. Perkins has for the past three years had charge of the vocal department of the Sherwood Music School and is rapidly making a name for herself throughout the country. She possesses to an unusual degree the faculty of imparting knowledge, and as she possesses a complete familiarity with the best methods of vocal instruction, her work has produced excellent results.

Mrs. Perkins is also one of the best accompanists in the country. Her fine playing is an inspiration to her pupils, and she arouses and holds their enthusiasm and never fails to impel them to put forth their best efforts.

Mrs. Perkins was born in Cleveland, Ohio, in 1867. She comes from a family which numbers among its ancestors soldiers of the war of the revolution and men prominent in other walks of life. Mrs. Perkins' brightness and geniality have won for her a large circle of friends.

MRS. GERTRUDE GROSSCUP PERKINS

A SHORT HISTORY OF THE APOLLO CLUB

This organization, of which the importance may be gauged by the frequent mention it has required in our brief sketch of Chicago's musical history, is undoubtedly the leading choral body existing today in the United States and would take leading rank with any similar body in Europe. It is not suffering from any extreme youth, for it was as far back as 1872 that George P. Upton, the eminent Chicago newspaper man and quondam music critic for the Chicago *Tribune,* at the suggestion of Silas G. Pratt, formed the choral society which has since assumed such large and important proportions. The organization it is interesting to note, was perfected in the temporary store of Lyon & Healy, then located— little of the South Side was left by the great fire of the year preceding—in the little wooden church at Sixteenth street and Wabash avenue.

George P. Upton became the society's first president, and Silas G. Pratt, who is now in New York, was appointed its first director. The latter was succeeded by A. W. Dohn.

C. P. VAN INWEGEN

PRESIDENT OF APOLLO CLUB

The work attempted was not of any ambitious order, and consisted chiefly of part songs. The thirty charter members are certainly worthy of recognition and are here given: S. G. Pratt, C. T. Root, Edwin Brown, F. A. Bowen, C. C. Stebbins, E. H. Pratt, Theo. F. Brown, Harry Gates, William Sprague, John A. Lyndon, Frank G. Rohner, J. S. Marsh, S. E. Cleveland, Warren C. Coffin, Philo A. Otis, J. R. Ranney, C. C. Curtiss, Louis Falk, A. L. Goldsmith, A. R. Sabin, William Cox, F. B. Williams, W. W. Boynton, C. V. Pring, A. B. Stiles, Fritz Foltz, F. S. Pond, W. H. Coulston, H. Rocher, C. C. Phillips, W. R. Allen, L. M. Prentiss, George P. Upton.

The first officers were: President, George P. Upton; vice-president, William Sprague; treasurer, F. A. Bowen; secretary, C. C. Curtiss; librarian, W. C. Coffin; music committee, Fritz Foltz, S. E. Cleveland and Philo A. Otis.

Satisfactory progress was made and a female auxiliary organization suggested by Mr. Dohn, who was evidently a capable leader. Schumann's "Paradise and the Peri" was given in 1874 in McCormick Hall. The following year Carl Bergestein became conductor and the club gave one concert, a few part songs, the sextet from "Lucia" and some solos by local singers. Previous to this concert a number of members not blind to the failings of the club had been considering the possibility of securing William L. Tomlins as director. It was finally so arranged, and at once the wisdom of the choice became apparent. Mr. Tomlins was a strict disciplinarian and at the very commencement of his association showed that those members who would not work could be dispensed with. Part songs were the feature of the first concert, but these songs were so splendidly rendered that music lovers were more than satisfied. The club became one of the city's most popular institutions and year after year greater triumphs were obtained. Frequently it became necessary to repeat concerts, as McCormick Hall could not accommodate the crowds that gathered.

The Apollos had been satisfied to remain as a male chorus, but Mr. Tomlins was already a convert to the female auxiliary idea and merely waited a suitable time to bring it forward. At last, with a mixed chorus, Gounod's cantata "By Babylon's Wave" was given and wondrous enthusiasm was aroused. The position of Director Tomlins was assured and there was no member of the Apollo Club but recognized in him both guide and friend.

Handel's "Acis and Galatea," was then essayed and followed by "The Messiah" and Mendelssohn's "St. Paul," the public being at last brought to appreciate the great artistic possibilities of choral music. The twentieth anniversary of the Apollo Club's existence was celebrated in 1892 with a three days' May festival. To take part in the celebration Edward Lloyd came from England, Amalia Joachim from Germany and William Ludwig from Ireland. "The Creation" and "Requiem Mass" were given on the first day; "Acis and Galatea" and "The Hymn of Praise" for the second, and Bach's "Passion" on the final day. The occasion was a memorable one in the history of Chicago's musical progress.

In the spring of 1878, in the old Tabernacle, now the basement of the wholesale house of J. V. Farwell & Co., a festival was given by the club and portions of Handel's "Israel in Egypt" included. New laurels for the Apollos were the result. Berlioz' "Te Deum," MacKenzie's "Dream of Jubal," Sullivan's "Golden Legend" and Becker's "Reformation" cantata were given for the first time in this country, and the splendid concerts during the World's Fair, both in the Festival and Music Halls, were such as to establish high estimation for the Apollo Club wherever on the civilized globe good music is honored.

The list of its productions is a long one, but certainly claims a place in any sketch of what has been achieved by this organization. Of the following either one or more performances have been given:

Handel's "Acis and Galatea," Max Bruch's "Fair Ellen," Haydn's "Seasons," Berlioz' "Te Deum," Mackenzie's "Rose of Sharon," Bach's cantata "I Wrestle and Pray," Gade's "Crusaders," Hoffman's "Cinderella," when the Central Music Hall was dedicated, selections from Wagner's "Tannhauser," Dvorak's "Specter Bride," "Requiem Mass," Gounod's "Third Mass," Rheinberger's "Christophorus," Paine's "Oedipus," Schumann's "Manfred," Sullivan's cantata "On Sea and Shore," Sullivan's "Golden Legend," Becker's "Reformation" cantata, Grieg's "Bergliot" (with reader), Gleason's "Commemoration Ode," at the dedication of the Auditorium, Berlioz' "Messe des Morts" and Bach's "Passion," Saint-Saens' "Samson and Delilah," Horatio W. Parker's "Hora Novissima," Max Bruch's "Arminius," Goring Thomas' "Swan and Skylark."

"The Messiah" has been given over twenty-five times, and the following each on several occasions Haydn's "Creation," Handel's "Judas Maccabeus," Berlioz' "Damnation of Faust," Mendelssohn's "St. Paul" and "Hymn of Praise," Massenet's "Eve," Mendelssohn's "Elijah," Rossini's "Stabat Mater" and Bruch's "Frithjof."

The performances during the World's Fair must not be forgotten, Handel's "Messiah" four times and Rossini's "Stabat Mater," Mendelssohn's "Elijah" and Bach's "Passion."

What wonder is it that an organization that has done so much for Chicago's music and has at the same time given such generous support to whatsoever was for Chicago's good should possess such popularity and universal respect among all sections of the community.

This sketch of the Apollo Club would be entirely incomplete without some reference to Angus S. Hibbard, its popular and able late president. Unquestionably his open and liberal policy, his bright business ideas, and the public confidence his energetic and persistent demand for all that was best in music, had created, did much to place the Apollos in the last two years on a far firmer basis. Mr. Hibbard is an old-time member, and the interests of the club have always been dear to him. For some time when business took him to New York, the connection was severed, but no sooner did he return to Chicago than he once more made himself active for the welfare of the club and of Chicago music. It would almost be as impossible to disassociate Mr. Tomlins from the achievements of the Apollo Club as to forget all that is owing to Angus S. Hibbard.

To the present president also, Clarence P. Van Inwegen, who has been unanimously re-elected to the position he so worthily filled last season, the Apollo Club is very greatly indebted. A man of keen discrimination and rare business and administrative faculties, with an unusual capacity for making and retaining friends, and first and before all, an abiding and enthusiastic faith in the possibilities before the Apollo Club, Mr. Van Inwegen makes an ideal presiding officer. His policy is earnest and fearless; he is an indefatigable worker and his determination has already done much and will assuredly do more toward popularizing one of Chicago's best musical institutions, the Apollo Club.

The present officers of the club are as follows: President, Clarence P. Van Inwegen; vice-president, Nathaniel Board; secretary, Louis Evans; treasurer, Arthur Heurtley; directors, Franklin C. Hollister, George L. Cragg and Charles H. Blatchford.

MAURICE ROSENFELD

PIANIST

FREDERICK W. ROOT

The name is at once suggestive of musical talent of a high order. Both paternal and maternal ancestors for several generations back were famous in music. Dr. George F. Root, his father, was known and revered by all lovers of song. Frederick W. has won fame as a teacher of vocal music and is widely known as a conductor, writer, lecturer and composer.

His musical education began when he was only six years old. At fifteen he was placed under the instruction of Mr. B. C. Blodgett, who is now director of the musical department in Smith College. Later he studied the piano with Dr. William Mason in New York and also received instructions in organ playing under James Flint.

In 1863 Mr. Root came to Chicago to accept the position of organist in the Third Presbyterian Church. A year later he resigned to officiate at the new organ in the Swedenborgian Church, a position which he held until 1884.

Meanwhile in the winter of 1864-65 Mr. Root resumed his technical studies, concluding with a series of lessons from Robert Goldbeck. In vocal culture he had been a pupil of his father and of Carlo Bassini. In 1869 he went abroad and spent eight- een months in study and travel, receiv- ing instructions at Florence from Vannuccini. In 1893 he again visited Europe with his family and closely observed methods of teaching voice production in England and on the con- tinent. His observations have since been of the greatest practical value to him, for one respect in which he has won distinctive success has been the practical value of his instruction. In every undertaking with which he has been connected he has achieved distinction; in his conduct of ladies' chorus or church work or as exam- iner and lecturer Frederick Root is one of the foremost names in the mu- sical history of Chicago.

FRANCES A. ROOT

A season of study with William Mason in New York City had kindled the ambitions of Frances A. Root in her youth to play and teach the piano. Circumstances diverted the directions of her musical talents to vocal instruc- tion. She came to Chicago in the au- tumn of 1859, after having taught mu- sic two years in the Judson Female Institute, Marion, Ala., and one year

in Maplewood Institute, Pittsfield, Mass. At Chicago at that time she found greater call for vocal than for advanced instrumental work and en- tered into choir and incidental sing- ing, equipped with only natural, un- trained ability. Soon after she took voice lessons of Hans Balatka, whose high musicianship contributed much to her musical knowledge and appre- ciation. The two years from 1864 to 1866 she spent in New York, re- suming her studies with Dr. Mason and taking musical lessons from An- tonio Barili, the half brother of Patti, then a popular teacher in New York. The Italian language as a helpful means of voice training was thus opened to her.

Returning to Chicago, she resumed her choir work. She has sung in the First, Second and Third Presbyterian churches of Chicago, and last and longest in Grace Episcopal Church. In 1876 she spent a year of rest and recreation in Europe, hearing the mu- sic of France, Italy and Germany, and studying the characteristics and lan- guage at each, taking also lessons from Madame Viardot-Garcia. This was followed by another ten years' work in Chicago, then musically far in advance of former days.

In 1887 she studied in London with William Shakespeare, whose method of releasing voices from all constraint of false muscular action gave her new light. During the following year her pupils were given lessons in physical training by Miss Annie Payson Call, of Boston, author of "Power Through Repose," and she took a course in Delsarte exercises from Mrs. Frank Stuart Parker, all confirming her belief in the principle of relaxing unnecessary muscular action in order to concentrate on true efforts, whether in singing or in other physical energies. She has since studied the methods of Madame Marchesi, Madame La Grange, Alfred Blume and other celebrities, by personal conference, through their writings and by their artist pupils, and she believes that the evolution in music has brought to this country and to Chicago a high and intellectual plane in voice culture comparable with that of its progenitors across the sea.

ELLA DAHL-RICH

Ella Dahl-Rich came quickly into the position which she now holds as one of the leading pianists of the west. This recognition was given her soon after her return to Chicago from extended instruction abroad. Though not a native of Chicago, she claims this as her own city, for when yet an infant she was brought here by her parents, and in Chicago she received her earlier education. At a very early age she showed signs of pronounced musical aptitude and, her talent being recognized, she was placed in the care of some of the leading local teachers.

In 1890, Mrs. Rich, then Miss Dahl, went to Berlin, where for two years she was a pupil of Oscar Raif. She then studied for two years with Theodore Leschetizky, of Vienna. Her progress was thus attested by that instructor in a letter: "Miss Dahl is by nature very musical and possessed of talent for interpretations, and has made, during the two years she has studied with me, remarkable progress in technique and expression. I must, therefore, believe that as a public performer she will achieve the real, true success through her poetic instinct, and also that as a teacher she will be capable of attaining the highest results."

Returning to Berlin Miss Dahl played with great success in various concerts, notably at the Singacademmie. She traveled, and at Vienna, Dresden and other European cities where she appeared she received enthusiastic praise from the critics. Her playing was described as of a highly musicianly order, brilliant and at the same time exceedingly sympathetic. The *Berliner Tageblatt* said of her: "Miss Dahl belongs to that class of pianists, which because of their clean,

clear technique and graceful, easy style, one is always glad to hear."

Returning to America Miss Dahl renewed her old residence among Chicago friends. Her artistic attainments were revealed in a concert given at Chicago soon after her return, and at which she achieved a notable success. Speaking of this performance the Chicago *Tribune* said: "Finish in performance, repose and genuinely musical temperament were evidenced by the young artist." "The player," commented the Chicago *Inter Ocean,* "was in thorough sympathy with the composer's ideals, and brought her audience to her state of mind." Since then the appreciation of her most excellent work has been steadily extending not less notable than her playing being her fine teaching powers. Mrs. Dahl-Rich has proved herself a splendid instructor, as her large class testifies.

EDITH V. RANN

There has seldom been a more conspicuous example of success being the proof of merit than in the case of Miss Edith V. Rann, the pianiste. Coming to Chicago ten years ago an entire stranger, she was at once engaged to teach at the Chicago Conservatory, where she remained five years. At the expiration of that time she opened a studio of her own, as her class was sufficiently large to justify her in so doing. As a concert player Miss Rann was extensively known, but relinquished all professional playing when she decided to devote her entire time to teaching, for which she possesses special qualifications. Her aims and ambitions are of the highest and her success with pupils has been very great. One of Miss Rann's characteristics is the ability to interest her pupils to such an extent that it is not unusual to find pianists who have commenced with her remaining until such time as they could enter the profession. Several pupils at present with Miss Rann have been studying with her over six years. She enjoys the respect

and esteem of the most prominent Chicagoans, many of whom have sent their daughters to her for instruction. A number of Miss Rann's pupils are occupying very responsible positions as teachers in schools and colleges in various parts of the country. Every season teachers from other cities come to Chicago to study with this pianiste, who is known for her thoroughness of piano art. This season Miss Rann has her very prominent pupil, Miss Zoe Tuthill assisting her by taking the younger pupils and preparing them for Miss Rann's class. Miss Tuthill is a charming pianiste, and evidenced talent of a high order at a recent recital.

An American by birth, Miss Rann is descended from an old French family. Her studio is now in the Fine Arts Building. Broad-minded and progressive, Miss Rann works on legitimate, straightforward lines, taking the best from all methods and claiming for no particular one exclusive superiority.

HANS VON SCHILLER

CLARE OSBORNE REED

Clare Osborne Reed early in life gave evidence of decided musical talent. As a child she attracted attention as a pianiste, which resulted in her removing from Plymouth, Ind., to Chicago. She entered the Chicago Musical College and at once became Dr. Ziegfeld's most talented pupil. As she progressed she gained the highest medal in each class, and upon her graduation was offered the position of assistant teacher to the president of the college. She filled this post with great credit until a desire to acquaint herself with European methods of music study influenced her to sail with her mother for Germany to again become a student. On reaching Vienna she was fortunate in securing lessons with Leschetiszky, that prince among concert piano instructors, while in composition she placed herself under the tuition of Dr. Kane Nawratie. Here she remained a year and a half.

At this time her attention was called to the work and methods of Oscar Raif. Upon investigation she became deeply interested, and began a course of musical study under this celebrated teacher. To this day she is a firm believer in many of his advanced musical theories and forms of technical development. After three years she returned to Chicago, and was at once re-engaged as a leading teacher at the Musical College, where many pupils testify to her ability. Intellectually she stands in front rank among the musicians of Chicago. Her lectures on musical history are a feature of the college course, and although her teaching occupies her first thought she is often heard in the concert room, where her programs are of high artistic rating. To her guiding hand and mind many owe their success musically. She works for art, not for public applause. Probably no teacher in the West, in a quiet unpretentious way, exerts a stronger influence for the better things in music. She is a teacher of music, not piano playing alone, and as such helps to make a permanent musical standard for American art.

MISS MAMIE L. SHERRATT

Miss Sherratt is one of the younger musicians of Chicago who is rapidly making a name for herself as a concert pianiste.

Leopold Godowsky, with whom she studied for several years, has predicted that she may become one of the greatest women pianistes in the world.

A recent article in the Magazine "Music" says of her:

"She is a very talented virtuoso, having enormous force and sustained power. She has also many other musical qualities, and every indication points to her becoming a pianiste of celebrity and of a distinction long to be remembered."

Her playing is noted for its brilliancy and powerful bravura as well as for artistic finish.

She has all the qualities requisite for a successful concert artist, a remarkably well developed technic, immense power and entire self possession.

MRS. NELLIE BANGS SKELTON

Mrs. Nellie Bangs Skelton was born at Lacon, Ill., and at the age of seven began the study of music, composing and publishing her first composition when she was eleven years old. At the age of sixteen she moved to Chicago, where for five years she pursued her musical studies under the direction of Madame De Roode Rice. Her progress was so great that she then became solo pianiste with the Litta Concert Company, a position she held with marked success for two years. After this she was at the head of her own concert company for a year, and from that time until the present she has been located in Chicago devoting herself to teaching, local concert work and composition. She has published several compositions which have been well received by the public, principal among which are the Ripple Gavotte in E minor and the Trifler. Mrs. Skelton holds a foremost place as an accompanist and devotes much of her time to the coaching of prominent singers.

ALLEN SPENCER

Allen Spencer has been prominently identified with music in Chicago for a number of years.

Coming to the city in 1890 he gave his first recital in November of that year and received the commendation of the press and the profession. Soon after Mr. Spencer was engaged by the School of Music of Northwestern University to teach part of each week, giving private lessons in Chicago on the remaining days. Mr. Spencer's public playing attracted the attention of Mr. John J. Hattstaedt, who engaged him as a member of his faculty at the American Conservatory, where he has since remained.

Mr. Spencer has given a series of recitals every season covering a wide range of piano literature, and his audiences have always over-run the seating capacities of the largest recital

ALLEN SPENCER

certs and recitals. Still more may be expected in this line of work in the near future, for he is each season in increasing demand. Mr. Spencer has been prominently connected with the Illinois Music Teachers' Association and has been for three years the soloist and adjudicator for the Hutchinson (Kan.) Musical Jubilee. All the time that is available for teaching is taken by a class of enthusiastic young pianists, who come from all parts of the country for lessons from Mr. Spencer.

As he is a severe student and prefers friendly criticism to praise, Mr. Spencer's progress in his art is constant each succeeding year. Not only is more expected from this really good artist, but every hope is being fully realized.

halls. He has also been much in demand outside of the city for con-

CLARA MURRAY

A beautiful woman, it has been said, never looks more beautiful than when playing the most graceful of musical instruments, the harp. It would be difficult, indeed, to find a better exemplification of this statement than in Clara Murray, whose evident ambition it is to become to the harp what Madame Marchesi has long been to the voice—one of the best known of the women instructors.

It was as a child of seven that this accomplished woman, Clara Murray, began the study of the piano, and two years later the harp was taken up also. Both instruments were continued until she graduated. At this time vocal music was also added, and she received instruction from a number of leading teachers, among whom may be mentioned Sig. Barili, a half-brother of Patti.

Mrs. Murray was twenty years of age when she placed herself under the skillful instruction of John Cheshire, the distinguished English harpist, intending to embrace the profession of harpist, and for concert and teaching

purposes. Though supposedly by this time thoroughly equipped for the profession, Mrs. Murray made a close study of the teaching methods used by other masters.

Her success as a teacher was immediate and most pronounced, and a very large number of pupils are attracting notice on the concert platform. Not less great has become her career as a soloist, in which capacity all the principal cities in America have been visited at different times when Mrs. Murray was on tour with Mme. Genevra Johnstone-Bishop, Miss Maud Powell, Marie Decca, Mrs. Scott Siddons and latterly with Mme. Clementine De Vere. At all times Mrs. Murray's appearance has been the occasion of an ovation, and the press of several cities has unhesitatingly declared her to be the greatest woman harpist ever heard.

The exceptional advantages of her musical education are certainly well manifested. Her command of the instrument is perfect and the smoothness of her pedaling is most notice-

able. Passages of the greatest difficulty Mrs. Murray accomplishes with
ease, and artists delighted with her
work have said that her tone production is perfect, her technic extraor-
dinarily clean and her phrasing finished.

WILLIAM H. SHERWOOD

It might have been accepted as a
probability that with his illustrious ancestry William H. Sherwood would
have won a success in whatever career
his talents and tastes might have led
him.   As director of the Sherwood
Piano School, as piano virtuoso, composer and teacher, he is one of the
most important factors of music in
Chicago.

His paternal ancestry goes back to
the family of "Sherwood's Forest"
fame in Robin Hood's time. The American branch settled in Bennington, Vt.,
and one member of the family was a
captain in the Revolutionary Army.

Lyman Sherwood, grandfather of William H., was a prominent senator and judge in Wayne Co., N. Y. Lorenzo, a great uncle, was a senator and judge in Texas, and Leman, another great uncle, was a judge and signed the R. Bates, a maternal uncle, served as major of a volunteer regiment.

William H. received his early musical education from his father, from Pychowski, who died this year, William Mason and Edward Heimberger.

WILLIAM H. SHERWOOD

charter of the city of New York. Rev. L. H. Sherwood, father of our subject, founded Lyons Musical Academy, Lyons, N. Y., the second musical institution in America. Edgar H. Sherwood, the well-known musical composer, uncle of Wm. H., volunteered at 17 in the Civil war, and John He was recognized as a boy prodigy and at 17 went abroad, studying music for five years under Theodore Kullak (principal of Royal Conservatory of Berlin), Weitzmann, Dippe, Doeppler (who died in 1900), Scotson, Clark, Liszt and other masters.

After a most successful debut in

Berlin and other foreign cities, Mr. Sherwood in 1876 returned to America and has here won high fame as a musician. His methods of interpretative technique and musical analysis and artistic delivery are of international reputation, showing the most modern research in such directions. Mr. Sherwood furthers in every way possible the advancement of art in America.

Besides the direction of his own Sherwood Piano School in The Fine Arts building, Chicago, and his numerous concert tours, he has for twelve years conducted a summer department, with recitals and lectures, at the original Chautauqua Assembly,

Chautauqua, N. Y., and has also been associated with the Toronto Conservatory of Music as examiner since its establishment twelve years ago. He is president of the Manuscript Society of Chicago, an honorary member of the "Orpheus Club," of Boston, Mass., and of the Clefs Club, of Toronto, of the Manuscript Society, of New York, and of the "Sherwood Club."

One notable event inseparably connected with the name of W. H. Sherwood is the fact that he opened Hershey Hall with two piano recitals and that he also closed that hall in a similar way several years after.

ADA MARKLAND SHEFFIELD

Among the singers rapidly coming to the public notice is Mrs. Ada Markland Sheffield, the soprano. A native of Indianapolis, Mrs. Sheffield commenced her career in that city as a pianiste, being educated for this branch of the profession. She began

teaching the piano at the age of sixteen and continued in this work until she came to Chicago, when having discovered she was the possessor of a beautiful voice she began studying vocal culture with L. G. Gottschalk, with whom she remained four years. Since that time she studied with Mrs. Magnus. Mrs. Sheffield is

an excellent linquist and has a large repertoire in German, French, Italian and English, a repertoire which will stand comparison with that of any well known vocalist. During the past season she has been engaged very considerably in concert work, having given recitals in many of the prominent clubs in Chicago, while her appearances in other cities have been mostly honored by return engagements. Mrs. Sheffield has sung in Crawfordsville, South Bend, Elgin, Goshen, Joliet, Oskaloosa and in Ontario with unvarying good results. For the past three years Chatauqua work has been part of Mrs. Sheffield's summer work, her capability for this class of work being evidenced most thoroughly at all the assemblies she has attended. In her teaching she has obtained remarkable success, having had this season all the pupils she can possibly manage. An indefatigable worker, Mrs. Sheffield deserves all the good that has come to her. Indomitable energy, much talent, a beautiful lyric voice, united to fine musicianship and one finds in Mrs. Sheffield an unusual type of artist. She has held several good church positions, notably Christ Church, where she was soprano for two years.

MISS HELEN PAGE SMITH

Accompanying as a fine art has been of comparatively recent development. Miss Helen Page Smith, daughter of Dr. Julia Holmes Smith, of Chicago, has made a thorough study of this much-abused, but all-essential branch of music, and after long and patient study and broad experience is now counted one of the best accompanistes in the city.

After six years of piano work with Mr. William H. Sherwood and before that work with Madame Eugenia De Roode Rice and Mr. Seeboeck, it is unnecessary to say that she is a thoroughly good pianiste. During four years of this time she studied ensemble playing with Mr. Adolf Weidig, and is now accompaniste for Mr. Clement Tetedoux. Miss Smith has played often for Bicknell Young, Signor Janotta, Karleton Hackett, Adolf Weidig and Jan Van Dordt. She read at sight one evening many songs for Mrs. Katharine Fisk, who was enthusiastic in her praise. Miss Smith has enjoyed great success with her many pupils, and in her chosen profession of accompanying her success is an assured fact.

HENRY SCHOENEFELD

Mr. Schoenefeld, who is a Milwaukeean by birth, has been identified with music in Chicago since he returned from study in Europe in 1879. In the contest instituted by the National Conservatory when Dvorak was head of that institution, Mr. Schoenefeld took the prize for the best symphony by an American. This work found hearty favor in the estimation of Dvorak, who strongly urged its author to continue in the musical way he was then going, and predicted ultimate success and eminence for him. Another sonata, which last year was crowned in Paris, is in three movements, and contains the rhythms which are found in negro music, and which Mr. Schoenefeld has used with marked success in his Suite Characteristique and his concert overture, "The Sunny South." These rhythms, he maintains, are the only tangible elements we possess from which to form a music that has in it something characteristic of the country, and which may in a measure be considered American.

LUCILLE STEVENSON

A young singer, gifted with a voice of beautiful quality, a true soprano whose tone production is excellent and who sings with both taste and expression, is the concert artist, Miss Lucille Stevenson. It was five years ago that she decided upon Chicago as a field for her work, and in that time her success has been remarkable. A few months after her arrival in Chicago she was given the appointment as soloist of the by the leading musical institutions of Chicago, and also brought her into request in other cities. Her vocalizing is intelligent and satisfying, her purity of tone and the sympathetic and dramatic quality of her voice, together with its evident splendid cultivation assuring her as a favorite with her audiences wherever they may be.

Oratorio, however, is probably Miss Stevenson's strongest accomplish-

New England Church, twelve months later accepting a similar position at the Forty-first Presbyterian Church.

Another twelve months found her at the Hyde Park Presbyterian Church, where after a short while the offer was made her of .the soprano work at the Plymouth Congregational Church, thus holding, one following the other, some of the most important church positions in this city.

The reputation she has won is by no means local, the excellence of her work having secured her engagements ment, and the work to which her special gifts have been best suited, for in addition to her exceptional voice, she possesses in the highest degree musical interpretation and feeling. Already a factor in the city's musical life the promise of the work Miss Stevenson has already accomplished presages a foremost place among the artists of the West. At present she is soprano at the famous Second Presbyterian Church, which has always been filled by the leading Chicago sopranos.

MUSIC AND THE CHURCH

The musical culture of a city may be very correctly estimated by the character and value of its church music, for, while all cultivated music lovers may not take an active part in the service, they still retain their musical ear, which, having been once attuned to harmonious sound, demands as hearers musical intelligence and some degree of skill.

Although Chicago has at present four times the number of churches that existed before the fire, the number of good choirs is not so great, and the music of a much inferior grade. In fact, in this great city the choirs which demand even recognition can be counted upon a single hand. Even the small suburb of Evanston has a better musical rating, for while nothing can be claimed for high excellence, there is a uniform attempt at fair rating, which gives better musical average. In recalling the choir lofts immediately preceding and following the great fire, we find a list of church choirs and singers whose ability was and is unquestioned. They were the musical foundation and culture of the city. Such names as Fannie Root, Mary Holden, Hope Glenn, Jennie Dutton, Mrs. George B. Carpenter, Ella White Custer, Mrs. O. K. Johnson, Mme. Hastreiter, Mrs. J. A. Farwell, Mrs. Seymour, Mrs. McGuire, Mrs. Balfour, Charles Herbert Clark, Ben Goldsmith, Charles Knorr, Jules Lombard, Horace Sloan, Robert Howard, John Hubbard, Albert Sabin, William Sprague, Charles Barnes, Alexander Bischoff, and Fritz Foltz, with many others of whom space forbids mention, give a faint idea of what good musically came out of the churches.

At that time the church choirs took the lead in all musical events. They were engaged as quartets, and not individually, and not a few had as large a secular repertoire as sacred. I recall the opening of the organ of the First Presbyterian Church (Twenty-First and Indiana avenue), when the First, Second and Fourth Presbyterian church choirs were the attraction, so well known were they as organizations. The Second Presbyterian Church choir enjoyed a reputation for a number of years in the concert field throughout the western circuit. I do not wish to be understood as stating that churches no longer employ musical talent to assist in their services, but I do not hesitate to assert that, with but few exceptions, the compensation is not enough to cover the cost of weekly lessons. At the present time many of the New York churches are employing Chicago talent, who were unable to obtain even a living salary in their own city. Those who have not followed this example stay because ties of a domestic character bind them. The empty seats in many churches tell a story of waning interest, which might in a measure be averted by better music to brighten the service. Poor music will soon degrade the standard of the church service. Some will endure the music for the sake of what comes after if the pastor happens to be a man of strong intellect and oratory, but even this is an injustice to the speaker, for if he be at all musical, with an ear sensitive to tune and harmony, he cannot be in as good a mental or religious frame of mind for his sermon, nor his hearers in as receptive condition as they would be after hearing music of emotional or inspirational character. The greatest compliment I ever received as a singer, was from a celebrated divine, in whose church I had the pleasure of singing. I always sang my solo directly before the sermon, and one day he came to me after the service and said: "I can always preach better after hearing you sing." Environment adds much to the impressiveness of music, and few singers sing frivolously in church, although often accused of such a fault. If churches feel that the desire "to draw all men unto me" is the keynote to religious growth, more attention and money must be invested in the choir loft. The pious man will go to church from sense of duty, no matter how poor the preaching or singing, but the sinful wanderer (for whom churches are built and maintained?) must be attracted. No soul is so lost as not to be touched by the power of music (not noise). A cheap choir of singers, with more enthusiasm in their souls than music in their voices or sense of pitch in their ears, can hardly raise a depressed mind above earthly incompleteness to heavenly fulfillment. Praise God with becoming reverence by filling the church with celestial music. The churches have made the standard so low that there is a common idea afloat that any one can fill a church position. This is daily proven by would-be musical students applying to teachers for positions. They say: "If you could secure me a church position to pay my way I would study. "But," comes the query, "have you had any experience or culture?" "Oh, no." "Can you read music at sight?" "No, but I guess I could fill a church position."

They have this impression from what they hear in churches. Churches generally are run on a financial basis and business principles, but include the music in the list of charities, without supporting the charity. In fact, there seems to be a lack of principle in this connection, business or otherwise. I know of a church that has been accepting the service of soloists for the last six months, with the understanding on the part of the singer that it was a trial for the position, when really they had no idea of employing any one. Many of the applicants were in woeful need of the remuneration, and the car fare used was a strain. It would have been a charity to have paid them for the use of the voice God had given them, even though by so doing some heathen who is content to worship his idols should go to face his Maker without the light of Christianity in his soul, for God will never destroy an unenlightened soul, and some of these struggling, deceived mortals may lose their souls at the church door. The organist of this same church has not been paid for five months. Few men in any church would recognize any firm doing business on such a basis. The world calls them "dead beats." Many churches hire one man to take entire charge of the music, on a limited salary, he furnishing the singers. If he paid a fraction of a living to his singers he would have nothing for his own labor. Thus the church encourages spongeing or misrepresentations. Every churchman who is qualified to be on the official board can count two and two and know the result; therefore, if they award a contract for $1,000 worth of labor for $400, they know it can't be done, and done honestly. Chicago is rich enough in its churches to pay a fair living rate for good music, yet no city is quoted so low.

Local singers have themselves to blame, in a measure. They should not sing on trial even without compensation. Voices can be heard outside the church, and when selected for trial should be paid, engaged permanently or not. There are enough reputable teachers in Chicago who could supply all church demands and would be only too glad to furnish the grade demanded. One church in Chicago always has and always did have good music. The reason is, they keep the singers together for years, pay good salaries and secure excellent talent, and make music an important factor in the church service. Long association gives the choir an opportunity to acquire finish and even tone balance besides cultivating a personal interest in the church and pastor which creates a unison of thought in the service. It is not showy nor operatic singing, as some fanatical ministers prate, but churchy, devotional, true in sentiment, yet meritorious from musical standpoints. If you doubt it, spend an evening at the Second Presbyterian Church and be convinced. Every church should feel proud of its choir and the singers should be selected for ability, not favoritism. There is an old saying: "A man may be a good fellow, but not able to run a hotel," which may with truth be applied to singers.

After losing so many churches by fire, an economical plan had to be adopted for some years to enable the houses of worship to once more rise from the ashes. Habit has thus been formed which makes it impossible for singers to gain any financial footing. Episcopal choirs make use of the boys' voices, and many other denominations run choruses, but the choir, outside the surplice, which gives dignity to a church service, is a well-trained quartet of cultured singers. The church that supports such a choir respects itself and its congregation.

At the present time I know of not over a half dozen who can congratulate themselves as really praising 'God in a respectful manner. The rest? Well! I wish to be charitable and will say with "Deacon Jones":

"Now I may have spoke too open,
But 'twas too hard to keep still,
An' I hope you'll tell the singers
'At I bear 'em no ill-will;
'At they all may git to glory
Is my wish an' my desire;
But they'll need some extry trainin'
'Fore they jine the heavenly choir."

ANCELLA M. FOX.

THE SPIERING QUARTET

Of all the musical organizations in Chicago none holds a higher place in public esteem than the Spiering Quartet. Its members, all of whom have been associated with the Chicago Orchestra, are artists of the highest ability. It was during the World's Fair that this organization first came into existence, and on account of the desire of many prominent patrons of music that chamber music should be brought into more prominent notice. A series of concerts was first given in Kimball Hall, Chicago. From the beginning the work of the quartet was of so high an order that it attracted the interest of a very large number of music lovers. The next season it took a still greater leap into public favor by extending its concert field to the principal cities of the west.

The members of the organization are Theodore Spiering, first violin; Otto Roehrborn, second violinist; Adolph Weidig, viola, and Hermann Diestel, violoncello.

When the Spiering Quartet was first organized its members also belonged to the Chicago Orchestra, but all of them have since resigned, in order to give their attention entirely to the rapidly increasing work of the quartet. Not only has the Spiering Quartet performed at its concerts the standard works of the classic composers, but it has produced for the first time in Chicago many of the novelties in chamber music of both European and American composers. Constant association has done its utmost for these performers; indeed, it is not too much to say that Mr. Spiering and his comrades are entitled to a place in the front rank of those who bring to the interpretation of chamber music the highest qualities of understanding and refinement. They have attained a complete unanimity of feeling, of phrasing and of style, and these excellent qualities are not obtained by a sacrifice of individuality, nor is it possible to detect the predominance of any one player's manner of interpretation. It seems as though a common inspiration had guided the four players to precisely the same way of regarding the passages they play.

This quartet has given over fifty concerts in one season, the principal ones being a series here and also in St. Louis, and single concerts in New York City, Brooklyn and Ithaca, N. Y.; Toronto, Canada; Minneapolis, Minn.; Memphis, Tenn.; Lawrenceville, N. J.; Columbus O., and Detroit, Mich.

THEODORE SPIERING

Theodore Spiering is one of the first performers on the violin in America. He was born in St. Louis, Mo., in 1871. He was fortunate in having his parents give him every encouragement and assistance to make for himself a career as a musician. When he was

ing also organized a quartet in the Hochschule, which remained together until he returned to America. During a visit of Brahms to Berlin, a concert was given in his honor, on which occasion the Joachim Quartet and Muehlfeld played Brahms' clar-

five years of age his father (a distinguished violinist and for many years concert-master of the St. Louis Symphony Orchestra) gave him his first instruction in violin playing. At fifteen, Mr. Spiering entered the Cincinnati College of Music, where he studied for two years under Herr Schradieck. He then went to Berlin, and was a pupil of Joachim for four years in the Hochschule. While in Berlin he made a number of appearances with the Barth trio. Mr. Spier-

inet quintet. Mr. Spiering and his colleagues played the string quartet in G major, op. 111, and Brahms himself conducted a performance of his D major symphony. Mr. Spiering has a photograph of Brahms, on which the famous composer has inscribed: "In remembrance of the two quintets and the 11th of December, 1891. —Johannes Brahms."

Mr. Spiering returned to America in 1891, bringing with him a strong letter of introduction and recommendation from Joachim to Theodore Thomas. He settled in Chicago and became a member of the Chicago Orchestra. He remained with this orchestra for four years, resigning his position in order to devote more time to the work of the Spiering Quartet, which he had organized in 1893.

W. C. E. SEEBOECK

A great pianist, a latter day genius, whose special gifts, and in many ways peculiar to himself, have gained him an immense following among the musical people of the city, is this representative musician. Mr. Seeboeck's talents are evidently inherited, for his mother was an accomplished singer who spent considerable time under Marchesi while the latter was residing in Vienna. His early training was in every way the best obtainable, for among the instructors of this fine artist were Nottebohm, Leo Hill and Herman Gresedeuer. Fortunate in a college education he took up the active study of music, and after a year and a half spent in St. Petersburg, Russia, to complete his studies, came to Chicago in 1880, at which time the city was possessed of only half a million inhabitants. Growing up with Chicago he has impressed the city with his own very distinct individuality, and both as pianist and composer has, during that whole period taken foremost rank. As teacher too, no one has been more successful, and the large class Mr. Seeboeck now possesses evidences there is no diminution in the regard in which his talent is held. He has given a great many concerts, not only in this city but also throughout the country. The chief characteristics of his playing are remarkable delicacy, shading, finesse and the beauty of tone produced. A great feature in his recitals has been the educational character, and here his extensive repertory and his careful thoroughness and attention to detail have interested in the strongest way possible all piano students. Mr. Seeboeck's compositions are too well known to need any extensive notice. Their originality and thorough musicianship have served to make his name known throughout the country. Great, too, is the variety he has displayed, his songs, piano pieces and minor works have won very decided favor. As for his more ambitious efforts, of his two quintets for strings and piano, one was given on two occasions by the Bendix quartet and himself, and one by the same quartet and Mrs. Lapham, at the Amateur Club. Another of his compositions, the Concerto No. 2 D minor, was played by him in 1896 with the Thomas Orchestra, and a very notable success achieved. Altogether it may be said, without fear of contradiction, that no musician is a greater factor in the musical life of Chicago than Mr. W. C. E. Seeboeck.

CLAYTON F. SUMMY

An account of music in Chicago would be incomplete without a notice of the work done by Clayton F. Summy for the advancement of music.

It is just twenty years since Mr. Summy came to Chicago, and he immediately entered the Sarah Hershey School, where he had as his confreres Frederic Grant Gleason, Clarence Eddy and other at that time well-known people.

With the Hershey School Mr. Summy remained two years and then went to Lyon & Healy's. After a period of eight years he opened a sheet music business and music publishing house for himself, and in this business he has continued since. It has always been Mr. Summy's aim to assist musical artists in Chicago to the greatest extent in his power, and there are many artists today indebted for much of their success to Mr Summy's sound advice and superior judgment. He was the first to recognize the possibility of chamber music in Chicago, and for that purpose engaged the Bendix, Listemann and Spiering quartets to give concerts in Central Music Hall, thinking it would be a good plan to unite chamber music interests and create an incentive to work and at the same time arouse a love for classic music in Chicago. He also instituted a series of recitals in Summy's recital hall, where young pianists of merit could make a public appearance. It was his intention to create a sort of school of criticism which would have beneficial effect upon the different pianists and also upon pupils, as doubtless it would stimulate ambition and lead to higher results if there were more public playing done by the worthy pianists of the younger generation. It is a great advantage for practically unknown pianists, but who possibly are talented, to have such an opportunity and one which should be eagerly embraced. Everything is provided gratis; hall, programs, advertising, and not only local pianists but those from a distance have often availed themselves of Mr. Summy's liberality.

In 1894 Mr. Summy, in addition to his rapidly growing publishing business, opened a piano house, he taking the exclusive management of the Chickering piano. From that time the increase of sales has been most marked, owing to the high principled methods which distinguish all his transactions. As a business man there is no one who stands higher in the trade or in the musical profession than Clayton F. Summy.

He has always aimed to handle only the highest class of publications; he is the Western representative of Novello, Ewer & Co., of London, and also represents exclusively some of the Eastern publishing houses. So far as the publishing department is concerned, it can be positively stated that those works accepted by Clayton F. Summy are meritorious, are musicianly and worthy a place in modern musical literature.

ANTHONY STANKOWITCH

This well known artist has won recognition both as a pianist and a teacher. He is an American by birth, but in 1887 at an early age he began his musical education abroad as a student in the Leipsic Conservatory. He remained at this celebrated institution for three years, and his success at the conservatory concerts and elsewhere was so marked that he continued his work still further at Vienna, studying with the best masters of that period. For several years he was the pupil of the renowned pedagogue Professor J. Dachs, master of De Pachmann, in the higher art of piano playing, while his theoretical studies were directed by that great contrapuntist, Anton Bruckner. During his sojourn at Vienna he appeared in public on various occasions and his artistic work was well received, critics unanimously praising his beautiful touch and artistic interpretation.

In 1884 Mr. Stankowitch returned to America, and since then he has devoted his energies to educational work, occasionally appearing in public as a pianist. He has played with distinguished success in the largest cities of the country and has everywhere been received with marked favor. Grace, delicacy and freedom in expression, with remarkable facility in execution, have characterized his performances and won for him enthusiastic praise, both from his audiences and from the critics. He lacks nothing in romantic temperament nor in definiteness of aim in his interpretations. His recitals have been educational in character and his large repertory, his earnestness and matured style have made his concerts of peculiar interest to piano students. Mr. Stankowitch is, therefore, a prominent solo artist, who appeals directly to schools of music, making exemplary programs and performances of piano music as an inspiration and stimulus to pupil.

His success as a teacher has been equally marked. His methods of imparting technic and interpretation are the most advanced, progressive and original. Dr. Edward Fisher, director Toronto Conservatory of Music, says: "As a musical educator Mr. Stankowitch ranks relatively even higher than as a performer, admirable though his piano playing is, and which speaks for itself in most eloquent language." His many pupils are enthusiastic in testimony of his good work.

RETTA JOHNSTEN SHANK

Not infrequently the highest exponents of music have been recruited from women who in society have won distinctions by the charm of their personality and by their eminent social qualities. Chicago owes the possession of one of her most promising and talented contralto singers to the surrender by the city of Tacoma of a leading society woman whom art beckoned to a more ennobled career.

Born in Ohio, Mrs. Retta Johnsten

Shank was reared in the best artistic atmosphere of her native state. Her unusual musical ability attracted marked attention at Cincinnati, where she spent much of her life. She has had the advantage of the best musical training and her deep devotion to her art has added to the development of her rare and gifted qualities. Her voice possesses wonderful volume and beautiful sympathetic quality. She sings with a peculiar pathos and warmth that reaches the hearts of her audience, and at the same time she possesses dramatic ability of a high order. These, with her charming personality, have won for her enthusiastic friends wherever she has sung. Mrs. Shank has appeared in concert and oratorio work with unvarying success, winning unstinted encomiums from critics, who have frequently expressed the opinion that her oratorio work will favorably compare with that of renowned artists.

Her interpretation of "Despised and Rejected," which she has sung on various occasions, has especially won admiration from those most competent to judge, who have declared that her manner of singing this glorious aria could not be surpassed.

In making Chicago her home, Mrs. Shank has chosen a field where her natural gifts will find scope and where opportunities are arising to secure for her great talent the recognition it deserves.

WALTER SPRY

Walter Spry was born in Chicago Feb. 27, 1868. He studied under Ziegfeld, Regina Watson and Clarence Eddy. In 1889 he went to Europe, where he spent four years in serious study under Leschetizky, of Vienna, and Rudorff, of Berlin. Later he went for two years to Paris, where he studied composition and orchestration under Rousseau of the Conservatoire. Returning to Chicago in 1896, he appeared in piano recitals as well as the chamber music concerts of the Spiering Quartet, and always with success. In 1897 he accepted the position as director of the Conservatory of Music at Quincy, Ill., and has through his artistic and energetic management raised the standard of the school so that it now is one of the best institutions of its kind in the West. Mr. Spry's thorough preparation and broad musicianship place him in the front rank as a musical educator.

HENRY L. SLAYTON

Henry L. Slayton was born in Woodstock, Vt., May 29, 1841. Four years later his father moved to Lebanon, N. H.

After attending the district high school he entered Kimball Union Academy and pursued a three years' course, with the intention of entering Dartmouth College, but the breaking out of the war in 1861 led him to modify his plans. Accordingly he entered Norwich University for one year, taking a special course. Upon leaving the university he was employed by the state of New Hampshire to organize and drill her volunteers. Fulfilling his contract with the state he went before the military board at Washington, D. C., of which Major General Silas Casey was president. As a result of the severe examination for which this board became famous, Cadet Slayton received a commission on the 24th of September, 1863, as first lieutenant in the Second United States Colored Infantry, ranking with regular army officers. His service in the army was principally confined to the Gulf States and Florida, where the Confederates boasted of having orders to take no colored soldiers or white officers in colored regiments alive as prisoners of war, but to kill them at sight without quarter.

HENRY L. SLAYTON

Being mustered out of the service as commanding officer of Company K at Washington, D. C., in January, 1866, he was offered a commission as captain in the regular army. This he declined.

Soon after returning home he entered the Albany Law School, graduating from that institution the following year; was admitted to the bar and began the practice of law in Chicago in the fall of 1867, and continued in active practice until the great Chicago fire, when he accepted a position as superintendent of public schools in Texas. His efforts in building up a system of colored as well as white schools in that state, made for him many enemies. Some of his colored school houses were burned and his life frequently threatened, but he stuck to his post for two years, and after the free school system had triumphed over all opposition he resigned and returned to Chicago. In March, 1874,

Mr. Slayton was married at Philadelphia, Pa., to Mina E. Gregory, of Northfield, Vt. At the time of her marriage Miss Gregory was studying elocution and laying the foundation for the fame as Mina G. Slayton, which she subsequently achieved as one of the most successful of public readers. Mr. Slayton's marriage had a material influence in changing his life work, and he accordingly gave up the law and set about the establishment of the Slayton Lyceum Bureau, which is the oldest institution of its kind in the West and one of the largest and most successful in the world.

Mr. and Mrs. Slayton's only son Windell has been secretary of the bureau since 1894 and has proved a most competent and efficient officer.

As a manager Mr. Slayton is courageous but not recklessly enterprising in the truest sense, but sufficiently conservative to avoid the dangers which others encounter.

MARY PECK THOMSON

As a soprano Miss Mary Peck Thomson has won an artistic success which is very gratifying to her many friends. She possesses those magnetic and sympathetic qualities which grace a charming personality as well as tend to artistic success.

A native of the Northwest, the education of Miss Thomson has been of the highest American standard supplemented with two years in Europe with Henschel and Sbriglia. She has studied with that diligence and masterful application which always attain renowned appreciation. The character of her professional work has met with signal favor. Her repertoire is quite extended. It includes oratorios, song cycles, song recitals and arias in French, German and English. Miss Thomson has sung in many cities throughout the West; held splendid church positions, and is now soprano at Christ Church. The career of Miss Thomson should be one long continued triumph, both as singer and teacher, as in addition to her many gifts as a vocalist she possesses in a splendid degree the ability to teach her art.

CATHARINE ELMA THATCHER

Catharine Elma Thatcher (nee Hall) is a native Virginian, her parents being New Yorkers. Her ancestors for generations have been musical, and she comes naturally by her talent.

She began the study of the violin at a very early age and was doing some public work at the age of nine.

She had the advantage of a brother's instruction, who watched her carefully in the beginning, since which time she has enjoyed the teaching of J. Fred Zimmerman, Henry Hahn, Max Weil and for five years has been under the care of Bernhard Listemann.

Naturally, she has gone through a large amount of violin literature, and has had great success in her public appearances.

She is a good quartette and trio player, reads readily, draws a strong bow, and there is warmth and life in her playing.

BERTHA TITUS

A traveled western woman of high culture, whose gifts are as varied as her personality is charming. This representative Chicagoan is making a name in devious ways. Her chief study in music has been to become an accompanist. Mrs. Titus possesses all the qualifications for the proper performance of her chosen vocation. She has a sympathetic, warm touch, intelligence of a keen order, and understands the art of subordinating herself in following the requirements of the artist she accompanies. Mrs. Titus' principal work was done with Mr. Emil Liebling, the eminent pianist and teacher. Her playing is marked by much refinement and careful attention to detail that so often is lacking in accompanists. Many well known artists speak in terms of high praise of Mrs. Titus' work and fine temperament. Lately Mrs. Titus has gone in for lecturing and this season fulfilled many club engagements. Her subjects are most entertaining.

CLARA G. TRIMBLE

Another American singer who is just entering upon what promises to be a brilliant career, is Mrs. Clara G. Trimble. Mrs. Trimble is possessed of all the qualities of an artistic singer. She is magnetic and has the artist temperament. A beautiful, pure, highly cultivated soprano, of warmth and sympathy is her voice and she is blessed with brains and beauty.

During the past season Mrs. Trimble has been making a series of splendid successes at the different festivals. She is soprano at the First Presbyterian Church, Chicago, a position she has occupied for several years.

WILLIAM L. TOMLINS

Teacher, artist, composer, the possessor of a subtle magnetic power enabling him to hold in check, stimulate and at the same time bring out all there is best in the voices under his command, is this distinguished Chicago musical representative, William L. Tomlins.

He is a Londoner, born there February 4, 1844. In his early education music took a prominent part. While a boy of nine he sang in a church choir, and later attended the classes of the Royal Academy of Music, where in harmony he was a favorite pupil of Dr. Macfarren. Mr. Tomlins became so proficient on the harmonium and organ that at an early age he acted as organist, and when but seventeen years old he conducted a performance of Handel's "Messiah," with soloists, chorus and orchestra. Soon afterward he was made examiner and inspector of certificates for the teachers of music in the London board schools.

At twenty-two he became one of the managers of the Tonic Sol Fa. Coming to New York in 1870, he obtained various positions during the next two years as an organist, and with the Ritchings Bernard Old Folks Company, managing the Mason & Hamlin orchestral organ, which no one else was able to properly illustrate. The latter occupation brought him to Chicago, and he obtained an opportunity to show his abilities as a vocal conductor in the Mason & Hamlin rooms. The Apollo Musical Club was lacking a leader, and the post was offered to Mr. Tomlins.

This was in 1875, when that musical body was at its lowest ebb. He accepted the offer, and by the most careful training, by absolute labor—daring difficulties for the delight it gave him to conquer, that club has been made one of the most competent in the musical world today, and unquestionably is at the head of all choral societies in the United States. This was the result of twenty-two years under his direction, and as his has

been the work, to him must be given the praise for the artistic result which obtained through the years he was connected with the institution. At the first setting out he felt circumscribed by the methods in which he had been taught, but the originality of his mind came to the fore, and his attempts at a wider and more general form of training have borne wondrous fruit. His primary experiments were with adults, but while unsatisfactory, there was sufficient result to assure him he was working in the right direction. He became "convinced that the musical instinct is well nigh universal and that the song voice is a common heritage." In 1879 his attention was turned to children, and following out his theories, every advance opening new discoveries, he saw at the end of three years success was won.

Theodore Thomas heard his chorus of 200 voices at this time and admitted that he had never heard anything like it. Mme. Christine Nilsson after hearing Tomlins' chorus in 1884, gave equally generous indorsement.

In 1887 Mr. Tomlins, whose Chicago work had obtained such recognition, was invited to take the conductorship of the Arion Musical Club in Milwaukee, then vacant, and was able to achieve equally valuable results until that organization is today beyond all doubt one of the finest choral bodies in America. In 1888, the heavy nature of his other duties and his desire to carry out some highly important special work in Chicago, led Mr. Tomlins to resign the Milwaukee Arion Club leadership. In June, 1893, the members of that club attended the World's Fair musical festivals, singing under the direction of Theodore Thomas and their old conductor. Shortly after this Mr. Tomlins was again induced to assume his old position.

His method of conducting is interesting. No baton is used; characteristic gestures of the hand, expressive mimicry and an occasional undertone command rouses every singer to his best efforts. The training of the choruses of the May festivals have been done by him. As a chorus master he has evinced positive genius, and where the best interests of the city musically have been concerned Mr.

many engagements in the East and West for these lectures, which are replete with educational and musical qualifications.

The new phase of Mr. Tomlins ability, and in which his remarkable powers are demonstrated, has created a desire to know further about the

WILLIAM L. TOMLINS

Tomlins has always been ready with his active co-operation and his absolutely invaluable assistance. Both as a musician and as a man William L. Tomlins possesses a high place in the estimation of Chicago.

A few words must be given to his lectures, which at present are attracting widespread attention. He has

musical culture of children, which William L. Tomlins has done more to develop than any other man in the West.

He has now broadened his field of work, and to the regret of Chicago, William L. Tomlins has become identified with New York.

THEODORE THOMAS

THEODORE THOMAS

Perhaps the World's Fair brought Theodore Thomas permanently to Chicago. The musical spirit of the Western metropolis caught the inspirational keynote of that exposition and made the city the center of music. Yet to all acquainted with the musical happenings for many years anterior to that epoch in the city's history the name of Theodore Thomas was a most familiar one, and his forceful character and strong power were thoroughly understood. Throughout the history of music in Chicago he necessarily frequently appears and since 1891 has been creatively and permanently associated with the Chicago Orchestra of which the ninth season closed in April, 1900.

Theodore Thomas was born in Essen, Hanover, October 11, 1835, and when a boy of ten years he came to America. Here his musical education was obtained, chiefly by self help. Becoming a violin virtuoso he was in 1855 the leader of the Thomas-Mason chamber music concerts. For fourteen years this famous quintet remained a vital musical entity and during that period the whole catalogue of chamber music was absorbed. His career was already well defined. The work of this quintet excited a deep impression upon the musical world which it touched and vivified. Its masterful interpretations, its wonderful finish and precision molded the public taste and also carved deeply and clearly the outlines of the talented young leader's musical character. He soon became the head of an orchestra and in 1866 conducted a series of summer concerts in New York, from which grew a series of symphony concerts during the winter months.

About 1870 Mr. Thomas made a tour with his full orchestra through the country. His May festivals at Cincinnati attracted the attention of the musical world.

Since coming to Chicago in 1891 the nine seasons of concerts in the Auditorium under his direction have been truly remarkable in range and variety and in uniform excellence. He is a natural leader, born to command, yet of gentle manner, unwilling to impose upon others tasks which he himself will not assume. He has introduced many masters and many compositions to the western world and as an educational force ranks with the world's greatest musicians.

GEORGE P. UPTON

Through the history of music's progress and advancement in Chicago one man has always been among the foremost—George P. Upton, the writer, newspaper man and leading music critic.

He was born at Boston, Mass., October 25, 1835, and is of old-time American descent. His education was received at Brown University, Providence, R. I., from which he graduated in 1854. The following year he came to Chicago, and two days following his arrival, October 29, 1855, his journalistic career began, which has continued uninterruptedly to the present time. The first paper with which he connected himself was the Chicago *Native Citizen*, but six months later he engaged with the Chicago *Journal,* with which he remained in the latter portion of the time as music critic, until 1862, when he accepted an editorial position on the Chicago *Tribune.* Few newspaper men have had more thorough or more varied experience. At different times he served as city editor, commercial editor, night editor, war correspondent, art, music, dramatic and literary editor. Altogether for thirty years, notwithstanding what other position might be his on the papers, he remained as music critic on the *Journal* and the *Tribune,* and to him the distinction is acknowledged of writing the first music criticism in Chicago. Mr. Upton was the founder of the Apollo Club, of which organization he still remains an honored member. It was founded in 1872, the year following the fire, with George P. Upton as first president and A. W. Dohn as conductor.

Not merely has he been known as a newspaper man and a most able music critic, he is also a writer of considerable note. His musical articles in the magazines have been many, and Reprinted from the Musical Courier.

he is the author of the following musical books: "Woman in Music," "Standard Operas," "Standard Oratorios," "Standard Cantatas," "Standard Symphonies," and the following translations: "Life of Haydn," "Life of Liszt," "Life of Wagner."

When the musical department of the Newberry Library was being organized to Mr. Upton was assigned the task of making out the lists of necessary books. The library is said to be the most complete in that particular on this continent. Mr. Upton has a splendid private musical library of about 2,000 volumes.

CONSTANCE LOCKE–VALISI

the best teachers of this city, and being musically talented, necessarily in music, received special attention. The result of her sound training and well recognized abilities was seen in her appointment some years ago as one of the instructors of the American Conservatory of Music. So great was her success as a teacher and accompanist that later she felt justified in placing her services before the public as a high class teacher of the piano, and she opened a studio on the South Side of the city with most satisfactory results. Ill health, however, forced her to leave Chicago, and she is now located in St. Paul, Minn., where she is meeting with remarkable success.

A native Chicagoan, musically gifted, a very capable teacher and a sympathetic and gifted accompanist is this Norse descended lady, who has so well demonstrated the possession of the perseverance and energy which are typical characteristics of her race.

Madame Locke-Valisi studied under

As pianist and accompanist, Madame Locke-Valisi has a high reputation—in the latter regard, possessing few rivals in the West. Musically, she is never at fault, her reading at sight is a gift; instinctively she appears to grasp the necessities of music placed before her and at the same time to possess a sympathetic power, enabling her to sink self and make seemingly the sole interest the soloist for whom she is playing. In this regard her familiarity with German, French, Italian and English music is to her of infinite service. Wherever she has appeared, public and critics have united in their praise of the musician as well as the charming woman, and during the present season her engagements have been very numerous and success most pronounced. Her energy has found its fair reward. She has unquestionably accomplished what she set herself to do, and has obtained an enviable reputation among musicians.

JAN VAN OORDT

Decidedly one of the most notable artists in the concert life of the coming American season will be Jan van Oordt, the young Holland violin virtuoso, who has just been engaged as director of the violin department of the American Conservatory.

Mr. van Oordt may be said to be just entering upon his American career, since, with the exception of a very few engagements with the prominent orchestras three years ago, he has preferred to remain in retirement, working constantly on a concert repertory which literally embraces every serious work for the violin known to contemporary musicians.

Mr. van Oordt, after two years of such study, has just returned from The Hague, and established himself in the Western metropolis. He will fill numerous important concert engagements, besides devoting a portion of his time to teaching and composition.

Without dwelling upon Mr. van Oordt's remarkable student experiences, it may be stated that he comes of an old Holland family, and was graduated from the Conservatoire Royale de Musique in The Hague at the age of sixteen with the highest possible honors, namely, the gold medal with "special distinction" and the "wreath of laurel." Later, he spent five years under the great master, Cesar Thomson, to whom he owes his great technical and chaste style of playing.

Mr. van Oordt has made a signal success of his teaching, as well as his concert engagements, which have been very numerous the past season.

JOSEPH VILIM

His engrossing duties as instructor and teacher have cut short, for the present at least, the public appearance of Joseph Vilim in concert. He is a well known solo violinist of Chicago, and for two years played with Theodore Thomas as first violinist. Mr. Vilim is a native of Chicago. He was born in this city January 18, 1861. His family was musical, and early in boyhood his art education was commenced under the instruction of his brother, and continued under local teachers. Entering Prague Conservatory in 1880, he graduated two years later. In 1884 Mr. Vilim became teacher of the violin at the Chicago Musical College, continuing two and one-half years, and then assumed the directorship of the violin department of the American Conservatory of Music, which position he resigned to open a school of his own. He manages two orchestras, mainly for his pupils, and the latter are sought as teachers, soloists, chamber music players and orchestra players. One of his pupils is now first violinist with Thomas Ondricek, the famous Bohemian violinist, who says of Mr. Vilim's teaching: "I can congratulate America that it has such a fine teacher." The Vilim trio has played with marked success wherever it has appeared. Mr. Vilim met with a gen-

erous success in concert work before his work as teacher so absorbed his time.

ELENA VARESI

It was in 1887 that Signorina Elena Varesi was introduced to a Chicago audience as assisting prima donna in the Gilmore concerts. Her reception was most generous, fitting prelude to her many reappearances, fitting sequence also to her splendid career in Europe. Her parentage accounts in part for her wonderful talent. Her grandmother was a contemporary of Malibran, and like her adored during a long career. Her father, the great baritone, Felice Varesi, was the artist expressly for whom Verdi wrote the operas of Rigoletto, Traviata and Macbeth. Her mother was one of the first teachers of Italy, and her aunt was the celebrated Boccabadati, artist and teacher. From them she received her musical education, and she made her debut as a prima donna in Florence. A continuously successful career in grand opera followed throughout Europe, and for two seasons she was with Col. Mapleson at Her Majesty's Opera in London and in the principal cities of Great Britain. Her voice is thoroughly sympathetic, her intonation faultless. Finish, feeling, delicacy and refinement she richly possesses. An unrivaled exemplar of the genuine, pure, divine singing of the

Italian school she has won unstinted plaudits wherever she has been heard. Miss Varesi retired from the stage several years ago and is now one of the foremost teachers of the country, and her concerts are among the most successful and artistic given in Chicago.

THE VIRGIL PIANO SCHOOL OF CHICAGO

This school is devoted exclusively to the study of the piano, and Mr. A. K. Virgil, the inventor of the clavier, in the fall of 1896 made a special trip from London, England (where he had been very successful in the introduction of the clavier and method) for the express purpose of introducing the work in Chicago. He founded the school here, where the work is conducted on the same lines as the London, Berlin and New York schools.

The instruction is the famous Virgil Clavier Method. During the past years it has been most clearly demonstrated in America and Europe, that a conscientious application of this method of technical instruction will result in the most satisfactory advancement in much shorter time, and, consequently, at less expense than by the usual methods or modes of instruction. This system of technical instruction is clear, logical, and most thorough. The mental faculties are brought into play, and the brain is trained to do its share in the acquisition of technic.

A feature is the complete separation of the mechanical or technical from the musical or emotional, which is made possible and thoroughly practical by the correct use of the Virgil Practice Clavier in conjunction with the piano.

In artistic playing it is positively necessary to have the fingers, hands and arms under perfect control; the Virgil method takes full cognizance of this fact, and from the outset the course of study is shaped with that end in view, and as a natural consequence rapid progress is the result.

Special attention is devoted to physical development, and hand massage for the purpose of securing control and perfect freedom of the playing muscles and good physical conditions, which are so necessary in accurate and easy playing movements and nimbleness of fingers, wrists and arms.

ADOLPH WEIDIG

Mr. Weidig declined a prominent court position at Munich a few years ago in order that he might come to America and in the inviting field of Chicago find wider opportunities for his musical talents and aspirations, a choice which he has not regretted.

Born at Hamburg, Germany, Nov. 28, 1867, his musical predilictions found early encouragement, for his father was a well known musician, for thirty-one years a member of the Hamburg orchestra at the Conservatory of Hamburg. Mr. Weidig was instructed in violin by Carl Bargherr (a pupil of Spohr), and in theory by C. P. Gardener. After the latter's death he became the pupil of Dr. Hugo Reimann, one of the greatest living theorists, and from him received also instruction in piano.

In 1884 he became a member of the celebrated Philharmonic Orchestra, having the good fortune to play under Bulow, Brahms, Rubinstein, Tchaikowsky and others. While yet a pupil in the conservatory he produced various creditable compositions, and in 1888 won over twenty-one contestants the Mozart prize, given by the Frankfort Singing Society, the works required being a string quartet and a vocal composition. Thereby he was obliged to continue his studies under Rheinberger for composition and Abel for violin. At Munich Academy he conducted many orchestral performances, and in 1891 graduated with highest honors. The position of assistant court conductor, offered him by Baron von Perfal, intendent of the Munich Court Theater, he declined, in order to come to America, where he became one of the principal members of the Thomas Orchestra, remaining several years with this organization. His teaching work and concert playing requiring time he gave up the orchestral playing, but in such high regard is he held as a musician that only a short time ago one of his works was selected by Mr. Thomas to be played by the Chicago Orchestra at the tenth concert of the season.

FRANZ WAGNER

Franz Wagner came to Chicago a few years ago, but in the comparatively short time he has been here he has made an enviable reputation as a 'cello soloist, as an ensemble player, and as a teacher. He has been connected with two quartet organizations, and for several years has been teaching in the Chicago Musical College, and at the same time taking charge of the ensemble classes. His pupils have been more numerous and have been quite as prominent, if not more so, than those of other 'cellists. For a time he was one of the leading players with the Chicago Orchestra under the baton of Theodore Thomas, and only left the organization because of an excess of engagements elsewhere.

His education was completed in Germany, and after leaving his native land, in which he made a pronounced success, has toured this country with various concert companies, the last four years with the Listemann Quartet.

REGINA WATSON

Mrs. Regina Watson was born in Breslau, Germany, where at the age of five years her musical studies began for the first three years under the instruction of Fraulein Bertha Bial, a renowned pianiste of the time. Later, her precocity warranting the change, she was at the age of eight years, placed under the tuition of the great organist, Adolph Hesse, with whom she made such remarkable progress that she became his show pupil, and was pronounced by him a child gifted with extraordinary talents. During the three years she studied with him she played from memory the best known sonatas and trios of Haydn and Mozart, a good deal of Bach, all the earlier sonatas of Beethoven, many compositions of Hummel, Schubert, Chopin and Schumann. Upon this splendid classical foundation, when, at the age of eleven years, she came with her parents to America she built up such a musical structure that it was thought best to send her back to Europe; and five years later she returned to place herself under the guidance of that great master, Carl Tausig, with whom she remained two years, studying theory and score reading under Prof. Carl Weitzmann. During that period she played repeatedly at the Tausig matinees with great success, and several times with orchestras at larger concerts. Upon returning to her home in Detroit, she soon took prominent rank in the musical profession, playing much in public, and teaching. After her marriage to Dr. L. H. Watson, she moved to Chicago, where she has lived ever since. The first few years of her life in Chicago she played frequently in concerts, and also with the Apollo Club and Beethoven Society as soloist. As the duties and obligation of teaching became more and more absorbing she retired from the concert field and devoted herself exclusively and enthusiastically to this most congenial branch of the profession, and it is in this field that her pronounced success has been won until she is recognized today as one of the leading teachers of America, and has been so pronounced by men like Rubinstein, Dr. Hans Van Bulow, Eugene D'Albert and Otto Lessmann, who have endorsed her in the strongest terms. In 1881 she established her "school for the higher art of piano playing," modeled after the famous school of Carl Tausig of the same name. This school, which is known all over America for the thoroughness and finish of its pupils, is often quoted in foreign musical journals as one of the leading pianoforte schools of this country, and Mrs. Watson's name stands for all that is noblest and highest in her art. Mrs. Watson possesses great magnetism, and has the faculty of inspiring her pupils, and instilling into them the respect and reverence she herself has for the noble art of music. Their playing, too, is conceded to compare very favorably with the playing of the pupils of any European teacher.

Aside from her labors as a teacher, Mrs. Watson finds time to give lecture recitals with musical illustrations, upon various fascinating topics connected with the history and literature of music. She has also written a number of songs of a strongly dramatic character, which are soon to be published.

GENEVIEVE CLARK WILSON

Mrs. Wilson has been singing publicly five years, during which time she has
appeared in all the large cities of the North and East, and also
as soloist for the principal oratorio societies

HARRISON M. WILD

The accepted and perfunctory mode of biographical mention will never do in writing an estimate of Harrison M. Wild's life work. The cursory notice of hackneyed data as to birth, early training, gradual development, sensational incidents, or perchance romantic adventures, seem out of place when dealing with one who is essentially the

many partial failures has served him well; whatever he has undertaken he has carried out to a successful issue; he has not only created opportunity, but developed already existing enterprises to unexpected proportions; the esteem and unlimited confidence which he inspires has practically raised him to a position of unique importance,

man of the hour and possesses a personality sufficiently strong to ignore the past, discount the future and revel in the accomplishment of the present epoch. With Wild everything is built on exact lines, yet without sacrificing ideal aims; his very appearance is characteristic of the man; spare and lithe of figure, quick of thought and speech, a glance from his steel gray eye shows that the decision is made and that it is irrevocable. The very versatility which is the cause of so

power and comprehensiveness. Mr. Wild directs the music at Grace Church, and this work is done on so high and exalted a plane that the immense edifice does not begin to accommodate those who are inspired by the grand service. As director of the Apollo Club he has shown a mastery of vast musical forces, orchestral as well as vocal, which is attracting national attention, and under his skillful training the Mendelssohn Club has achieved triumphs which have marked a new era in the history of that association.

In the light of these achievements it seems trite to add that an organ recital by Wild is the realization of all the probabilities and resources of that noble instrument, that he is an able writer on musical topics, and that a large and devoted band of piano and organ students owe to him their present position in the musical world.

A man of sterling worth, not easily approached, but once won a life-long friend, of rare musical attainments coupled with great executive ability, Harrison M. Wild fills a distinct niche in the galaxy of Chicago artists.

E. L.

ALFRED WILLIAMS

Among the younger singers of Chicago, Alfred Williams, in addition to his recognized ability, has the further distinction of being one of the very few exponents at Chicago of the tone graduation methods of Sbriglia, the talented master of Paris. Mr. Williams has received a certificate from that renowned artist, attesting his full comprehension of his teacher's principles and his ability to teach them to others.

Mr. Williams was born in Plainfield, N. J. From his brother, Wardner Williams, now director of the musical department of the Chicago University, he received the elements of his training. He also studied voice production and oratorio with Mr. Whitney of Boston. He graduated at Alfred University, N. Y., and completed a post-graduate course at the Chicago University. Mr. Williams then went abroad, studying for a time with

Shakespeare in London, then becoming for a year the pupil of Sbriglia of Paris.

Returning to America, Mr. Williams opened a studio at Chicago. He is the bass soloist of the First Presbyterian Church, possessing a mellow voice of exceptional richness. As a teacher he communicates to his pupils his own enthusiasm, and elicits their best efforts. Mr. Williams contemplates a resumption of his studies with Sbriglia in the near future with a view to operatic work, a course which his many friends most heartily commend.

WARDNER WILLIAMS

Mr. Wardner Williams, the instructor of voice at the University of Chicago, has had charge of the musical interests there since its opening. Mr. Williams is a descendant of Roger Williams and son of the Rev. Dr. Thomas R. Williams, a man of more than local reputation as a metaphysi-

·cian. It is doubtless to his father's mental traits that Mr. Williams owes that analytic faculty which Dudley Buck noted in writing of him a few years ago. This analytic power is not necessary to the forming of a good musical performer, but it is the *sine qua non* that goes to the making up of an eminent teacher. This faculty, together with his powers as a performer, Mr. Williams has trained under some of the most eminent teachers in this country and Europe. To his talents as a teacher and organizer Mr. Williams adds a musical taste that is almost perfect and poetic sensibility that rarely goes with more practical gifts. This poetic feeling is manifested in the just interpretation of the more subtle effects in such master works as Chopin's.

Mr. Williams has had wide experience as a conductor of chorus and orchestra. Among other works rendered under his direction at the University of Chicago were the "Messiah," "Elijah," the "Hymn of Praise," Grieg's "Cloister Gate," Mendelssohn's "Athalie," and an overture for orchestra written for and dedicated to the university by Carl Gustav Schmitt, of Auckland, New Zealand.

Mr. Williams is not only conversant with the best musical interests of America, but of Europe as well, and has made special study of the great conservatories and musical centers of both England and the Continent. Among 'some of Mr. Williams most eminent teachers were Sherwood, Larker, Zerrahn, Dudley Buck, Numa Augnes and Alexandre Guilmant, of the National Conservatory of Paris.

HOWARD WELLS

Mr. Howard Wells is one of the best representatives of the rising musicians of Chicago. He was born in Rockford, Ill., and received his early musical training there. Then he studied for five years in Chicago, and taught two years in Rockford College. At the expiration of this time he received the flattering offer from Leopold Godowsky to serve as one of his assistant teachers in Chicago.

Mr. Godowsky has recognized Mr. Wells as one of his most intellectual pupils, and also as one of the ablest exponents of his own methods. Mr. Wells' work in Chicago both as a pianist and teacher has been remarkably successful. His playing is notable for its intellectual breadth and refinement. His ensemble work reveals a thorough musicianship unusual in so young an artist. He has a well developed technic, an individuality and brilliancy of style which characterizes the work of Godowsky's pupils.

Mr. Wells' study has been so orderly, conscientious and thorough, and the mechanical and expression so well proportioned, that the unfoldment is creditable alike to master and pupil. This uniform and steady advancement promises for Mr. Wells an exalted and

enviable position. He possesses a good command of touch, has a retentive memory, is a ready reader and has a fluent technic.—*Music, Chicago.*

MRS. STACEY WILLIAMS

A secret of success enjoyed for several years past by Mrs. Williams is her extraordinary capacity for hard work and her thorough studentship. She is essentially a student, she thinks while she works, and it has been said that it is just this very seriousness that separates her from the ordinary and which will, with her talents and voice, possesses unusual dramatic ability. In the art of singing Mrs. Williams is an ardent disciple of William Shakespeare. With her pupils she has been singularly fortunate, many voices having been trained entirely by her with splendid results. Mrs. Williams excels in tone placement and voice development, while interpretation is also

place her in the front rank of vocalists and teachers. Although practically a newcomer to Chicago, her methods and merits have become fully recognized. A woman of fine education, cultivated and charming, Mrs. Stacey Williams has in a short time established a large class, and is fast winning here the prestige she has for many years held in Milwaukee. Mrs. Williams' voice is a big dramatic soprano, capable of doing remarkable work in opera. Such roles as Adalgesa in Bellini's Norma she interprets with much force and intensity, for she a strong feature of her work. The essence of art has so thoroughly permeated her own life that she is thoroughly recognisive and ready with help toward young and struggling musicians. The work done by Mrs. Stacey Williams in opera and concert has won the indorsement of some of the best critics. Every year Mrs. Williams goes to Europe, where she spends the summer months in studying the newer methods as well as in perfecting her own system with the different European masters.

SYDNEY LLOYD WRIGHTSON

The promise of a musical ancestry is nicely fulfilled in the personality of —Sydney Lloyd Wrightson, a recent acquisition to Chicago. His maternal grandfather, James Harris, was conductor of the queen's private orchestra and for many years director of the Drury Lane Grand Opera Or-

1869. His introduction to music was as choir boy, in which capacity he served eight years. At sixteen he began an extensive tour, visiting almost every country in Europe and spending two years in Australia. In 1890 he first came to America, and he began his career in boy choir work, rapidly

chestra. Sir Joseph Harris, a great English composer and organist of Worcester Cathedral, knighted for musical ability, was his great uncle. Herbert Gresham, organist of the Liverpool Parish Church pro-Cathedral is his cousin. His paternal ancestry was equally illustrious. The family all have excellent voices and musical tastes and his sister is a fellow of the Royal College of Organists.

Mr. Wrightson was born in Stoke-Newington, near London, England, in

winning an enviable reputation. For two years he was choir master of the diocese of Fond du Lac, Wis., and throughout that state, of which he was for seven years a resident, no name perhaps is better known in musical circles than his. In 1897 he organized in the First Congregational Church of Appleton, Wis., the first boy choir in any sectarian church in that portion of the country, and perhaps the largest choir of its nature in the world. It consisted of 106 men and boys, and Mr. Wrightson achieved marked success in the good work he thus accomplished.

Last year Mr. Wrightson decided to abandon boy choir work and in October, 1899, he came to Chicago, where his work and ability have won merited recognition. In voice culture he is an exponent of Shakespeare's method of breathing, and he has achieved distinction in oratorios and American and English ballad singing. He possesses a baritone voice of two and one-fourth octaves. He is connected with the Fullerton Avenue Church, where he has the direction of a choir of fifty voices. He is also vocal director of the University School of Chicago. Almost every summer since his arrival in the United States Mr. Wrightson has gone abroad to study with his teacher, William Shakespeare. As a conductor, teacher and vocalist no future could be filled with higher promise.

ALBERT R. WINDUST

Mr. Albert Windust, who was born in this city March 21, 1874, is a genuine Chicago boy. An artist by profession he has had much success in illustration and it was only through accident that his voice was discovered by his instructor, Mr. Kowalski, of Kimball Hall. During the past two years he has devoted all his spare moments to serious study and thought along musical lines with the hope of one day making a name for himself on the concert and oratorio stage, for which branch of the stage Mr. Windust appears to be especially adapted. His voice is a lyric tenor of over two octaves in range and is of splendid quality. His musical temperament is decided and has the power of holding the attention of his audience while singing. Mr. Windust has before him a great future if his physique becomes more robust, as his instructor predicts for him a fine musical career.

HERMAN L. WALKER

For several years Mr. Walker has been a teacher of singing at the Chicago Conservatory of Music, a position for which his thorough instruction so eminently fitted him, and to which he has brought marked ability. He was born and educated in New England, and coming from a family of decided musical tastes and talent, received from his mother and uncle his earliest artistic instruction. In 1880 Mr. Walker entered the New England Conservatory of Music at Boston, studying under John O'Neill, Nordica's teacher. Mr. Walker continued under the same master after the latter left the conservatory. He was also for a time with Charles R. Adams. After teaching for two years, in 1888, he went abroad, visiting England, Belgium,

Germany, Switzerland and France, hearing many artists. The same year he attended the Wagner performances at Bayreuth, hearing Parsifal and Meistersinger.

and also studying at Florence, Italy, spending some time also in London. In 1893 Mr. Walker became a resident of Chicago, where he has since continued, one of the city's highly

HERMAN L. WALKER

In 1890 he again went abroad, studying with Wm. Shakespeare at London and Sbriglia at Paris. Returning to America to fulfill teaching engagements he in 1891 made his third trip to Europe, remaining until 1893, continuing instruction under Sbriglia

appreciated, artistic instructors, whose aims and ideals are of the highest order. He enjoys the esteem of his colleagues both as a man and an artist. Mr. Walker has a beautiful lyric tenor voice, and sings in a thoroughly refined, artistic manner.

MR. AND MRS. BICKNELL YOUNG

Mr. Bicknell Young received his musical education in London, although he is an American by birth. He made an especial study of oratorio and its interpretation, and for several years before returning to America sang in concerts and oratorio performances in London and the provinces. His master was Visetti, a well known Italian teacher, but his training was quite as largely in French and German songs as in English and Italian, so that he sings in these languages with a beautiful accent and almost perfect diction. He is one of the few professional singers who really enjoy the work of teaching. He is a profound student of the voice and an expert in voice production. Through his years' of experience he has acquired a knowledge of it that enables him to point out the cause of voice defects and suggest the remedy. He is, for this reason, consulted by many singers and teachers from various parts of the country, especially during the summer months. Mr. Young is a firm believer in American teachers and thinks that they are not only the most conscientious, but the best instructors in the vocal art.

Mrs. Young was born in Italy, and had every advantage in education and surroundings. She is well known as a composer, although she has published little. One prominent musician remarked upon hearing one of her compositions: "It is strange that Mrs. Young, being an Italian, should compose with the seriousness and solidity of a German." As a teacher of harmony and composition, Mrs. Young is highly successful. In addition to private pupils she has charge of classes for pupils in rudimentary harmony and sight reading, as it is the intention of these artists to graduate only such students as are thoroughly equipped singers, both in perfect use of the voice and in musical knowledge.

Mr. Young is a well known and highly successful oratorio singer, and he and Mrs. Young give many recital programs selected from their exceptionally large and varied repertoire.

Mr. and Mrs. Young's studio in Kimball Hall is one of the largest and most artistic teaching rooms in the city.

FANNIE BLOOMFIELD ZEISLER

(See page 50.)

BERNHARD ZIEHN

Bernhard Ziehn was born in January, 1845, at Erfurt, in Thuringia. After receiving a common school education he went through the "Schullehrerseminar" (normal school) and for three years taught school at Muehlhausen. In November, 1868, he came to Chicago to serve for two years more in the same capacity. Like Schubert, he seems to have taken but little delight in teaching school, and about 1871 made music his profession. While Mr. Ziehn, in common with all German schoolmasters, had received some instruction in music, it is still from this date that his music study began, and with such results that he is ranked, both here and abroad, among the foremost theorists.

In 1881 were published (Pohle, Hamburg) his "System of Exercises for Pianoforte" and "A New Method of Instruction for Beginners." The idea underlying this work is that one hand being, so to speak, the inversion of the other, the exercises must be so arranged as to bring out this important point. As a consequence, a great part of the exercises are in contrary motion, so as to involve the same key positions for the hands.

The work on which Mr. Ziehn's fame will rest is his "Harmonie und Modulations Schore" (Sulzer, Berlin, 1887). It is the result of many years of patient research. The old theory, in many points not a reflection from living works, but the imaginary guide for composition invented by dry old pedants, is here set aside and all the points taken are illustrated by examples from the masters. Among those quoted most frequently are Bach, Bee-

thoven, Liszt, Wagner, Chopin, Schubert, Franz, Mozart, Berlioz, Jensen, Grieg, Heller—altogether over ninety composers are quoted, and it will be admitted that a work that cites Astorga and d'Albert, Bach and Brahms, Beethoven and Berlioz, Cherubini and Cornelius, Gluck and Grieg, Kirnberger and Kirchner, Rameau and Raff, Scarlatti and Schumann, Weber and Wagner, is not one-sided.

The most astounding feat of musical criticism Mr. Ziehn accomplished was when he (this time attacking the Bach biographer, Smitta) proved that the "Lucas passion" was not written by Bach. This scholarly article prevented the adoption of this spurious work into the "Ausgahe der Bachgesellschaft," and made Mr. Ziehn the recipient of a most flattering letter from Dr. Robert Franz, the Bach student and scholar.

A close study of two years made Mr. Ziehn an unsurpassed master in the correct execution of the embellishments in classical works. (See Nos. 1 and 2 of "Alte Klavierstucke," Pohle, Hamburg.)

In conclusion it should also be mentioned that Mr. Ziehn is a great friend of nature, and is especially versed in botany. Last summer he published in one of the Chicago dailies a detailed account of the numerous places in the Chicago parks and suburbs where poison ivy grows. The attention of the Department of Agriculture in Washington was called to this article, and Mr. Ziehn in consequence received several flattering communications from the department.

Reprinted from the Musical Courier.

EARLY OPERA IN CHICAGO

If the composer of American opera had been in Chicago half a century ago he might easily have become saturated with Aborigine atmosphere by lingering about the blockhouse of old Fort Dearborn. There is no necessity for a discussion of Indian music or the making melody of primitive peoples, which has been determined by the musical doctors as an analysis of harmony.

The first theater in Chicago was known as the Rialto (on Dearborn street) opened in 1838, one year after the incorporation of the city. Concerts had been given in the taverns prior to this time, but the first operatic concert was given upon this stage.

It has been erroneously stated that Chicago first heard grand opera in 1860, when Strakosch brought a company to McVicker's led by Patti and Brignoli. The fact is that seven seasons of opera and numerous concerts had been enjoyed in this city prior to that time.

The inaugural of opera in Chicago was a performance of "La Sonnambula," in Rice's theater, July 30, 1850. The leading singers were Miss Briente, Mr. Manvers and Mr. Lippert. The season if brilliant was certainly brief, for the house burned down the night after the first performance. The chronicler of the time states that the loss was $4,000 and the insurance $2,000, so neither the theater nor the opera company represented a very heavy investment.

Two years later opera was attempted on a more elaborate scale, for the second opera season opened Oct. 27, 1853, and continued two weeks. Signor Ardita was the conductor and the principals were: Mdlle. De Vries, Mdlle. Seidenbourg, Signors Pozzolini, Saffanalli, Barratini, Cándi and Coletti. This year was quite brilliant in the concert line. Adelina Patti made her first appearance at the Tremont House, April 21, with Ole Bull, Amelia Patti and Maurice Strakosch. Annie Thillon, Anna Bishop, Henry Squires, Teresa Parodi, Signora Balbrina and Paul Julian were all heard in concert that season.

The third opera season opened Sept. 27, 1858, by the English Opera Company, of New Orleans. The leaders were Georgenia Hodson, Miss Durand, Miss King, Messrs Swan, Lyster, Trevor and Arnold. A season was given later by Strakosch, his company enlisting Cora Wilhorst, Amelia Patti, Signor Brignoli, Squires, Amodio, Nicolo and Barilli.

December 5, of the year 1859, Parodi opened a season of Italian opera in Metropolitan Hall, and Lucy Escott, Fanny Kemp, Kate Duckworth and Boudinet opened against her with English opera at McVicker's.

Adelina Patti came on her first farewell tour June 19, 1860, at the Metropolitan Hall, and gave a concert in the Wigwam, where Lincoln was nominated on June 28. Clara Louise Kellogg made her debut in Chicago this year on November 12 in the Colson concerts.

The opening of the war put a quietus on operatic enterprises that was first broken by Carl Anschutz' German opera season. In 1862 Caroline Richings was largely responsible for the operatic renaissance in the West. Her company was organized in New York in 1865, and was early devoted to carrying operatic gospel into one night stands. Jessie Bartlett Davis was the child wonder of this organization. In 1869 C. D. Hess organized an English opera company with Parepa Rosa as the star, including Rose Hershe, Zelda Seguin, William Castle, Shed Campbell, Edward Seguin and others. The succeeding season the Parepa company was combined with that of Caroline Richings. The organization had a repertoire of thirty-nine operas, and in their three weeks' season at Crosby's Opera House changed the bill at every performance.

In 1873 Hess pooled issues with Strakosch and had a company, enlisting Clara Louise Kellogg, Annie Louise Cary, Jennie Van Zandt, Joseph Mass, George Conley, Henry Peakes, Gus Hall and W. T. Carleton. Mr. Hess was a Chicagoan and was the first manager of the Crosby Opera House.

The old-timers proudly assert that these early days were the golden era of opera, and boast of the seasons at Rice's and North's and Crosby's as unsurpassed by any later-day achievement. The meager records of the times do not leave much testimony for argument, as the fire swept all accounts of the operatic early days out of existence.

The writer's personal memories of music extend back to 1882, and since that time Chicago has certainly had the best that the operatic impressarios could provide. This history, however, is so recent that it need not be repeated. The interest in music was almost coincident with the beginning of things in Chicago as a city.

While the recent operatic season was not successful, it does not argue that the depressed conditions will continue long. Of course Chicago will have grand opera next year as usual, notwithstanding invidious comments of envious and rank outsiders to the contrary.   CHARLES E. NIXON.

THE CHICAGO MUSICAL COLLEGE

An Historical Sketch by George P. Upton

The Chicago Musical College, organized in 1867, has entered upon the thirty-fourth year of its long and successful career, under the auspices of its president and founder, Dr. Florence Ziegfeld. It first opened its doors when Chicago was a city of about 200,000 people, and it has grown with the municipal growth and strengthened with its strength. It is now the musical educational center of a city of over a million and three-quarters of people, and in all its departments it has kept even pace with the marvelous growth of this western metropolis. It long ago passed the tentative stage, and has now become a permanent educational institution, holding the same prominent position in music as the University, the Art Institute, the Academy of Science, and the Field Columbian Museum in their respective departments of educational labor.

Looking back over its long and brilliant career—a career which covers almost the whole space of music in Chicago—and considering its humble beginning in the ante-fire days when its home in the Crosby Opera House was the musical center of the city, comparing its present distinguished array of teachers and professors, its

generous equipment and comprehensive curriculum, embracing not alone music in the abstract, but the arts allied with it, with the modest beginning of 1867, one realizes that it has kept even pace with the material growth of the city, and has satisfied every demand of musical culture. Dr. Ziegfeld, looking back over these thirty-three years of labor, has every reason to congratulate himself upon the success which he has achieved, and the great and lasting work he has done for music. His musical children are now numbered by thousands. Some of them have taken places upon the lyric stage, many have become distinguished teachers and professors, while others who have gone into active business life, or into society, have carried with them the knowledge and skill acquired under his tuition, and added to their own pleasure as well as to the delight of those in their circle with the musical attainments of voice or instrument secured in the Chicago Musical College.

In 1867 this institution was a little local school. In 1900 it is one of the vigorous educational forces of Chicago, enjoying national and international reputation, summoning its pu-

CHICAGO MUSICAL COLLEGE

pils from every part of the Union, and calling upon the United States and Europe for professors and teachers of the highest class. Its influences are boundless, for its graduates are teaching in every state of the Union. No better certificate is needed than the diploma of this college. Its graduates are accepted without question as past masters in the art of music.

The history of this college in its different locations, for the demands of growth have several times necessitated change of site, is well known to the public. It was humble in its beginning in the Crosby Opera House in 1867; not even its most sanguine friends anticipating its remarkable growth, but in 1871 Dr. Ziegfeld had to secure more commodious rooms at 253 Wabash avenue. Then came the great conflagration, when "the daughters of music were brought low," but the Chicago Musical College rose Phœnix-like from the ashes of that monumental disaster within three weeks. It apparently bore a charmed life. It was supposed that music would be the last thing to receive attention in the reconstruction of the city, but in this short time the college doors opened, the teachers had resumed their duties, and the new quarters at 800 Wabash Avenue were filled with pupils so speedily that more commodious school-rooms were sought at 493 Wabash Avenue, where the college remained until the Central Music Hall building was erected.

In that conspicuous structure it had its headquarters and its home—for there is no other musical institution in the United States more homelike than the Chicago Musical College—until last year, and from this busy hive have swarmed thousands of graduates carrying with them the influence, the information, the graces and educational facilities of musical culture obtained within its walls.

But, ample as the accommodations in the music hall building appeared to be, the college outgrew its home; more room was needed to accommodate its rapidly increasing list of scholars, and improved facilities for the accomplishment of their work. After careful scrutiny a new location was found, which is admirably adapted for the purposes of the college, and it is now housed in the Chicago Musical College building on Michigan Boulevard, between Van Buren and Congress streets, and may boast the most elegant structure devoted to musical uses in the United States, if not in the world. Its massive facade is a triumph of architecture, and its stately entrance invites one to an interior which throughout its entire six stories, and in all of its forty rooms, its spacious corridors and its artistic and commodious halls is perfectly adapted to the purposes of a college of this kind. Each of these rooms, which are as sumptuous in their appointments and decorations as private parlors, has been fitted up not only with special reference to the duties of teaching, but with an eye to artistic effect, so that the student shall literally dwell in an art atmosphere. Even the location itself may be said to be artistic, for on the one side is a noble structure filled with artists' studios, nearly opposite is the Art Institute, a few doors away is the stately Auditorium, and a near neighbor is the new Library.

It is removed from the noise of the busy streets, it fronts the lake, and, therefore, has a superb outlook to the east and a fine view of the city from all sides. It is amid such environments as these that the College has established its new home, and there it will remain for years to come as one of the art monuments in which Chicago justly takes pride.

While no expense has been spared in decorating and furnishing the rooms of the College so that its material advantages shall meet all requirements, equal attention has been paid to its educational demands. Every branch of the faculty has been strengthened. * * * Every department has been made as perfect and complete as possible by the engagement of tried and successful teachers. With such a staff of instructors, with such a new and elegant home, with such a constantly increasing patronage, Dr. Ziegfeld should be a happy man. He stands at the head of an institution which is unique in its appointments and in its success.

During the past thirty-three years of labor the college has been the center of musical activity, impulse and influence. Thousands of young men and women have been graduated, and now look back upon it as their Musica Mater. A full generation of teachers has gone out from its pleasant walls to give back in turn to others the instruction they have received there, and the second generation of pupils will soon follow their example. Every year has been filled with pupils' and faculty concerts, and the annual commencements have come to be among the most brilliant musical events of the season. The influence of such an institution as this can hardly be estimated. It is an educational force of a decided nature, and an institution therefore which holds the same high place in its department of labor as the university or libraries of the city in theirs. It has come to be something more than a school or a college of music. It is one of the institutions of the city with a far-reaching outspread of influence, and as such its officers and directors and its magnificent array of teachers are to be congratulated. That their labors are appreciated is demonstrated by the munificent patronage of their college. It has largely dominated the concert world also by the unusual number of artists it has given to the stage. It has taken a place among the great conservatories to which eminent teachers from abroad are glad to transfer their services.

The college catalogue bears testimony to the completeness of this great school of musical learning, both in the list of the faculty, composed of experienced teachers and many virtuosi of international reputation, and the system of instruction and arrangement of courses which represent the outcome of thirty years' experience. No school of its kind offers such comprehensive advantages; no institution requires more complete or satisfactory examinations; hence, a diploma of the Chicago Musical College means that its possessor has a well-rounded and complete education and is fitted for the department of musical labor which he or she chooses to occupy.

Dr. F. Ziegfeld stands at the head of the College as its president, the post of honor he has occupied since it was organized, and gives to every department the artistic supervision it may require, and the invaluable aid of his advice and long experience. With him in the active management are associated two of his sons, Carl and William K. The former is secretary and treasurer, and has shown such executive ability in developing the methods of his father that his administration of business affairs has won for him an enviable reputation and has contributed in no small degree toward the maintenance of the institution's high standard.

William K. Ziegfeld holds the responsible position of manager, and has conspicuously demonstrated his ability to meet all the demands of his post. Having had the advantage of extensive travel the world over, with its added advantage of personal acquaintance and knowledge of affairs, he brings to his work, besides superior business talent, a fund of musical and general knowledge which is of inestimable value. The Board of Directors for 1899-1900 includes the following well-known gentlemen: Rev. Dr. H. W. Thomas, Hon. Richard S. Tuthill, Dr. F. Ziegfeld, William M. Hoyt, Edwin A. Potter, Alexander H. Revell, A. E. Bournique, Alfred M. Snydacker, Carl Ziegfeld, and William K. Ziegfeld.

The Chicago Musical College may claim with all confidence that it is completely equipped in all its departments with one of the largest and most brilliant faculties ever brought together in a conservatory of its kind, and with a curriculum that includes every department of musical study as well as the allied arts.

Among the faculty are such distinguished representatives of musical progress as Vans Von Schiller, Dr. Falk, William Castle, Charles Gauthier, Herman De Vries, Bernhard Listemann, Mrs. O. L. Fox, Arthur Friedheim, Herman Klum, Rudolph Ganz, S. E. Jacobsohn, and Hart Conway, director school of acting.

DR. FLORENCE ZIEGFELD

President Chicago Musical College

WM. K. ZIEGFELD

CARL ZIEGFELD

MISS EMMA E. CLARK

This pianiste and able teacher has established a studio of artistic pianoforte playing in one of the handsomest suites in the Fine Arts Building. She is a descendant of a colonial family of Revolutionary fame, inheriting her love for music through her father, who, though a lawyer by profession, was identified with Dr. Mason's choir

of Boston and other musical organizations.

Miss Clark's studies began at the age of four. Before she was out of her teens she had acquired a reputation in Detroit as a musician. In 1891 she went to Berlin, and was accepted by the distinguished Professor Barth, of the Royal Conservatory, who, upon hearing her play a movement of a Beethoven sonata, complimented her highly. Then Miss Clark spent some time under other teachers and famous pianists, gaining the best methods. Herr Wilhelm Berger, the "composer-pianist," speaks of her as "his most conscientious worker. Her heart and soul are full of music."

The manager of a musical college at Chicago, while in Europe securing artists, engaged Miss Clark. In two other musical institutions of Chicago she has been at the head of the piano department. Then she has had the honor of being chosen by outside schools as one of the judges of pupils in contests.

She has pupils from nearly all the states in the Union, and some who have been under renowned masters abroad have placed themselves under Miss Clark upon returning. Many of her pupils are holding good positions as teachers, and she is constantly receiving letters of commendation.

Miss Clark's life is a busy one, and has been productive of more than ordinary success. She has received flattering offers to return to Berlin and teach, but she prefers America, which is the true birthright and spirit of a "Daughter of the American Revolution." She is president of the Schumann Club.

FRANK S. HANNAH

In Mr. Frank S. Hannah, the senior member of the firm of Hannah & Hamlin, directors of musical artists, Chicago has found a gentleman peculiarly well adapted to the necessities of a very difficult business. He fears not the responsibilities of his position, although he thoroughly recognizes, for he is a singer of more than ordinary ability, and his honest dealing and earnest attention to the interests of all his clients are prominent characteristics.

Born in Missouri, the youngest son of Judge John F. Hannah, a prominent jurist of that state, Mr. Hannah inherits his musical talent from his mother, who taught both music and languages. In January, 1895, he came to Chicago and joined the choir of St. Paul's Universalist Church, where he has since remained, and is now tenor soloist and choir director. He was also tenor and manager of the Sherwood Quartet, as well as director of the Glee Club of the Central Department of the Chicago Young Men's Christian Association. Very fortunate was his connection with the Sherwood Quartet as it enabled him to make the acquaintance of our well-known Chicago soprano, Miss Jenny Osborn, who later consented to a life partnership. They were married while on tour in Kansas City.

German Lieder, presenting the *"Dichterliebe"* of Schumann and the *"Schwanengesang"* of Schubert by that sterling artist, Mr. Chas. W. Clark. He also introduced here Miss Clara Butt, the English contralto. Since Jan. 1, 1900, when Mr. George Hamlin was admitted to the firm, quite a number of attractions of a very high order have

FRANK S. HANNAH

Having become established as a manager for musical artists Mr. Hannah determined to use original lines and to give the musical public of Chicago an opportunity not only to hear prominent artists, but also compositions new and unheard here. Quite early in the season of 1898-99 the "Persian Garden" was presented, a work at that time practically unknown. The following season Mr. Hannah opened with two classical recitals of

been presented. A grand Wagnerian description concert on the "Ring," by Mr. Walter Damrosch, with selections from the operas sung by Mme. Gadski, Mr. George Hamlin and Mr. David Bispham, crowded the Central Music Hall; Mr. Wm. Shakespeare, the voice specialist in two lecture recitals, Mme. Schumann-Heink and many others. Such methods as Mr. Hannah used could have but one result. He is the leading director for musical artists, enjoys a lucrative business, has a host of friends and possesses the confidence and respect of the city's leading musicians.

Mr. and Mrs. Hannah spend their summers in Europe, the latter enlarging her repertoire of French and German songs and Mr. Hannah seeking for artists to present to the American public, for he is a firm believer in the necessity of a manager, knowing by personal observation the ability of the artists he is recommending. The justice of his ideas in this regard are evidenced by the position he holds today in the musical life of Chicago.

INDEX

INDEX TO BIOGRAPHICAL SKETCHES

Index

PART V. PRE-PRODUCTION

CONTENTS

PART VII. POST-PRODUCTION

PART VIII. DISTRIBUTION

IX. CONCLUSION